Earley Days

An illustrated account of our community's development

Earley Local History Group

Earley Days

An illustrated account of our community's development

Earley Local History Group

The Kennet swift for silver eels renowned
The Loddon slow with verdant alders crowned

The Rivers, A. Pope

Earley Local History Group
2000

Published by
Earley Local History Group
48 Harcourt Drive
Earley
Reading RG6 5TJ

ISBN 0 9540041-0-8

Designed and printed by the
Department of Typography & Graphic Communication
The University of Reading

2001

Front cover

The Porter Institute, now part of St Peter's School
Dann/Lewis 636
© Rural History Centre, The University of Reading

Back cover

The Breadmore family, 1921
© William Breadmore

Aerial photograph of Earley, 1963
© Ordnance Survey

Aerial photograph of Earley, 1996
Aerial photograph reproduced with permission from Wokingham District Council, rectified with permission of Her Majesty's Stationery Office
© Crown Copyright, N/C/00/1037

Cover designed by Clair Georgelli, a student in
The Department of Typography & Graphic Communication
The University of Reading

Contents

This book is dedicated to

Ray Harrington-Vail

and

Joe Pettitt

(1909–1999)

Acknowledgements

Julie Boulton, Grahame Hawker, Liz Vincent and Elaine Watts are the main authors and Graham Parlour supplied many of the postcards. We are indebted to the following people:

All the staff at Earley Town Council, particularly Richard Raymond, Kay Martin and Diana Collins, for their help, support and great patience.

Earley Town Council, Awards for All, Millennium Fund, Wokingham District Council, Berkshire Carpets and Tech 2K for financial support.

The book was designed and printed in Earley at the Department of Typography & Graphic Communication, The University of Reading, the production staff for the book being Mick Stocks, Jennie Welsh, Andy Cross, Geoff Wyeth and Neale Smith.

Corridor Press; M. Bott (The Library, The University of Reading); Ordnance Survey; Berkshire Records Office; Reading Local Studies Library; Earl of Macclesfield; Wessex Archaeology; English Heritage; Phyl Pettitt for the use of the Joe Pettitt archives; Gordon Rowley (Whiteknights); Brian Cook (Woodley Hill House); Bernard Moles (Ideal Windows); Ted Anderson (Earley Power Station); Brian Stone (Maiden Erlegh School); Lilian King (MICE); Roy Pike (Scouts); Mrs B. Hutch (Guides); Margaret Erith (WI); Eric Jefferies (Earley Carnival); N. Wright (East Reading Horticultural Association); Sutton's; Maiden Erlegh Outdoor and Whiteknights Bowling Clubs; Peter van Went (Holme Park/Bluecoat School); Tim Newell-Price (Leighton Park School); Henry Hawes (Shinfield Players); Ian Boyd (Crosfields School); Bill Clayton (Earley Home Guard); Valerie Ayres (Methodism); Martin & Pole, Nicholas (Estate Agents); *The Reading Chronicle* and *The Evening Post*.

Additional background material was supplied by all of Earley's schools, churches and museums, the European Centre for Medium Range Weather forecasting, the Meteorological Office, Dinton Pastures, The Lions, Rotary and Round Table.

Brian Kemp, Julian Vincent and Bill Watts for proof reading the text.

Preface

In George Orwell's *Coming up for Air* the hero is shocked to see the changes that have occurred in the town of his birth. His remembrance of the town is caught in a time warp and he has difficulty in reconciling the new base lines set by the people who have come in recently. Those of us who have moved into Earley have our own individual base lines. By listening to older residents, reading recent histories of Earley and delving into documents and maps of Earley's past we have tried to peel back the houses, roads and railway lines to produce a common starting point from which to understand the development of Earley. This book sets out to document and celebrate the long and varied history of Earley over the last millennium: from before the *Domesday Book* to the development of Lower Earley.

It is an opportune time for such a project for a number of reasons. First, it is over half a century since the last history of Earley was produced. Second, Earley's structural development is nearing completion now that almost all of the available land between Reading and Woodley and the Thames, the Loddon and the M4 has been built on; and third, it is an excellent time to find out where we have come from as we commence the next millennium.

Whilst we have endeavoured to include as wide a subject matter as possible within this book, we face many of the constraints that faced Ernest Dormer over 50 years ago when he produced his historical account of Earley, as he stated at the start of his book:

> *The scope and size of the book have been conditioned by prevailing circumstances; there is still much in uncharted records that would make a further volume about the parish, but the necessity to go to publication in [time for] the actual [millennium] year has been one of the limiting factors in the production* (Dormer, 1944).

The intention has been to produce a book that covers as many aspects of Earley's history as possible in separate sections, and to intersperse the text with a large number of old photographs, postcards and maps. It is hoped that this approach will introduce to many of the newer residents of Earley a flavour of the area's rich historical heritage and that their appetites will be whetted for a more in depth look into Earley's past. We also hope that it will encourage more of our older residents to write down their reminiscences of life in Earley.

Of the authors, three of us are not native to Earley but have developed an interest in the area and have become curious about what Earley was like before the houses, industrial estates and business parks were built. We wanted to know what was there before. Why was that street so named? How and why these estates/industrial areas/business parks developed where they did? Who owned the land before? Who lived there? How did they live? Why did they sell? And so on. So many changes have taken place that we felt that it was necessary to record them and people's reminiscences before they had forgotten what the place was like before the changes. Many of the features mentioned throughout the book can be referred to on a map at the end (page 244).

Finally it is the hope of the authors that other residents of Earley will be enthused and stimulated to continue the research necessary to produce a larger and more in-depth successor to this book.

1 Setting the Scene

Introduction

Few places have changed as rapidly as Earley over the last century and particularly in the last 25 years. At the turn of the last century Earley was a rural place on the eastern outskirts of Reading. There was no real centre and to anyone's knowledge there had never been one. The few dwellings that existed were mostly tied to one or other of several large estates and farms in the area. This situation changed rapidly when the large estates were broken up and sold, mainly to builders who built houses for the people attracted to work in the ever-increasing number of industries in and around Reading. This meant that Reading expanded into the surrounding communities. The reasons for breaking up the estates were varied – inability to afford the upkeep of a large estate, preferring to live in another property, the family line dying out, profiteering, etc. Whatever the reason estates were easily sold in Earley as the builders were keen to buy.

The modern town of Earley is hourglass-shaped and stretches 3 1/2 miles from the Thames in the north to the M4 in the south. It is bounded by Reading and Shinfield to the west, the Thames and Oxfordshire to the north, Sonning, Woodley, Winnersh and the Loddon to the east, Shinfield, Arborfield and Newlands, Winnersh and the M4 to the south.

Physically the town stretches from its lowest point by the Thames (125 feet above sea level) to its highest point on its western boundary (the Earley Water Tower, 263 feet above sea level). The soils are river gravels near the rivers, heavy clays at the highest points and mixed gravelly-sandy soils in the middle.

The Reading Beds cover the chalk and are hidden by alluvium and gravel. They consist of clay although important beds of sand occur. The clay is often mottled, red, blue, orange, etc. Beds of pebbles occur in places and vary from 70 to 90 feet in depth. Good supplies of water are obtained from the sands. On the highest points London Clay overlays the Reading Beds (VCH, 1923), see map 1. Its basement bed is 10 feet thick and consists of green coloured sands and clays with bands of calcareous stone and some pebbles: the Mockbeggar Brickfields are fossiliferous throughout with marine snails such as *Pectunculus* and *Cardium* being found there. The London Clay is wholly clay, uniform and practically impervious to water.

The area would have been vegetated with mixed oak woods above the

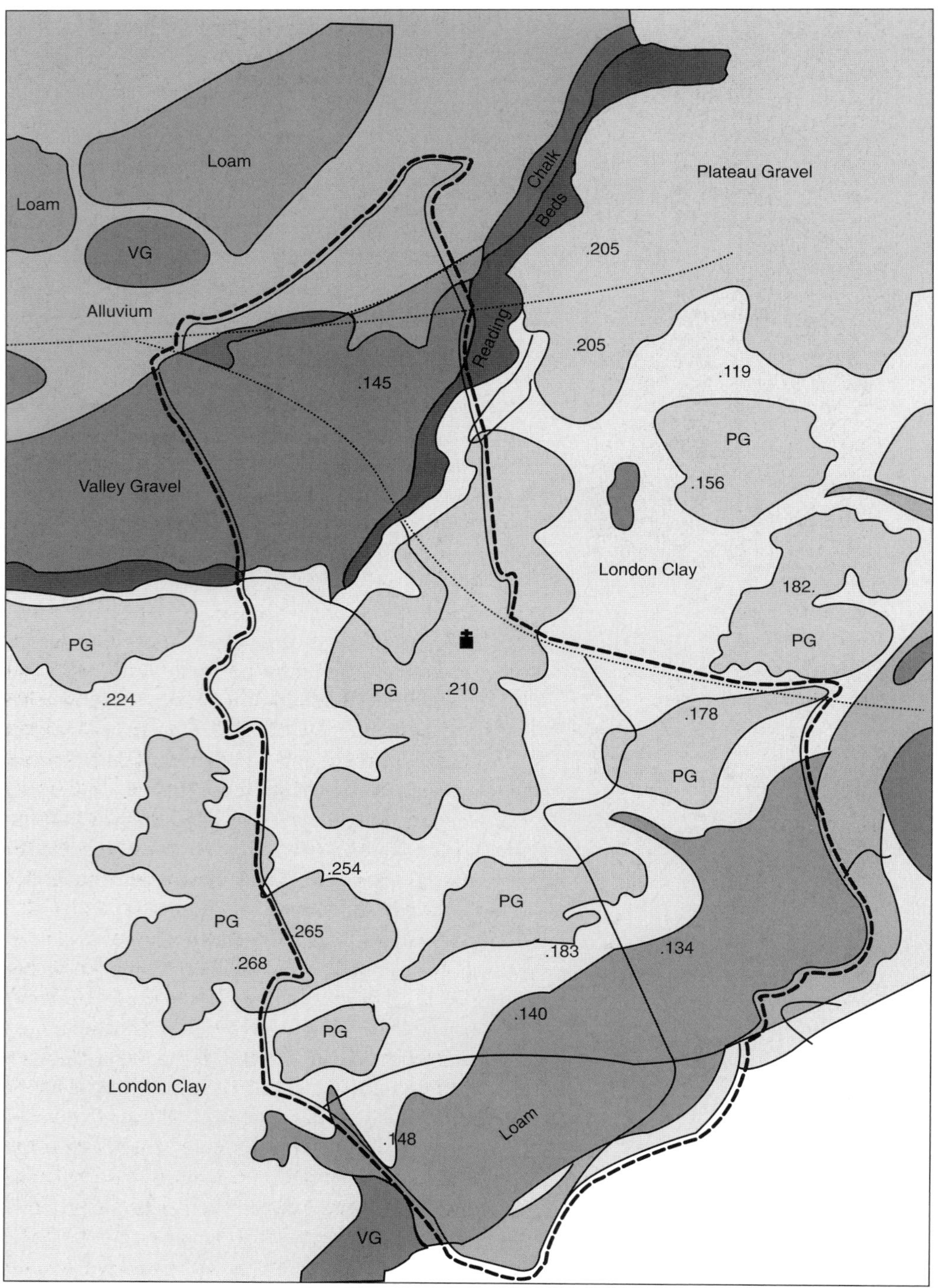

Map 1: Geology of Earley
based on an original by Bruce Sellwood

Development of Earley from prehistory to the year 2000
© *Trust for Wessex Archaeology*

flood plains of the Thames and Loddon; wet woodlands in the valleys; and heathland in the middle.

In 1887 Earley Rise and the eastern part of Newtown became part of Reading; nearly one hundred years later the second reorganisation of boundaries took place when the M4 became the southern boundary.

For most of its existence Earley has been one of the four Liberties under the jurisdiction of the Parish of St Andrew's, Sonning. In 1844 Earley gained its own Church of St Peter's, and St Bartholomew's was consecrated in 1870 to meet the needs of the burgeoning area of Newtown. The Civil administration of the Liberty was under the control of the Reading and Earley Education Boards, the Wokingham Sanitary Authority and the Wokingham Poor Law Union. The many civil bodies dealing with education and sanitation were brought under the control of the Rural District of Wokingham in 1887 when the new Civil County of Berkshire and the extended Borough of Reading were brought into being.

The 1894 Local Government Act transferred the civil responsibilities from the parish vestry to new civil parish councils. It is believed that Earley Civil Parish dates from 1866 (Youngs, 1979). However the Minutes of Earley Parish Council, held at the Town Council Offices, date back only to 1974.

Many people think of Earley as a 1980s housing estate but as this book shows, Earley has a long and rich history. The first chapter, *Setting the Scene* describes how Earley came to have its hour-glass shape, when it took on its modern boundaries, and the possible origins of its name.

Very Early Earley starts with a time machine ride back 600 million years to a time when life was just beginning and the creatures to be seen in the area we now call Earley were small strange looking animals unlike any of those on the Earth today. At this time Earley was close to the South Pole! As our story moves forward in time fish, amphibians, reptiles, dinosaurs, birds and mammals all begin to appear; Earley gradually drifts northwards to take up its present position on the earth. At the end of this journey, one creature appears that will have a very dramatic impact on the way Earley looks today – man. Man's history in this area is traced through the Palaeolithic, Mesolithic, Neolithic, Bronze Age, Iron Age, Roman, Saxon and Viking periods.

The rest of the book concentrates on Earley's documented history from 1066 onwards. The next 800 years of Earley's history are dominated by the large ancient manors, country estates and parks of the very rich. Initially much of the land was owned by the monarch and granted to valued servants of the king. Later owners of these lands were wealthy landowners and the entrepreneurs who moved to the Earley area, like many people in recent times, because of its proximity to Reading, London and England's major east-west transportation routes. The story of Earley's upper class origins is told in *Manors and Estates*.

The story of the development of Earley as we know it today is told in the fourth chapter, *Development*. The rapid change from a small scattered hamlet set against an agricultural back-drop to a large, densely-populated commuter town on the edge of Reading took over 150 years, with most of the growth happening in the last 40 years.

The heart of any community is its communal buildings, its public houses, its churches, its educational and administrative centres, etc. It is in these buildings that the residents of Earley interact and bond. The history behind these culturally important centres is told in chapter 5, *Community Buildings and Institutions*.

True community spirit isn't generated by buildings alone and chapter 6, *Community Groups*, explores the history of just a few of the many community groups that form part of the rich tapestry that weaves the separate lives of the individual residents of Earley into one cohesive community.

A high proportion of the people who live in Earley have houses near its borders owing to its elongated shape. Their immediate neighbourhood is all around their homes and does not stop at some invisible boundary. It is for this reason that we have included a chapter called *History on the Edge* which relates the history of some of the more interesting buildings and areas of land that lie within a few minutes walk of Earley's borders.

Every town and village in Britain has its own story to tell of the war years, and Earley is no exception. In *Earley at War* we tell the history of the Earley Home Guard and a few of Earley's civilian residents tell their own fascinating tales.

In *Earley from the Air* and *Earley on the Ground* we have included a number of aerial photographs and local maps to enable you to piece together the story of the changes immediately around your own house.

Earley is relatively unusual in that the vast majority of its development has occurred during living memory. This has given us the opportunity to record much of its history through the memories of local people. It is hoped that the *Living Memories* chapter will not only add colour to this book and thereby make it a more enjoyable read, but also give you a more in-depth understanding of everyday life in twentieth-century Earley.

Finally we include some of our thoughts on Earley's future. This of course is pure speculation, but it will be interesting to see, in the next book produced on the history of Earley in fifty years' time, just how accurate we were.

The Changing Boundaries of Earley

For the purposes of this book, we are defining the extent of Earley as the area that is currently administered by Earley Town Council. However, it is important to keep in mind that the boundaries of Earley have changed over time. Therefore, where appropriate, we have stretched the boundaries of Earley to include those areas that were once within Earley and have subsequently been taken over by neighbouring authorities.

Whilst some of its current boundaries meander mysteriously through the centre of individual buildings, many of the boundaries follow easily identified features such as the Rivers Thames, Kennet, Loddon and the Reading to Guildford railway line and the M4.

The first map that we have seen which shows the whole of the Liberty of Earley is the 1756 map *A Plan of the Lordship and Liberty of Earley of the Manor and/Court Leet and Court Baron of Early Regis alias Early Whiteknights as also of the Manor and Court Baron of Early St. Bartholomew within the several tythings thereof situate in the Parish of Sunning in the County of Berkshire belonging to Sir Henry Englefield Baronet* (BRO D/EBb/P1). This map gives the complete outline of the Liberty of Earley but shows only the holdings of Sir Henry Englefield.

The parish of Sonning consisted of four Liberties: three in Berkshire (Sonning Town, Earley and Woodley) and one in Oxfordshire (Dunsden and Eye). The Mother church (St Andrew's) was situated in Sonning. Each of the Liberties was in effect a separate parish having its own overseer of the poor and, where there was a church or chapel, its own churchwarden, but all came under the Mother church. The Parish must have been one of the largest in the land. A parish was the ecclesiastical division, whilst the Hundred was the civil and legal division. Earley was in the Charlton Hundred, the other three Liberties were in the Sonning Hundred, after 1224 (Perkins, 1977). In the 19th century the new parish of Earley St Peter's was formed, its boundaries extended into Bulmershe, down to Loddon Bridge and Sindlesham Mill and westwards to Lower Earley.

In the past the people of Earley would have had a greater awareness of where the exact boundaries of Earley were than the present day residents. There are two records of beating the bounds, one in 1785 (BRO D/EDO E23) and one in 1840 (see chapter 3 for a full account). Any attempts to change the boundaries were noted and rectified. These boundaries had been in place for hundreds of years and were designated by ditches and natural features. Dormer (1944) talks about a ditch between Reading and Earley being incorporated into the back gardens of houses in Cardigan Road and a ditch between Earley and Woodley near Worlds End off Pitts Lane.

The boundaries of Earley have changed considerably over the years causing sudden dramatic increases and decreases in its population. In 1887, the Corporation of Reading which had always been land hungry (*the Town Council have an earth hunger … what Bulgaria is to Russia, Earley is to Reading* [Berkshire Chronicle 1886]) expanded its boundary to include the area between Cemetery Junction and Church Road, resulting in a large drop in Earley's population (see Chapter 4).

The history of this boundary change started in the 1850s when houses were built in Earley for employees of Huntley and Palmer's and Suttons. Suttons moved their nursery grounds to New Farm, London Road. The problem of drainage and sanitation brought Reading Borough Council and Wokingham Poor Law Guardians into conflict. In 1884 Reading Councillor George William Colebrook suggested that the Borough's boundaries should be enlarged to take in not only the developing urban/suburban fringes but also lands that could become building estates. The Poor Law Guardians of Wokingham opposed the boundary change. They administered the Poor Law in Earley and levied a rate for public health purposes as they were also the sanitary authority. Although they were under orders from the Thames Conservators to connect houses to a sewerage system, ten years later they had not carried out this order. In 1886 they started proposing schemes for drainage for Earley but only after a public meeting had come out in favour of moving into Reading. They then agreed that the Reading boundary should extend into this part of Earley as long as the Earley tax base was retained for Poor Law purposes. With this compromise Reading's private bill for incorporating part of Earley (and Tilehurst and Whitley) went to parliament unopposed.

After 1887 a number of abortive attempts were made to incorporate part or all of Earley into Reading. In 1907–1911 there was a proposal to take the whole of Whiteknights Park into Reading but nothing came of this proposal. In 1947 extensive plans were published that included extending the Reading Boundary to encompass Earley, Woodley and Sonning. The application failed when the Boundary Commission was abolished in 1948. Wokingham Rural District Council refused to provide Reading with the information that it requested in 1908 and 1948.

After the Second World War Reading was desperate for land for housing. A private bill to extend the boundaries was started in 1948 but was dropped when land outside the Borough boundaries was released for Reading tenants who paid their rates to one authority and their rents to Reading. Another attempt to move Reading's boundaries into Earley failed when a Royal Commission and the Maud Report superseded the Local Government Commission in the 1960s. In 1974 Reading lost its County Borough status (Alexander, 1985). With the reorganisation of Local Government on 1 April 1998 Reading regained many of its former powers.

In contrast the parish of Earley expanded its population on April 1st 1986 when its boundaries with Woodley and Shinfield were altered (*Reading Chronicle* 1985). The number of people living in Earley increased by about half as much again from its then population of 17,500, with the addition of 8,500 to 9,000 people to its electoral register. The principal additions to the parish of Earley at that time were:

- A small area north of the centre-line of the M4 motorway from Arborfield and Newland parish.
- The South Ward of Woodley parish.
- The area of Shinfield parish north of the centre-line of the M4 north of Pearmans Copse, east of the rear boundaries of properties fronting onto Shinfield Road and south of Shinfield Rise housing estate.
- A small area north of the centre-line of the M4 south of the Loddon and adjacent to Mill Lane from Winnersh parish.
- All the properties on the east side of Pitts Lane from Woodley parish.
- A small area south of the railway and north of the rear boundaries of properties in London Road and Shepherds Hill from Sonning parish.

(see map 2)

Having gone through all of these boundary changes over the years, one might expect that the present boundaries of Earley would be logically placed and that no future boundary changes would be necessary. There are, however, still a number of outstanding anomalies. These include a boundary that runs through the University of Reading Campus, another that splits the Thames Valley Business Park in two and one that cuts through the properties on Ryhill Way.

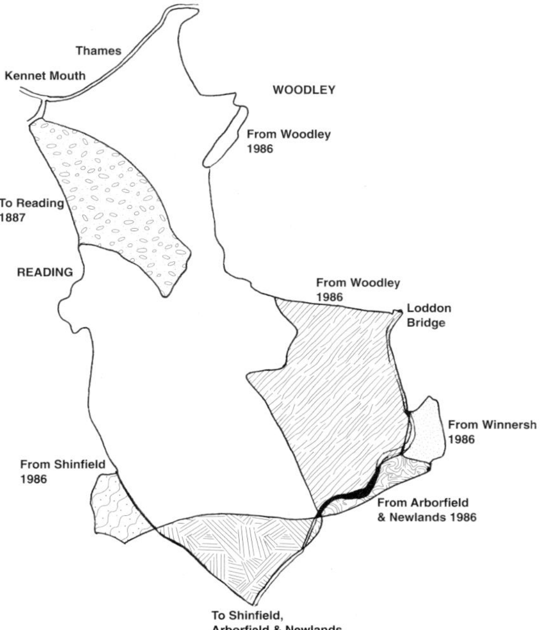

Map 2: The changing boundaries of Earley

What's in a Name?

These are some of the spellings of our town that have been recorded: Earley, Herlei, Arley, Erlegh, Erle, Ere, Arle, Ereleye, Early, Erleigh, Herlegh, Erlee, Harlegh, Herlie, Erley, Erleye … and there are probably many more.

Place names change with history. The current spelling of Earley has co-existed for the last century along with the older names of Erlegh, Erleigh and Early. Today three of these are in use as evidenced by place names such as Earley Hill Road, Maiden Erlegh Lake and Erleigh Road.

There is no correct way of spelling the settlement's name as all names have an equal place in history, but **Earley** is now generally accepted as the correct spelling.

The *Domesday Book* of 1086 records the name as Herlei and Erlei. This spelling could be a corruption of an original. Exactly what the name means is open to debate. Many hundreds of place names have ley or leigh within them, which, since it is Anglo-Saxon for wood or clearing, would apply to both Earley and Woodley. Er or ear could refer to eagles or gravel pit (Gelling, 1972). Both are possible. Birds of prey would have been a common sight in the Middle Ages and, whilst eagles may not have been common in Berkshire for many years, the term eagle may have been used generically to describe any large bird of prey. Interestingly Margaret Gelling (*pers comm*) also states that earn is an old Saxon name for the sea eagle.

More recently a golden eagle was shot in Berkshire in 1924 – the unfortunate creature became a focal point in Reading Museum at the time. A few sightings of white-tailed eagles were recorded in the county up until 1927. Today one occasionally sees a sparrowhawk hunting over Maiden Erlegh Lake and Redhatch Copse. Red kites have recently been re-introduced near Henley in Oxfordshire, so large birds of prey might one day return to our skies. Another meaning of er or ear is gravel. There are large gravel deposits in the north of the area but it is considered that Eagle Wood is the most likely meaning of Earley.

Two other possible origins are that Earley lies on the ground where Saxon farmers cultivated their corn or that Earley was the Earl's land. However, Paul Carvill from the English Place-name Society considers both of these suggestions to be impossible linguistically.

Topography

The history of any area is dependent on its topography. Between the low-lands of the Thames and the Loddon, Earley rises to a ridge running from Elm Road via Wilderness Road, Church Road and Pitts Lane to the

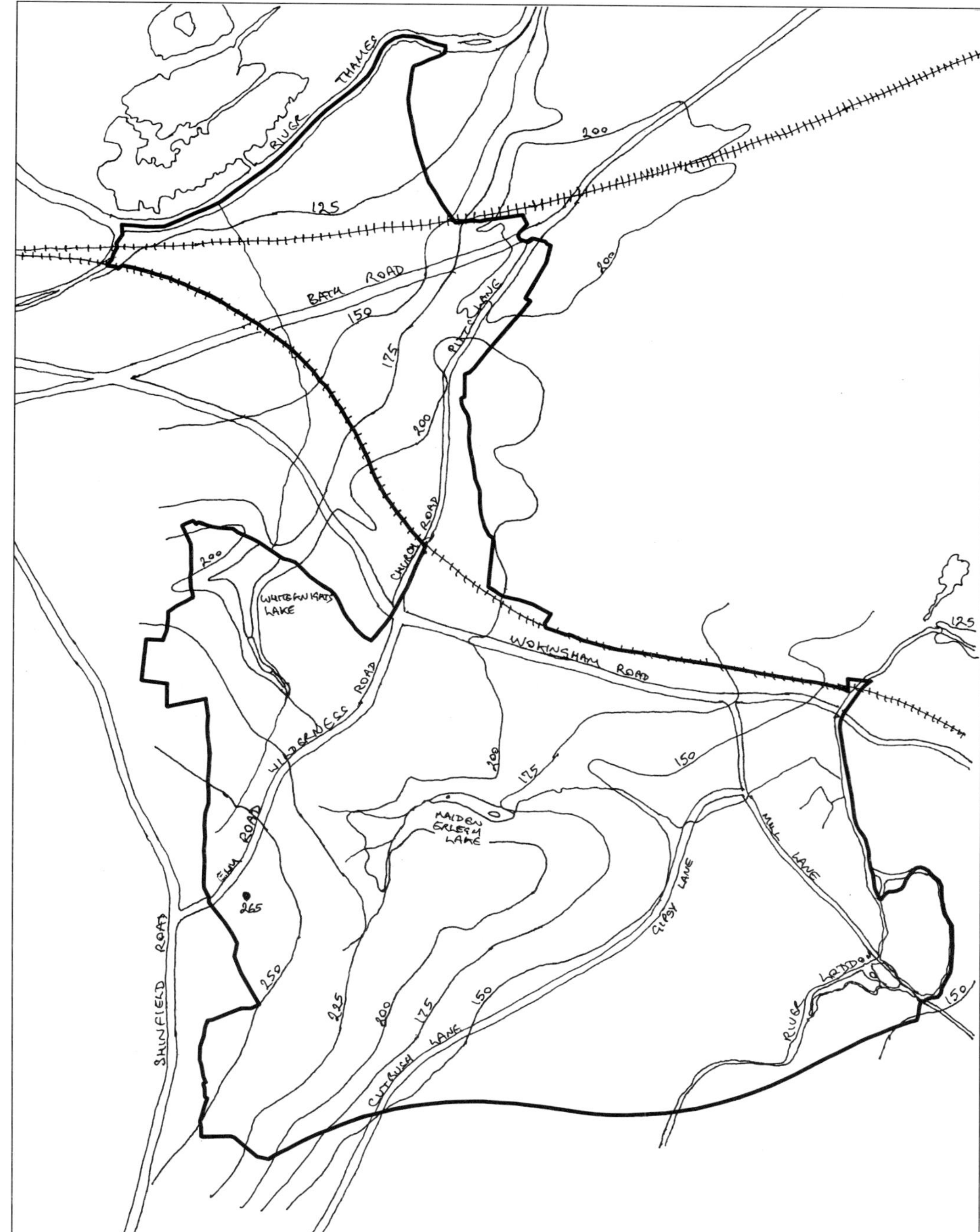

Map 3: The topography of Earley, dark line denotes Earley's 1985 boundaries

boundary with Sonning. There are high points at each end, formerly Noman's Land at the western extreme and Scotchman's Knob at the eastern end where the Great Western Railway begins its famous Sonning Cutting.

At Scotchman's Knob there were formerly two fields jointly called Comp Fields. These names are a survival of the Latin *campus* which means field (Gelling, 1972). The name *Scotchman's Knob* appears in the first edition OS 6 inch (County Map) c.1870, and its meaning is unknown.

North of this ridge the land falls to the Kennet. The northern region was almost entirely taken up with a cluster of 6 (possibly 9) open arable fields and Earley Common Mead. There were also four older enclosures: Shoulder of Mutton Mead by Kennet Mouth, Broken Brow by the Thames, Marquis of Granby and Shepherd's House at the foot of Shepherd's Hill.

The plateau lands of Earley and Bulmershe Heaths drain into north Earley thence into the Thames. Central Earley slopes north-west from the line of Church, Wilderness and Elm Roads. It is bisected south-west to north-east by a stream with three springs at the head of three tributaries making a deep valley (which continued to Culver Lane and so to the Thames and probably bottomed out as it reached the lane). This deep valley may have been Dean Field, covering what is now in part Whiteknights Lake.

South Earley slopes south from the spinal road to the Loddon. It is bisected west to east by a stream with three tributaries heading back to three springs. One rises from Wychwood Crescent/Reeds Avenue area, one from Redhatch Copse and one from Elm Lane which formerly had been dammed to produce a three-acre reservoir. The stream drains through the valley which was firstly dammed to produce a pond in what is now Old Ponds Copse and later to form Maiden Erlegh Lake. The stream drains into the lake and flows down to the Loddon (Pettitt, unpub).

2 Very Early Earley

Earley Before Man

Many people who have seen the changes that have taken place in Earley in recent decades may think that these changes have been dramatic, but they are minor compared with those that have taken place over geological time.

During the last 600 million years the area of land we now know as Earley has been near to the South Pole, on the equator and now 52 degrees north of the equator. The engine that drives this movement, continental drift, is still continuing and so Earley, and therefore your house is still continuing its slow journey around the world.

Also during this period, the Earley area has seen dramatic changes in climate and vegetation from baking hot deserts to frozen tundra, and from steamy tropical swamp forest to warm, clear, coral seas.

If you could travel in time you would be able to see all these amazing changes that have happened on the piece of land that is now occupied by your own living room. In addition you would also witness the amazing story of the evolution of life on earth.

In order to see all these dramatic changes for yourself you will have to leave the present behind, and use your armchair as a time machine, sit back and allow yourself to be transported back in time for a trip of a lifetime.

So close your eyes and brace yourself. As you rapidly travel back in time, the room around you becomes a blur and the year counter on the armrest of your chair starts to go backwards, slowly at first and then faster and faster – 2000 ... 1999 ... 1965 ... 1840 ... 1350 ... 650 ... 1000 BC... 20,000 BC... 1 million years ago (mya)... 100 million years ago... 200, 300, 400, 500, 600 million years ago. Now apply the brake!

We will start our journey from here. As your time machine judders to a halt and you open your eyes, you find yourself in a deep ocean trough on the edge of a large continent. You are now in the geological period known as the pre-Cambrian.

As you look around the dark watery world you find yourself in, you will notice that there is a lot of animal life around you but it consists of very small animals that are very different from the types we see today. If you were to float up to the surface and look towards the nearby Baltic continent, you would see that it was barren rock completely devoid of life. Whilst life had been developing and evolving on the earth for about 3,000 million years by this time, progress had been relatively slow.

By pressing the forward button on your time machine you will start your journey back to the present.

As you pass the 550 million-year mark, you are entering the Cambrian period. The spot you are standing on is approximately 40° south of the equator and the muddy waters you are standing in are cooled by currents flowing up from the Antarctic region. There has been an explosion of new life forms. Many of these are recognisable as similar to modern day corals, sponges, jellyfish, worms, sea urchins and shellfish, but others are less familiar, such as trilobites that scurry around your feet like giant woodlice.

As we move into the Ordovician period at 505 mya, you have drifted further north to about approximately where South Africa is today.

The sea you are in has become shallower and in addition to the Cambrian animals you are now surrounded by the first fishes. As you enter the mid-Ordovician period (450 mya) your head comes above water for the first time as the sea floor rises and the pre-Earley spot you are sitting on becomes dry land for the first time. This land known as the Midland landmass is again barren and devoid of any signs of life.

By the Silurian Period (438 mya) the land has sunk again and you find yourself on a shallow water coral reef. Around you is a dazzling array of corals, sponges and sea lilies. At times the seabed rises sufficiently for the spot you are sitting on to become a coastal seashore. For the first time you will notice that the very first of the land plants are appearing in the form of simple mosses and liverworts.

By the time you reach the Devonian Period (408 mya), Earley is once again dry land. You are now standing on a vast coastal plain divided up by huge river deltas. The climate is hot and wet and the shallow lakes that surround you are full of primitive fishes and surrounded by plants gradually colonising the land. By the end of the Devonian Period, real forests of plants such as ferns and club mosses have developed, the first amphibians have evolved from air-breathing fishes and the first insects have appeared. By this time you have drifted further north and are just south of the equator, on a continent that comprises present day North America and Northern Europe.

As the dial reaches 360 mya you enter the Carboniferous Period. You are now on the equator and as the sea floor in this area has started to sink again, you once again find yourself under water. This time you are surrounded by a myriad of slightly more modern-looking fish, bizarre-looking sharks and large ammonites (a shellfish related to the octopus).

During the latter half of the Carboniferous period the water became shallower and you are now in dense tropical forests composed of giant tree ferns, tree-sized mosses and horsetails, and early conifers. These forests were occupied by strange creatures. If you look to your right you

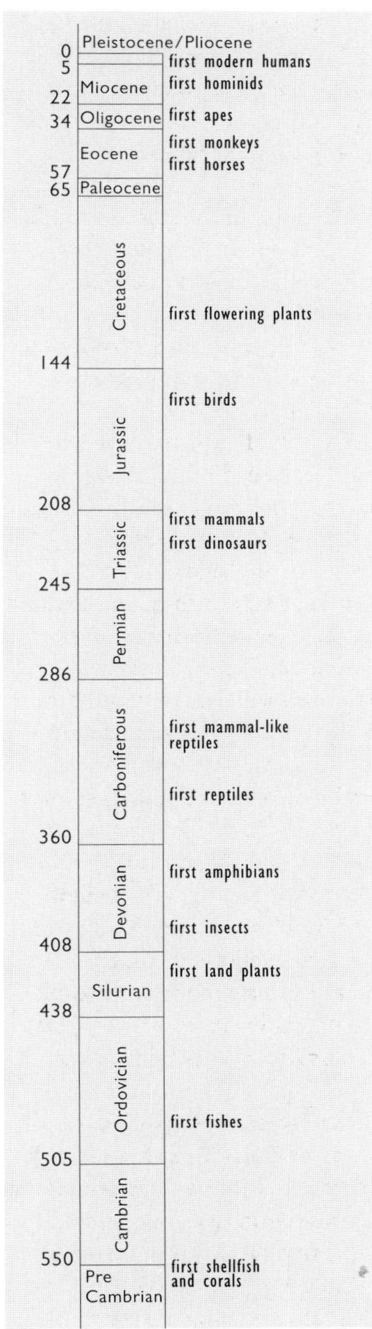

Geological time scale (million years ago) and major evolutionary events

can see a giant millipede over 6ft long and above you flies a dragonfly with a wingspan comparable to modern day seagulls. If we had time to sit and wait you would see many types of amphibians along with the first reptiles and mammal-like reptiles to walk the earth.

Unfortunately we must move on and, as you press the forward button once more, you arrive in the Permian Period (286 mya). Strong compression forces within the ground have forced the land to rise and the luxuriance of the Carboniferous Coal Forests has given way to a hot arid desert. All the continents have now collided to produce one super-continent known as Pangaea. The reptiles are better suited to these conditions than the amphibians, and, as you can see these are becoming dominant in this area. The next period you enter, the Triassic (245 mya), sees little change for our area except that towards the end of this period you may be lucky enough to see one of the first dinosaurs or even catch a glimpse of the first shrew-like mammals that hide away in the shadows to avoid detection by the dominant reptiles and dinosaurs.

Moving forward again you are in the Jurassic Period (208 mya). At the beginning of this period, life-giving tidal seas once again spread over Earley from the south. These seas are warm and clear and are probably similar to the seas around present day Bermuda. Along with the familiar array of fishes and shellfish, the seas that you now find yourself in are dominated by reptiles such as sea crocodiles, dolphin-like and Loch-Ness-Monster-like reptiles, and the squid-like belemnites and ammonites.

It is likely that the land mass to the north and east, the London Island, probably reached the Earley area from time to time and this would have brought the world of the giant dinosaurs to Earley. Whilst the air above you is dominated by flying dinosaurs, the very early birds also begin to appear at this time.

During the next period, the Cretaceous (144 mya), three major events happen. First, most of Britain subsides and is covered by thick deposits of chalk. Second, the first flowering plants appear and begin to displace the long dominant conifers. Third, America starts to separate from Europe as the Atlantic Ocean forms. The end of this period sees the extinction of many of the major groups such as the dinosaurs and the ammonites.

As your time machine transports you even closer to the present you pass through the period 65 mya. At this point you are entering the last six geological periods that represent the modern geological times known collectively as the Cenozoic. Britain has now drifted ever further north and you are on a point of the earth now occupied by present day France.

The environment you find yourself in is a deep muddy marine sea. The sticky goo at your feet is the start of the thick London clay which is gradually settling on the sea floor around you. Amongst the clay you can see a great variety of tropical plant and animal remains. These remains give you a tantalising glimpse of the nearby palmy shores and crocodile-infested swamp inhabited by large mammals and huge land birds now living untroubled by the recently extinct dinosaurs.

By 26 mya Earley has become dry land for the final time. You will notice as the time counter moves on that the climate of Earley changes many times from temperate to cold and back again. In the last 2½ million years of your time travel you travel through more than 20 cold periods. The last few of these cold periods have come to be known as the Ice Age. (They occurred as the Gulf Stream moved south and eastwards towards Spain and Britain's shores were washed by cold polar currents from Greenland. During these cold spells the average annual temperature fell to –6°C to 9°C).

During the most extensive of these glacial periods, the massive ice sheets that covered Britain came as far south as North London. As you look around you, however, you will notice that they never reach Earley, which instead becomes bare arctic tundra with permanently frozen ground.

If you slow your time machine down as you pass through one of these cold/ temperate cycles you will see that, as the climate begins to warm, the vegetation around you changes from arctic tundra, to coniferous forest to temperate forests, to sub-tropical grass-land, to temperate forest again, to coniferous forest, tundra and finally back to arctic ice desert. During some of the warm periods you will notice that the climate has become warm enough for Earley to be inhabited by hippopotamus, elephants and lions! In the colder periods you are more likely to see reindeer, woolly mammoths and cave bears.

As you pass through 10,000 years ago you will see the evidence of the last advance of the ice and by 5000 years ago the climate has become even warmer than it is today cooling down again slightly to today's climate. During this last 10,000 years you will see the tundra gradually giving way to thick, wild woodland.

As you travelled through the last 500,000 years you may have been lucky enough to catch an occasional glimpse of early man from time to time, but you will not have seen modern man *Homo sapiens* until the very end of your journey. At the same time as you see this species becoming more numerous you will notice that the thick, wild wood becomes thinner and thinner before disappearing almost entirely as man makes his presence felt on the landscape around you, chopping down most of the wood for fuel.

As your time machine judders to a halt at the present day, the familiar surroundings of your living room come slowly into focus once again. Sit for a moment to reflect on your momentous journey before preparing yourself a much-needed cup of strong tea.

Prehistoric Earley – Palaeolithic, Mesolithic, Neolithic and Bronze Age

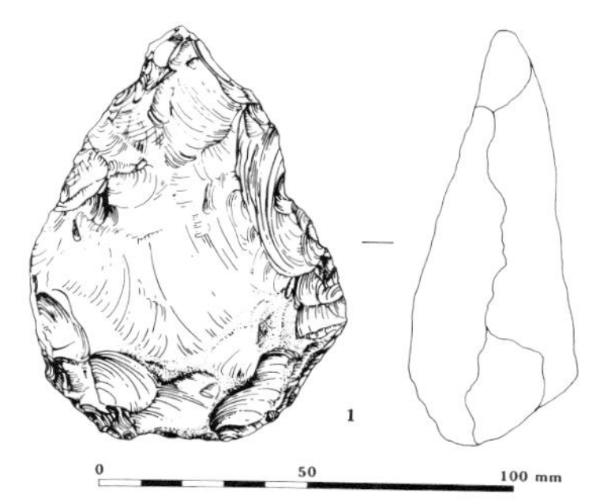

Hand axe found at Thames Valley Park
© *Trust for Wessex Archaeology*

It could be the case that humans from the Palaeolithic period – the Old Stone Age – (up to 400,000 years BC) were foraging for edible vegetation and grubs and hunting wild cattle, deer and elephant in the area now occupied by Earley. In 1961 a young man, Ian Skaife, found a small pointed hand-axe near Maiden Erlegh Lake near excavations at Instow Road.

Other finds include: a St Acheul-type Palaeolithic hand-axe found on the railway cutting in Earley, flint implements from a garden in Elm Lane, a large oval implement from the old brickyard at Kiln Farm, a stone hand axe found in Crockhamwell Road, in 1958 a cordate hand-axe of Late Middle Acheulean type at 12 Fowler Close and a mid-Acheulean cordate hand-axe from a garden in Silverdale Road. Numerous other finds have been made and these are recorded on maps kept for this purpose in Reading Museum (Underhill, 1981). Most finds are thought to come from the late Palaeolithic period around 35,000 years ago. These earliest flint tools include roughly shaped implements, many of which appear to have been used for chopping. Later tools became more sophisticated and included hand axes which were probably used for both meat preparation and hunting.

It seems hard to imagine Earley some 12,000 years ago covered with pine and birch woodland. As the climate warmed and the English Channel was created, the woodlands of southern England had succeeded to elm, alder, lime and oak. This period of history is known as Mesolithic or Middle Stone Age. It is from this time that the first evidence of human settlement and activity in the area is found. Traces of flimsy shelters, made from brushwood and probably covered in hides, have been discovered in north Earley on the site of the old Power Station at the Thames Valley Business Park; this is an exceptionally rare example. This riverside environment would have supported a small band of perhaps fifteen to twenty people on the resources of the area (fish, waterfowl and local edible wild plants) for many months before they had to move elsewhere. Along with larger tools this site also produced many tiny flint flakes known as microliths from the sieved soil which would originally have been hafted as barbs on arrows or spears.

Tools from this era have also been found within Earley including a Mesolithic flint blade found in the garden of 42 Silverdale Road in 1967. These people would have depended on the surrounding woodland for food through hunting animals and gathering edible plants such as nuts, berries and roots. During this period early humans began to change the landscape by the deliberate burning of the woodland. This would have created glades in the forest which would in turn have attracted wild animals to feed on the new growth and thus provided easy hunting. Hazel is known to benefit from increased sunlight to the forest floor which encourages flowering and nut production, thus providing another food source. It seems likely that whilst most of the population at this time were living on gravel islands along the marshy edges of the Thames in North Earley their hunting trips would have taken them into Maiden Erlegh and Lower Earley.

The clearing of woodland for agriculture and the keeping of domesticated animals started around 3400 BC in the Neolithic or New Stone Age with the arrival of ideas and people from the Continent. This clearance may have coincided with an outbreak of Elm Disease (Rackham, 1993). Indeed the spread of early agriculture may have hastened the spread of this devastating disease. Whatever the cause there is widespread evidence of a countrywide decline in elm at this time, a development quickly fol-

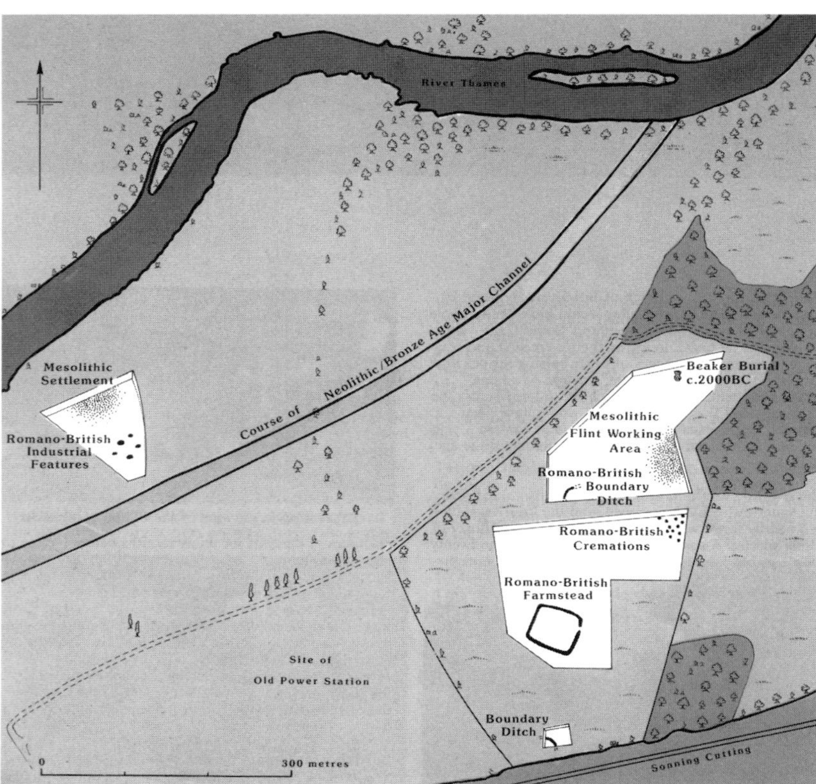

Archaeological features of the dig at the Thames Valley Park, 1988
© Trust for Wessex Archaeology

Above: Bronze Age remains: beaker
© *Trust for Wessex Archaeology*

Below: Arrowheads found at Thames Valley Park
© *Trust for Wessex Archaeology*

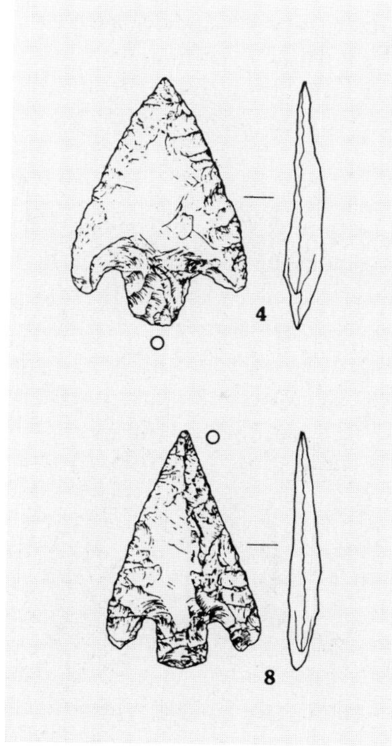

lowed by deforestation. Small areas of wild wood would have been cleared (using stone tools) for cereal growing and to create pasture for cattle, sheep, goats and pigs. The grazing of these animals would have also prevented re-growth from the tree stumps. Again artefacts have been found from this period including two flint blades at 160 Silverdale Road, a single barbed arrowhead at 35 Wychwood Crescent, a hollow scraper at 34 Moor Copse Close and a ground axe at 35 Aldbourne Avenue.

On the Thames Valley Business Park excavations a single broken leaf-shaped arrowhead is the only evidence of man's presence on the site during the Neolithic period. This is a reminder that even after the onset of farming, hunting may have remained an important way of life for many of Earley's residents.

There is archaeological evidence for continued human presence and settlement throughout the Bronze and Iron Ages on the site of the Thames Valley Business Park. It was possibly during the Bronze Age, 2400 – 750 BC, that large areas of Earley and Woodley were cleared for agriculture. The Bronze Age in Britain is best known for the development of the great ritual sites at Stonehenge and Avebury.

Archaeologists working at the Thames Valley Business Park site discovered a shallow scoop, which is believed to be the remains of a grave. The acid soil had destroyed the bones, but associated grave goods were discovered. These included fragments of a highly decorated distinctive type of pot known as a Beaker. These Beakers and the people named after them, the Beaker Folk, appeared in Britain shortly before 2000 BC. Variations of the Beaker pot are known from across western and central Europe, and the example found in the Business Park excavations is similar in style and decoration to others from central southern England and from the Rhineland in Germany.

Also found nearby was a collection of seventeen arrowheads. These had been finely worked and had been barbed and tanged for ease of attachment to a shaft. They were all laid with their tips facing to the south, presumably for some sort of religious reason. Whilst some of these arrowheads may have been produced specifically for the burial, at least two of them had broken tips suggesting some prior usage. A flint knife was also found with them.

The clearance of woodland for farming would have continued during the early Iron Age, about 700 BC, with improved tools such as iron axes and ploughshares. It is possible that much of England had ceased to be wild wood by 500 BC (Rackham, 1993).

On the lower terraces above the flood plain of the Thames an enclosure (0.25ha) covering the Iron Age-Romano-British period was found. Unfortunately a detailed investigation of the unenclosed areas could not be carried out, but it is considered that the field system originated in the

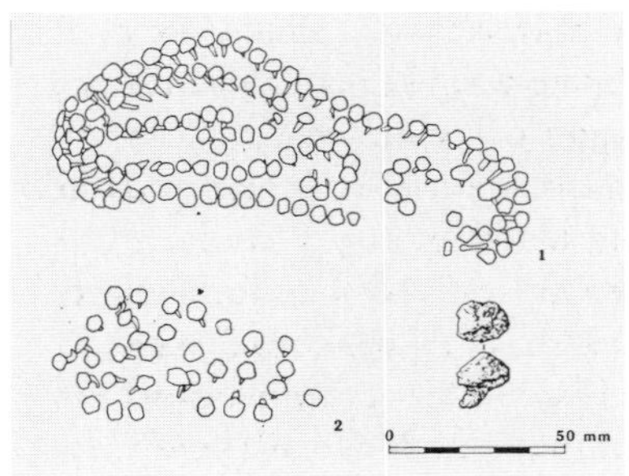

Hobnail boot, Thames Valley Park from the Romano–British period
© *Trust for Wessex Archaeology*

pre-Roman period. Within the enclosure a four-poster structure was recognised but no plan of any building could be reconstructed. From the plant remains (including spelt and emmer wheat and many cornfield weed seeds) and animal remains (butchery waste), pottery and loom weights, the absence of structural evidence and the low intensity of activity it was concluded that this was a seasonal settlement. The flood plain and lower terraces would have been subjected to flooding (Barnes, Butterworth, Hawkes and Smith, 1997).

Pits have been found which would have been used for storing small quantities of foodstuffs, including cereal but also perhaps dried or smoked meat in sufficient quantities for short-term temporary use only.

Other objects found give an interesting insight into everyday life at the site. These included remnants of cooking pots, quern stones for grinding corn, baked clay weights for tensioning loom threads and a simple kiln to supply most of the settlement's requirement for pottery. The sole of a hobnailed-boot from the Romano-British period contained 115 hobnails!

Romans, Saxons and Vikings

Roman pottery, Thames Valley Park
© *Trust for Wessex Archaeology*

The Romans came to England in AD 43, to a land with a fully developed agriculture. Despite the change of the ruling class the Roman conquest probably had an insignificant effect on rural settlements such as Earley. Among Roman artefacts discovered at a number of sites within Earley are a marble urn with a Roman inscription and some 2nd century Roman pottery which was unearthed during work on a building site off Meadow Road. The pottery was presented to Reading Museum by the builder, F. H. Crook, who named the site *Roman Way*.

Beyond the main area of settlement at Thames Valley Park, the archaeologists found evidence of at least three human cremations. These consisted of shallow pits, inside which the ashes were buried in pottery containers.

Although this was not a prestigious development, its occupants had by this time become rich enough to afford some examples of good quality imported pottery. These included French Samianware vessels, a glossy red pottery imported from central and southern France, and other fine tableware from around Lyon.

In addition, large storage vessels known as amphorae were discovered. These were similar to examples known to have been used to store wine from Italy and olive oil from southern Spain.

Further out on the flood plain, on an area of slightly drier land, archaeologists have found evidence for a Romano-British industrial area dating from the early Roman period. This consisted of a series of shallow pits, but, these pits were not of the shape normally used to dispose of domestic rubbish. Some of the pits had internal timber-reinforced steps, which have been preserved in the near-waterlogged conditions. From the quantities of burnt soil and slag found in these pits, it is thought that the pits were connected with small-scale metalworking.

Associated with these pits were the remains of a well, at the bottom of which the archaeologists found the remains of an iron ploughshare with part of its wooden beam attached. This has led to speculation that part of the flood plain had become dry enough by this time to allow some cultivation to take place.

Finds of distinctive 3rd and 4th century pottery suggest that the site continued to be occupied for some time, but it seems that the settlement was in decline during the later years of Roman Britain. By the time Roman rule ended, all traces of this settlement had disappeared and the area was effectively abandoned. During this time the nearest large Roman settlements were at London and Silchester.

In 1890 a cemetery of three levels found opposite the Jack-of-Both-Sides Public House (now the Upin Arms) was thought to be Romano-British followed by pagan and Christian burials, but it has now been shown to be entirely of the post conquest medieval period (Meaney, 1964).

During Saxon times, occupation moved to better drained land to the south of the flood plain and to the developing settlement of Reading. An Anglo-Saxon coin known as a sceatha was discovered in 1961 in a garden in Jubilee Road and a Saxon settlement, dating from about 600 AD, has been discovered near the confluence of the Kennet and Thames. These people were known as the *Readingas,* from which the town of Reading takes its name.

There is no direct evidence of Viking settlement in the Earley area, but it is almost certain that they would have at the very least travelled through Earley when they occupied Reading for a year in 871 and again when the Danish King, Sweyn, burned Reading to the ground in 1006.

3 Earley's Manors and Estates

The Manors of Earley

Whilst most people today have some knowledge of the ancient feudal manors, there is a lot of confusion over the term. This is not surprising as many large houses and their estates and parklands and even much smaller dwellings (such as the Manor House on Church Road) have over the years been somewhat incorrectly known as Manors.

> *The ancient manor as a geographical entity is difficult to map. The term referred to a parcel of lands granted to an individual and such holdings were frequently scattered over villages, or parts of villages, embracing cottages and farmsteads with the farming lands and lanes which related logically to them. The 'manor' as a mediaeval concept was associated not only with ownership and rights in commons, woods and open fields, but also with judicial and administrative authority, and cannot be equated with the concept of an 'estate' or 'park' – the term describing a 'country seat' of the late eighteenth and early nineteenth century. An additional complication is that of the constant process of exchange, purchase, gift, sale and lease of parts of manors and the effect of consolidation, by engrossment and enclosure over the centuries (Lloyd 1977).*

In the past the following manors have all lain partly or completely within the area of land now lying within the modern Earley boundary, Sonning Manor (parts of which became Holme Park), Earley Regis (St Nicholas or Whiteknights), Earley St Bartholomew (later Erleigh Court), Bullmarsh Manor (Bulmershe) and the Manor of Maiden Erlegh.

The Domesday Book states that:

In CHARLTON Hundred
Osbern Giffard holds EARLEY from the King. Dunn held it from King Edward in freehold. Then for 5 hides; now for 2 hides. Land for 7 ploughs. In lordship 1½ ploughs; 4 villagers and 7 smallholders with 2½ ploughs.
1 slave; 2 fisheries at 68d;
meadow, 20 acres;
woodland at 30 pigs,
The value was 100s; later 60s;
now £4.

(Morgan, 1979)

Erleigh St Bartholomew and Erleigh Court

During the reign of King Edward the Confessor, the area of land that was later to become Erleigh Court was held by a Saxon called Don. After the Norman Conquest the land was granted to the Giffords as overlords who held it until 1322 when John Gifford was executed.

The de Erleigh family, who were to become dominant in this area, leased the property from the Giffords. One member of the family, Thomas de Erleigh, is recorded as being keeper or verderer of the King's deer in Windsor Forest. The de Erleighs appear to have sold Erleigh Court to Robert de Charney round about 1320.

The property then passed through several owners, including Henry de Aldryngton before coming into the possession of the Fettiplace family in

1488. The manor came into the family when William Fettiplace, the fourth son of John Fettiplace, squire of Henry VI, from East Shefford in Berkshire, married Elizabeth, the daughter and heiress of Thomas Waring of Erlegh St Bartholomew.

The family continued to own the property, by now known as Erleigh Court, for nearly 220 years until 1708, when Sir Edmund Fettiplace sold it to Sir Owen Buckingham a wealthy merchant and a former Lord Mayor of London. He was Lord Mayor in 1705 and had made part of his fortune by establishing a sail cloth factory in Reading. His son, also called Owen, was a gentleman of the Privy Chamber to George I, and in several parliaments was elected Member of Parliament for Reading. He inherited the estate from his father in 1713 but his tenure was cut short when he was killed in a duel against Richard Aldworth at Stanlake Park in 1720.

The next owner was Richard Manley, an attorney from Cheshire who acquired the estate when he married Sir Owen's niece. He died in 1750. The following year his only daughter married Sir John Powell Pryce of Newtown Hall in Montgomery. Their ownership was not a happy one, however, as failing health and subsequent debts led to a long and complicated series of law-suites. The sorry outcome of all this saw Sir John Powell Pryce dying in a debtors prison in 1777 after losing his sight; his wife dying within the rules of the King's Bench in 1806, and their only son, Sir Edward Manley Pryce, dying in extreme poverty in a field at Pangbourne in 1791.

The final outcome of all this was the enforced sale of the estate at an auction held in one of the Court's own rooms. The successful bidder was a John Bagnall, who bought the property in 1766, but, because of legal complications the estate was not conveyed to him until after his death in 1802. Indeed, it was not until 1849 that a clear title was given to the property.

The Powell Pryces' downfall may not have been brought about by simple financial mismanagement but by a confidence trickster called Francis Skryme.

> *It soon transpired that Sir John's Welsh estate was heavily mortgaged to Lord George Bentinck for many thousands of pounds and when Sir John came to Erleigh Court to live his estates were virtually in the hands of the mortgagees. To remove some of these encumbrances on the Welsh estate, Dame Elizabeth consented to raise money by mortgaging Erleigh Court for £5000 and by another settlement conveyed the estate to two trustees – John Pottinger, Esq., and Richard Simeon, Esq., – for the purpose of preserving the equity of Redemption. Complications increased and Sir John had the misfortune to lose his sight.*
>
> *A certain Francis Skryme, by false and delusive promises of being*

> *able to introduce gentlemen having cash sufficient to help them out of their difficulties, so wormed himself into their confidence that they trust him with their affairs. Skryme then proceeded to … get Sir John confined in the King's Bench Debtors Prison, and while there Skryme, under pretence of getting Sir John's signature to a paper professing to be a security for money then to be advanced, induced this blind prisoner to put his signature to a document which afterwards turned out to be an authority to Skryme to sell Erleigh Court.*
>
> *…in 1766 Skryme, having arranged with John Bagnall, Esq., proceeded to sell. At the sale there were present John Bagnall, Esq., and two Quakers, and the sale taking place at short notice and held in a room at Erleigh Court, no other person but Bagnall bid for the property, and he was declared the purchaser at £9,250*
>
> (Antiquarian Notes of Berkshire, 1885).

After Bagnall's death his property was inherited by his two daughters. One of these daughters, Maria Anne, married Sir William Scott, a famous politician who became Lord Stowell. Under the terms of Bagnall's will the husbands of his daughters were devisees of his estate, thus, as Maria Anne pre-deceased her husband, Lord Stowell inherited Erleigh Court.

A contemporary description of Erleigh Court published in the Rusher's Reading Guide and Berkshire Directory for 1807 (No. VII) described the property thus:

Early Court, the residence of Sir William Scott, Judge of the High Court of Admiralty, stands at a short distance from the high Bath Road, and within two miles of the town of Reading; from which place the house and grounds are viewed as objects strikingly picturesque. The enclosures are not extensive, but disposed with much judgment and having lateley received a considerable augmentation. The house has no distinct character of architecture, but presents the comfortable aspect of a country gentleman's residence in the early part of the last century. A stable belonging to this dwelling is said to have been a free chapel of St Bartholemew, given to the provost and scholars of Queen's College, Oxford, by William Fettiplace Esqr. in 1526. Early Court, tho' not highly elevated, commands a fine view of the Oxfordshire hills, and of that part of Berkshire which skirts the Thames towards Pangbourn and Streatley.

Lord Stowell died at Erleigh Court in 1836 and, as his son had predeceased him, his daughter, Maria Anne (or Marianne) inherited the bulk of the property.

Maria Anne, Sir William Scott's daughter had first married Thomas Townsend, she married Viscount Sidmouth (Henry Addington) as her second husband in 1823. Henry Addington's first wife, Ursula Mary, died in 1811.

William Scott, Lord Stowell (1745–1836)

© Dormer 1912

William Scott was the eldest son of William Scott, a coal shipper of Newcastle upon Tyne. Because of the strife in the north caused by the Rebellion and the Pretender's army marching from Edinburgh to London, a route which took them through Newcastle, William's mother was sent to stay with her parents at her father's country house in Heworth in the County of Durham. William Scott and his twin sister, Barbara, were born there. William attended the Royal Grammar School in Newcastle and because he had been born in the County of Durham he became eligible for a scholarship to Oxford.

At Oxford he met Dr Samuel Johnson and they became lifelong friends, and he also met Henry Addington, who was also to become a friend. (Addington married Scott's daughter Maria Anne, after the death of his first wife).

William Scott's father died in 1776 and left him a considerable estate. He became a law student and went on to have a successful practice. In 1781 William Scott married Maria Anne Bagnall, the eldest daughter of John Bagnall of Erleigh Court. They had four children. William Scott was knighted in 1788 and later became a Member of Parliament, representing the University of Oxford.

He entered the House of Lords in 1821 on the coronation of George IV, taking the title Baron Stowell from Stowell Park, an estate in Gloucestershire which he had purchased some years previously.

As his health deteriorated he relinquished his various offices and from 1828 onwards he lived mostly at Erleigh Court, with Lord and Lady Sidmouth, his daughter, spending much of their time with him. Lord Stowell died on 28th January 1836 and was buried in Sonning Church. As Lord Stowell's son pre-deceased him the bulk of the property went to his daughter, Lady Sidmouth, for the rest of her life.

John Scott, Lord Eldon (1751–1838)

© Dormer 1912

John Scott, the younger brother of William Scott, was also educated at Oxford due to the generosity of his older brother, who persuaded his father to let him study there under his tutelage rather than stay in Newcastle and enter the family business. He became Lord Chancellor at the time of the Addington Government and it is said that he spent much time with his brother at Erleigh Court. He was a benefactor of the Royal Berkshire Hospital and there is a square near there named after him.

Lady Sidmouth pre-deceased her husband, he therefore inherited Erleigh Court from her. Viscount Sidmouth died in 1844 but the estate remained in the Sidmouth family until the 1930s, being leased to tenants. By 1932 Erleigh Court was empty and was demolished in 1935 after the estate was sold for building development. Regrettably the old chapel of St Bartholomew, which was in existence by the 13th Century and once stood to the east of the old mansion, has also gone. The advowson (the right to select the priest) had descended with the manorial rights which William Fettiplace had given to The Queen's College Oxford in 1526. The site of the old chapel of St Bartholomew and the Manor of Erleigh Court lay between Pitts Lane and London Road (approximately where Sidmouth Grange Close/ Hilltop Road are today).

The loss of this house was yet another part of the almost wholesale destruction of Earley's heritage that has taken place over the last seventy years. The charm and beauty that was lost when Erleigh Court was bull-dozed to the ground was accurately described and predicted by Ernest Dormer when he wrote in 1912:

> *The delights of the Court are perhaps more potent on a summer evening, and it is difficult to imagine a more peaceful scene or to check the pen in its too eager flow. When the sun is lowering in the west and the rooks call noisily from their high stations of*

Below: The front of Erleigh Court
Opposite top: The hall, Erleigh Court
Opposite below: Tapestry room, Erleigh Court
© *Dormer 1912*

immemorial antiquity in the park; when the windows throw back like deep dark lakes the golden glint of the sun and across the lands is borne the sound of the bells of Sonning Church to add a restfulness and seek a share in the pervading peace – then is the hour serene. For in the old parish church of Sonning are buried many of the long past proprietors of this manor house, and age has bred an affinity that time will not dispel until the Court and its neighbourhood lose their individuality in the demands of a growing community westward.

Earley's Lost Buildings: Erleigh Court – The House

The house called Erleigh Court stood on a ridge overlooking the Thames Valley, bounded by Pitts Lane to the south. Dormer (1912) suggested that a house had stood there since before the Norman Conquest. There is evidence that there was a house there when the Dean of Sarum came on one of his visitations in 1220 and commented on the Chapel of St Bartholomew that was near the house. The house with its long sloping roofs is shown on the 1669 map.

Dormer talked about the south side of the house being delightfully quaint and irregular. Parts of it dated back to Tudor times. Some time during the eighteenth century, the front of the house was repaired and altered. Bayed windows were thrown out on the east and on the north, a pediment was built up from the edge of the roof and a Georgian porch supported by four columns was constructed. The roof was re-timbered and re-tiled.

The photographs of the interior show a comfortable house that was not large. One of the rooms contained a tapestry woven at Mortlake depicting scenes in eastern countries. It is not known how the tapestry came to the house. In about 1905 the then owner of the house, Captain Rushby, had the panels carefully repaired and re-hung. The tapestry was removed in about 1932. Underneath was some 18th century painted pine panelling. Drawn in pencil on this panelling were pictures of 19th century lawyers and friends of Lord Stowell.

The house was approached from London Road by an elm lined narrow drive through white gates. The grounds of the Court covered all of what is now Chiltern Crescent, Delamere Road, Hilltop Road, Whitegates Lane, Byron Road, Milton Road and Erleigh Court Gardens (the site of the kitchen garden). On the south side there were tennis lawns, formerly a pond, connected with the farmhouse.

In 1935 the Erleigh Court Estate was purchased by a builder, Mr John Bridges, for residential development. The gardens were ploughed up, the walls knocked down, the lake drained and new roads built and Erleigh Court disappeared.

Sidmouth Grange

Sidmouth Grange, formerly Earley Court Farm, was next door to Erleigh Court. The house burnt down in the mid-1980s. Houses now occupy the site.

© *Berkshire Chronicle*, 10 May 1957

Bulmershe Manor – Woodley House – Woodley Lodge – Bulmershe Court

The early history of the Manor of Belvershall, Bulnassh, Bulmarsh or Bulmershe Court is unclear. It was probably formed partly out of the Manor of Sonning and partly out of the manor of Earley. The manor was not mentioned in the *Domesday Book* and would seem to have been carved from the old Earley Manor sometime during the twelfth century, when land at Buleneirs was exchanged between the Bishop of Salisbury and John de Erlegh. The de Erlegh family owned two manors mentioned in the *Domesday Book*, the Manors of Erlegh St Nicholas and Erlegh St Bartholomew (VCH, 1923).

The Victoria County History mentions *a manor of Belvershal called Bulnassh* in 1447 being in the possession of John Lovell who granted it to Richard Earl of Salisbury, and follows through its various owners until the 15/16th century when it was granted to Reading Abbey. The Manor of Bullmarsh was passed to the crown when the Abbey was dissolved and sold to William Gray of Reading in 1547 for the sum of £246.16s.8d. William Gray was Member of Parliament for Reading in 1547.

It is unclear as to the exact location and extent of William Gray's Bullmarsh Manor which included Mockbeggar. We can only speculate that it was the same location as the 285-acre estate bought by Henry Addington in 1789.

Henry Addington was speaker of the House of Commons when he purchased the estate; he was well connected with the political elite. He regularly entertained the Prime Minister, William Pitt, and many other well known statesmen of the day at his summer residence.

The manor house, Bullmarsh Court, was in a state of considerable decay so Addington decided to build a new mansion Woodley House on the western side of the estate.

Addington was active in setting up the volunteer force, the Woodley Cavalry, which consisted of three officers and fifty-four men with Addington in charge. The Woodley Cavalry had their barracks in a row of old cottages in Church Road, Earley, and met at the Three Tuns Inn to plan their many activities. The Cavalry contained representatives from many of the leading families in the county. George III, the Prime Minister William Pitt and most of the Royal family inspected the troops in 1799 and were entertained at Woodley House (Verey, Sampson, French and Frost, 1994).

In 1801 James Joseph Wheble purchased the estate which now went under the name of Woodley Lodge. The estate remained in the Wheble family until James St L. Wheble and his brother Major Tristram Joseph Wheble moved down to Hungerford Lodge in 1908 and Woodley Lodge was sold to Mr Rushbrooke of Bedford.

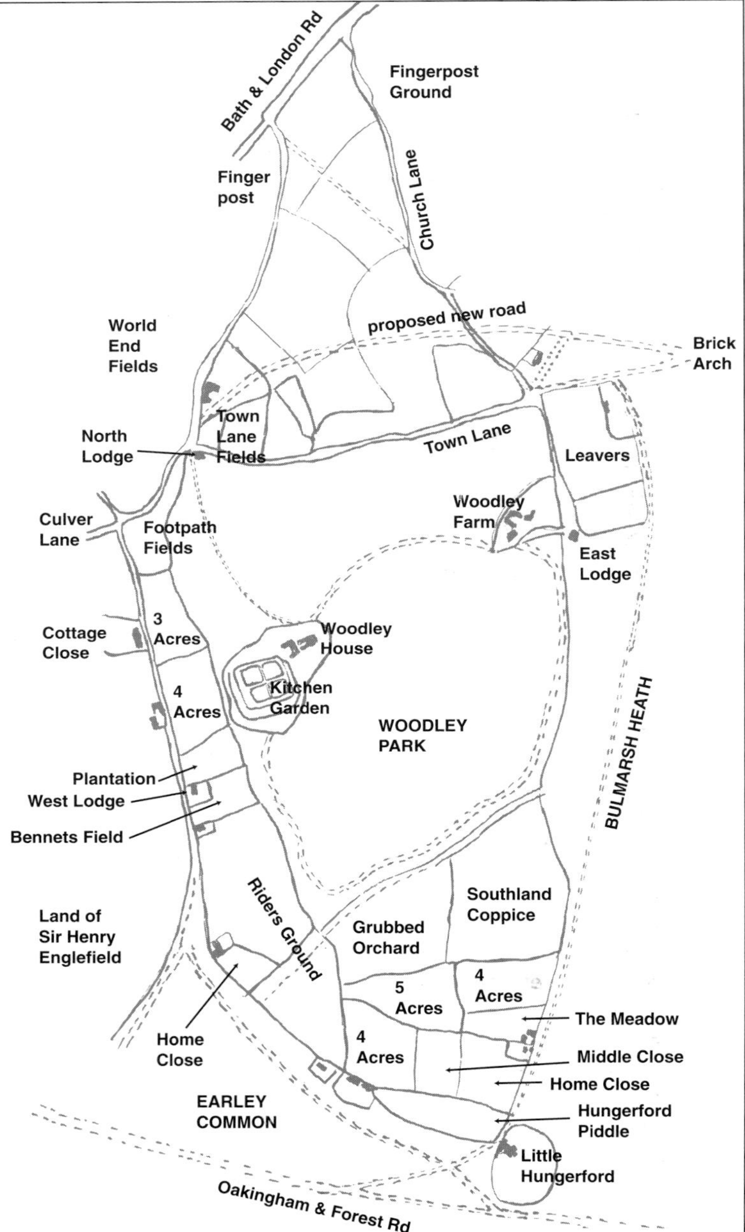

Map 5: Drawing from *Rough Draught of a Plan of Woodley Park, Lands and Woods adjoining situate in the Parish of Sonning, in the County of Berks, belonging to the Right Honourable Henry Addington. Taken by T. Pride, Surveyor.* BRO D/EDO P.2

Henry Addington – Viscount Sidmouth (1757–1844)

© Dormer 1912

Henry Addington was the eldest son of Dr Anthony Addington who had a medical practice in London Street from about 1744. Dr Addington married Mary Hiley, daughter of the Headmaster of Reading School. They moved to London in 1754 and Henry Addington was born in 1757.

Henry Addington was educated at Cheam, Winchester and Oxford. It is thought that he attended Reading School for a short while before going on to Winchester though there is no definite proof. On leaving Oxford, having taken his BA degree in 1778, he studied law. Henry Addington and Sir William Pitt had been friends since childhood and, under Pitt's influence, Henry Addington began to pursue a legal career and was elected MP for Devizes in 1784. When Pitt formed his first administration at the end of 1784 Addington was one of his greatest supporters, though he rarely spoke in Parliament. Addington was elected Speaker in 1789, an office he held for eleven years.

Addington spent much of his time away from Parliament at Woodley Lodge, which he had bought, and devoted much time to the Woodley Cavalry.

Henry Addington became Prime Minister in 1801, but it was only a brief reign as there was much political unrest at this time, the issue of Ireland and Catholic emancipation being the main sources of the domestic problems coupled with the ill health of George III. Addington was regarded as a dull and mediocre Minister and his administration was fraught with problems, which caused a rift in the relationship between him and Pitt, and he resigned in 1803. In 1805 he was created Lord Sidmouth. Later he was appointed secretary of the Home Department, a post he held for ten years. He was a stern administrator and there was much unrest at this time. He retired from office in 1821 but remained in the cabinet until 1824 and seldom attended Parliament after that. He continued to oppose Catholic emancipation and voted against the Reform Bill (1832) the last time he took part in a vote in person.

His first wife, Ursula, died in 1811, and in 1823 he married again, Maria Anne (Marianne) Townsend, widow of Mr Thomas Townsend and daughter of his good friend Lord Stowell of Erleigh Court. Lord and Lady Sidmouth spent much of their time with Lord Stowell at Erleigh Court until his death in 1836. Lady Sidmouth inherited the bulk of his property including Erleigh Court from her father. This great increase in wealth caused Lord Sidmouth to resign the crown pension which had been granted to him in 1817.

Lord Sidmouth's generous gift in August 1836 of four acres of land in London Road (on which stood an Inn called the Row Barge) from his Erleigh Court estate, became the site of the Royal Berkshire Hospital which opened on 27th May 1839. Although Dormer (1912) records that Miss Mitford attributes the gift as being from his wife, but that she told everyone that it was Lord Sidmouth's gift. He also contributed three acres of land for the site of Earley St Peter's Church and a donation of £500. His wife left £2,000 to the hospital and £1,250 towards the endowment of St Peter's Church.

Lady Sidmouth died in 1842; Lord Sidmouth lived to see the completion of the church, dying in 1844.

Although Lord Sidmouth owned Erleigh Court he spent much of his time at White Lodge, Richmond where he died. He is buried at Mortlake.

There are several streets near the hospital which are named after him.

The estate ran into difficulties before the First World War and by the time it went up for auction in 1926 most of it had been leased to a number of tenants.

Mr Bernard Short owned Woodley Lodge from 1930 and the Ministry of Defence used it during the war to house English and American troops.

The house was derelict by the time it was pulled down in 1962 to make way for Bulmershe College which is now part of The University of Reading. All that remains of the original building is part of the kitchen garden wall.

James Wheble

James Wheble bought Bulmershe Estate for over £27,000 in 1801. He is believed to have been on his way to buy a property in Wiltshire when he saw that Woodley Park Estate, as it was then known, was up for sale. It has been reported on several occasions that he bought the property that had once belonged to his father. The area of land inherited by his father in 1771 is unclear. It has been suggested that Richard Wheble purchased land in Sonning in 1760 and his son James Wheble of Kensington inherited it in 1771 and sold it in 1785. Dormer (1944) identifies the lands involved as being about forty-one acres in total situated in the Liberty of Woodley in Sonning, Berks, so whether the land bought by James Wheble in 1801 was the same as his father had inherited is unclear.

James Wheble and his family increased the size of his estate over the years, purchasing neighbouring land making his estate 1,081 acres, excluding Woodley Lodge and its kitchen and pleasure gardens. James had fourteen children, who were all christened in the Woodley chapel. He had five daughters by his first wife, Mary Talbot, between 1803 and 1812. Mary died in 1814 aged thirty-four and in August the following year James married Mary O'Brien. Between 1816 and 1829 Mary bore nine children, the last being a boy called Daniel O'Connell Wheble. Mary died five years later in 1834 aged forty-six. Both of James's wives were buried in Winchester Catholic Cemetery. During her time at Woodley Lodge the second Mrs Wheble suffered the loss of six children, four of James's daughters from his first marriage and two of her own. James did not appear to have taken much part in Woodley affairs, but did concern himself with vestry business in Earley. He was active in managing his business of land and property and negotiating the enclosure award, as well as managing his farm and supervising the landscaping and planting of his new park. His main contribution to the area was the founding of a Catholic Church in Reading; he donated the land on which St James' Church was built as well as the school beside it. The architect engaged in the design of the church was Welby Pugin. The church was not completed until 1840, the year James Wheble died. He was buried in Winchester alongside his wives.

There does not seem to be evidence to suggest James erected any significant buildings in Earley or Woodley other than those on his estate.

Top: The derelict Woodley Lodge before its demolition in 1962
Bottom: The Orangery, Woodley Lodge 1962)

Squire Wheble and Lady Catherine

James Joseph Wheble inherited the estate in 1840 and married Catherine Elizabeth, second daughter of the third Earl of Howth, in 1850. Catherine bore nine children between 1853 and 1869 and employed a large number of domestic servants. In 1851 there are reported to have been eleven servants resident in Woodley Lodge. James is reported to have taken a farmer's interest in local affairs and was present at all the vestry meetings held between 1854 and 1882. The Catholic Hierarchy Act of 1851 restored the Roman Catholics to full equality and in 1854 James Wheble was appointed High Sheriff of Berkshire. James developed a canal below his home farm for fishing and he regularly led his hounds.

In 1851 he added to his mansion house a billiard room, bought from the Great Exhibition in London. By the time of his death in 1884 James and Catherine had fully established the Wheble family amongst the land-owning gentry of the country. Catherine died in 1913.

Above: Drawing of the back of Woodley Lodge
Below: Hungerford Lodge, 1926 sales catalogue, Martin & Pole, Nicholas

Captain James St Lawrence Wheble

When James St Lawrence inherited the Bulmershe estate in 1884, it was almost completely self-contained. It had its own water-tower, blacksmith's shop, pump house and engine room, wagon sheds, granary, stables, coach-house and numerous other buildings as well as a gasholder.

Captain James never married and remained at the Mansion house until 1912 when he moved to Hungerford Lodge with his brother Major Tristram. He was a J.P. and saw active service in the First World War with the Royal Artillery. He was wounded and returned home at the end of the war with a limp. He remained at Hungerford Lodge with his brother until his death in 1925. When his brother died in 1926 Bulmershe Court and Hungerford Lodge were sold by auction.

In the Domesday Book it states:

EARLEY. Aelmer held it in free-hold from King Edward.
Then for 5 hides; now for 4 hides.
Land for 6 ploughs.
In lordship 1 plough;
6 villagers and 1 smallholder with 3 ploughs.
2 slaves; 1 site in Reading;
2 fisheries at 7s 6d;
meadow, 20 acres; woodland at 70 pigs.
Value before 1066, 100s;
later and now 50s.

(Morgan, 1979)

Earley Whiteknights (Regis, St Nicholas)

The de Erlegh family held Earley Regis, Earley St Nicholas directly from the King from about 1160 until 1362. The family, who also owned land in Dorset, Somerset and Ireland, were of sufficient status to hold a number of highly important offices under the crown. Henry de Erlegh, for example, in 1251 was sheriff for the counties of Dorset and Somerset, as well as being constable of the castles of Corfe and Sherborne.

John de Erlegh, who died sometime between 1161 and 1165 and was married to Adela, was the first of the family line to have possession of the Manor. He was succeeded by his son William, who was married to Aziria and is perhaps best known as the founder of Buckland Priory. There are also records showing that he was involved in land exchange deals in the Sonning Park area with the Bishop of Salisbury.

Their son, John de Erlegh, who married Sybil, received in 1197 a quitclaim from Robert de Erlegh's daughter Maud, for *two hides of land in Earley, Reading and Sonning*. He was succeeded by their son, yet another John, who died without issue in 1231.

John's younger brother, Henry de Erlegh, was the next holder of the Manor. The historical records get a little less clear here, and there may possibly have been a Richard between the Henry who inherited in 1231 and a Henry who died in 1272 leaving a son Philip and a widow Clemencia (VCH,1923).

The manor descended to Philip de Erlegh who inherited it in 1272. He died in 1275, leaving an infant son, John. Feudal law at that time meant that until John came of age the manor reverted to the Crown. This led to two Royal Orders being issued from Westminster. The first instructed the Crown's escheator to *assign a dower to Philip's widow, Roesia, subject to her taking an oath not to marry without the King's consent*. However, rather than comply with this Order, Roesia and Geoffrey de Wroxhale chose to pay a fine of £20 for their trespass in intermarrying without a licence. The second Order instructed the escheator to *take into the King's hands the lands of Philip de Erlegh, tenant-in-chief, to inquire as to their yearly value and to find the name and age of the heir.*

The manor did not remain empty, however, whilst the infant John de Erlegh was growing up. Thomas Cantilupe, a former Chancellor of the University of Oxford and the last Englishman to be canonised before the Reformation, was appointed as the Bishop of Hereford in 1275. In order that he would have a convenient place to stay on his many trips to London whilst on the King's business, he asked the King *to commit to him, until the heirs of Henry de Erley, tenant in chief, come of age, the manor of Erley near Reading* The King granted him custody in exchange for a fine of two hundred pounds and an annual payment of sixteen marks. Later Cantilupe was also given permission to include in his will *the custody of Erleye, during the minority of the heir, as well as his grain and goods in the said manor.*

Upon coming of age in 1292, John de Erlegh made his formal homage to the King, who instructed the Treasurer and Barons of the Exchequer to reinstate his inheritance.

John de Erlegh held the manor at the end of the thirteenth century and served under Edward I in the army in Scotland. He was known as the White Knight (*Johannas de Arle dictus Whythlenyght*), possibly because of the colour of the armour he wore and also to distinguish him from John de Erlegh who held Early St Bartholomew by 1316 and from a sub-tenant of the same name. And so the manor became known as Earley Whiteknights.

In 1314 he paid twenty shillings for a licence to transfer seven and a half acres of land to Richard Kymbale, parson of the Chapel of St Nicholas, Erle, and his successors; *to make provision for the celebration of divine service in the said chapel for all Christian souls.*

Whilst it seems most likely that the name Whiteknights originated from the nickname of John de Erlegh, a number of other charming stories as to the origin of the name also exist. The following account of the origin of the name is considerably more romantic and tragic than the more commonly accepted theory, but alas it does seem to lack authenticating evidence. A lack of documentary proof however, would be a very poor reason for depriving future generations of such a dramatic account.

> *Visitors strolling in at the Earley Gate entrance to Whiteknights must be puzzled by the two ruined fragments of brickwork they see on the right which stand incongruously beside the wartime build-*

Gothic chapel, Whiteknights Park
Postcard dated August 1909

ings that are now part of the University. Others may wonder at the name itself: were there really white knights, and what was their connection with Reading? It turns out that the name and the brick-work are interconnected, and to unravel the long and intriguing story we have to go back over eight centuries. For the full version you must consult the Reading Mercury and Berkshire County paper of 2 July 1904, as outlined by Ernest Dormer.

There he tells us how one of William the Conqueror's most highly regarded warriors, Gilbert de Montalieu, was granted possession of the manor of Herlie (Earley) and, later, the governorship of Reading itself. There he fell in love with Edith, daughter of a Saxon Chief, and, seeing her one day in the arms of another was so incensed by jealousy that he shot the man dead with an arrow. Alas, he turned out to be Edith's brother, and Gilbert's remorse was such that he laid down his arms forever and fled the scene, making a pilgrimage to Jerusalem as penance for his rash action. But he could never forget it, and years later he returned to die over the grave of Edith's brother, carrying a letter in which be begged to be buried in an adjacent grave and that a white column and chapel be erected on the site. Thus came into being the White Knight's grave and the chapel dedicated to St Nicholas that persisted on the same site for centuries, as is attested by various deeds relating to its upkeep. Opinions divide on whether the white refers to the chapel column, or to the costume of the knights of the period.

Where, then, was this ancient chapel, and does anything survive to support the legend? For an answer we must jump on ahead to a much later date when the manor and estate was in the possession of the Marquis of Blandford (later 5th Duke of Marlborough). In 1819 the Marquis commissioned a sumptuous account of Whiteknights by Barbara Hofland with illustrations by her husband Thomas (Soames, 1987)

The site of the ancient Chapel of White Knights…stands near the Wokingham Road lodge, on the highest part of the Estate. The Duke rebuilt the remains of the ancient edifice in the ornamental Gothic style, but very little of it now remains. A flint wall with a spectral window alone stands to mark the spot of the White Knight's Grave (Hofland, 1819).

Hoflland's admirable engraving shows this scene. It remains only to add that artificial ruins were fashionable at the time, and from contemporary maps it is clear that this represented a façade only, to be viewed in its semicircle of trees from the manor house, and was never a complete building. The Duke's chapel ruin survives to this day with loss of its surface stucco and other ornaments, and remains can be glimpsed in several old photographs. Local artist Reg Ford made a painting of it in the nineteen-thirties, when all that remained were two separate sections of wall in bare brickwork and three windows. Older readers familiar with Whiteknights in pre-war days may remember it in this form. The ultimate near disaster came during the war when the area was cleared to make way for the present buildings. One wonders who stopped the demolition in the nick of time, before the last clue to the location of the lost chapel of Whiteknights disappeared forever.

So as we gaze at this unprepossessing monument, we can foster the intriguing thought that beneath its stark brickwork lie the foundations of the original chapel, perhaps with its white column, too, and – who knows? – the mortal remains of the White Knight and the victim of his outburst of jealousy. Certainly it would seem to be a site worthy of investigation. An instrument survey was, indeed, undertaken as a student exercise in 1973, and gave promise of hidden revelations, but was never followed up. Or are we just pursuing a myth? Dormer himself added a final mystery. When he came to write the history of Earley in 1944 he made no reference to his account of the legend forty years earlier, and declares that the site of the ancient chapel is unknown! (Rowley pers. comm.)

John de Erlegh was succeeded by his son John upon his death in 1324. This John died in 1337, leaving a two year old son also called John! However, before his death he had granted the manor to Humphrey de la Rokele and his wife Maud for the duration of their lives.

In 1362 John de Erlegh, then aged 28 was given licence to *grant two messuages and 19 acres of land to Robert de Erlegh and his wife Joan, retaining a messuage and two carucates*. Fairly soon after this the lands appear to have been sold by him to Henry de Aldryngton.

Whilst fighting alongside the Black Prince in Spain, a John de Erleigh was captured and taken prisoner. The raising of the ransom demanded for his release is said to have impoverished the estate leading to its eventual change of hands to Henry Aldryngton.

Henry de Aldryngton already owned other properties in the surrounding area. Aldryngton's wealth was enhanced when he married the wealthy heiress, Elizabeth Loveday. Upon his death in 1375, his son John inherited the manor and chose to grant the reversion of the lands to John Olney of Weston and Richard Bruns of Harwell, subject to his mother's interest in it.

However, history followed another path. Henry's widow, Elizabeth, married John de Shilford three years after her first husband's death. Following Elizabeth's remarriage, John Olney and Richard Bruns renounced their interest in the manor in favour of Elizabeth, her new husband John de Shilford and the heirs of her son John. Unfortunately for Elizabeth and John this renunciation was made without first obtaining a royal licence and as a consequence they were compelled to pay the King a fine of one hundred shillings and sue pardon for the trespass they had committed before it could be ratified. In the same year they paid the King a further twenty shillings for a licence to settle the manor on themselves in fee tail (or entail: the settlement of lands on persons successively so that it cannot be bequeathed at pleasure). At this time they also made provision for the succession of the manor to their daughter Constance and her husband Thomas Overeye, a London clothier, and Constance's heirs.

In 1413, having no son, Constance and Thomas paid five marks for a licence to settle *the manor of Erlegh Whiteknyghtes upon themselves for life with remainder to their eldest daughter Agnes and her husband John Beke and the heirs of John.* So began a period of more than 150 years when the manor was passed continuously down the Beke's family line. This domination got off to a shaky start, however, with John Beke dying at much the same time as Thomas Overeye. This led to Agnes marrying her second husband, William Bisshopeston. In 1443, twelve years after Thomas Overeye's death, Agnes and her second husband renounced the manor in favour of John Beke's son Thomas. In 1446 Thomas Beke and his wife Isabel obtained a royal licence settling the manor on themselves and their heirs.

As well as having extensive land holdings, the Beke family also held a number of important positions in the area. John Beke had been in the household of King Henry IV and Thomas Beke was elected Mayor of Reading three times (1458–59, 1462–63 and 1476–77) and between 1451 and 1461 he was the Borough's Member of Parliament.

Thomas's heir, Marmaduke, did not live long enough to inherit, so upon the death of Thomas's wife, Isabel, the manor passed to his grandson, another Thomas. This Thomas was one of the Examiners, along with Abbot Hugh Faringdon, the Mayor of Reading and two other citizens in 1536; when a number of local people were thought to have had an involvement in the Pilgrimage of Grace – an event that according to historians was *so nearly disastrous to the throne of Henry VIII.*

Upon Thomas's death the manor passed to his son Mamaduke, who, having no heirs, in turn passed it on in 1552 to his nephew Henry. Henry died in 1580. There are two inscriptions dedicated to him in Shinfield Church. Henry had no sons and so the next occupiers were his daughter Elizabeth and her husband Hugh Speke. The Beke's family's association with the manor finally came to an end in 1606, when Hugh and Elizabeth Speke sold the manor.

The Manor of Erlegh Whiteknights was sold to Francis Englefield of Wootton Bassett in Wiltshire and William Wollascot of Brimpton for £7,500.

Sir Francis Englefield died 1596

Sir Francis Englefield was Lord of the Manor of Englefield and is said to have owned land in Whitley. Sir Francis, who had served under Henry VIII, was a devout Catholic. He served as Sheriff of Berkshire in 1547 and was made Knight of the Carpet at the Coronation of Edward VI. He became one of the chief officers of the household of Princess Mary, and was rewarded for his loyalty when Mary became Queen. When Mary died in 1558, Sir Francis refused to pledge an oath of allegiance to Queen Elizabeth I as he was a Catholic. He fled to Spain and in 1585 much of his property and other possessions were forfeited to the Crown, though he managed to retain his estate in Wootton Bassett.

His brother, Sir John Englefield, was Lord of the Manor of Wootton Bassett, Wiltshire.

Sir Francis was unmarried and tried to leave the Englefield estate to his nephew, Sir Francis, son of Sir John. However this failed as the estate had been forfeited. He died in 1596 whilst still in exile.

Francis Englefield of Wootton Basset died 1631

Francis Englefield was the son of Sir John Englefield of Wootton Basset, and nephew of Sir Francis Englefield who had lost much of his lands and possessions in his support of Mary Queen of Scots.

Sir Francis is recorded as living at Hartley Court, Shinfield from 1606 to 1609. In 1606 Sir Francis and William Wollascot purchased the Manor of Erlegh Whiteknights for £7,500. He later bought Sir William's interest in the estate.

He was created a baronet in 1611.

In 1630 Sir Francis built a house using bricks made from the clay from pits which were at the bottom of the Shinfield vicarage garden. This house was originally called Shinfield Park but later it became known as Goodrest. The house was next to (on the Reading side of) the old RAF station which is now the European Meteorological Centre, and now forms part of Crosfields School.

His second son, Francis, inherited the Wooton Bassett estate.

His third son, Thomas, married Mary, the daughter of William Wollascot.

Sir Francis died in 1631, leaving the Manor of Erlegh Whiteknights to his fifth son, Anthony.

Anthony Englefield d.1667

Anthony was the 5th son of Francis Englefield, he died in 1667 and was succeeded by his son, another Anthony.

There is a story that the Englefields, being Royalists, gave shelter to the King after the battle of Newbury (in 1643, during the Civil War). The King stayed with the Englefields at Shinfield Park and stated that he had had a good rest there. After this Sir Anthony Englefield re-named the house Goodrest. Dormer, however, does not accept this story.

The Englefields were an ancient family who can be traced back at least as far as the reign of King Egbert, early in the ninth century. They had held land in Berkshire for a long time and by the 12th century were the Lords of the manor of Englefield, living in Englefield House to the west of Reading. As the family were recusants, much of their property was forfeited during the reign of Elizabeth I.

Upon the death of Sir Francis Englefield in 1596 whilst he was still in exile, the line of succession passed first to his brother John, Lord of the manor of Wootton Basset in Wiltshire and then to his nephew Francis who had purchased Hartley Court in Shinfield. Hartley Court was built by Thomas Beke in about 1514 when a new farm was formed at Shinfield from lands belonging to the Abbey (Doble 1961).

Sir Francis and William Wollascott purchased the Manor of White-knights in 1606. In 1619 he bought Sir William's share in the estate for £5,600, thus becoming the sole owner of the estate. His fifth son

Anthony Englefield died 1711

Anthony Englefield was a lover of poetry and literature. In his time at Whiteknights he invited writers and poets to the house. William Wycherley, John Gay and Alexander Pope all visited Whiteknights. Pope, who lived in nearby Binfield was a frequent visitor.

Sir Anthony's daughter, Martha, married Lister Blount of Mapledurham and they had two daughters, Theresa and Martha, who were frequent visitors at Whiteknights, they were great friends of Pope and knew many of the other members of the literary world.

The Blounts of Mapledurham and the Wollascot, Hyde and Wheble families were all notable recusants. Anthony died in 1711.

Whiteknights, The Seat of Sr Hen. Englefield Bart. From an Originall Drawing by Govr. Pownall. 1776. © *The University of Reading*

Anthony Englefield inherited the Whiteknights estate. Dormer (1944) states that Anthony was the fourth son but Rylands (1907) records him as the fifth son; it seems to depend on the number of surviving sons at the time the information was recorded

The Englefields are recorded as being at Whiteknights in the 1640s and the estate remained in the hands of the Englefield family until 1783. Under their long stewardship, the development of the estate took a back seat to their main interests of religion, literature and science. The family were devout Catholics and maintained a Catholic priest. This devotion to a faith that by then was outlawed meant that they did not take an active part in local affairs and largely confined their socialising to other local families of the same faith.

When Henry Charles Englefield inherited Whiteknights his father's will stated that the manor should pass to his sons Henry Charles and

Sir Henry Englefield died 1780

Anthony Englefield (died in 1711) was succeeded by his eldest surviving son Henry. Henry died in 1720 and was succeeded by his son, also Henry (2nd)

In 1728, Henry (2nd) inherited the title held by his distant cousin, Sir Charles Englefield, succeeding him as sixth baronet. Soon after this, despite the establishment's anti-Catholic stance, he installed a chaplain at Whiteknights who surreptitiously also served the needs of the other Catholics in Reading and its surrounds.

It may have been during this Sir Henry's time that the Whiteknights estate was laid out with some formal gardens but little is known of the estate at this time.

Henry Charles Englefield died 1822

Henry Charles (3rd) inherited the estate from his father, Henry (2nd). He became the seventh and final Englefield baronet.

Sir Henry Englefield's interests lay in science and antiquities. He had the honour to be elected as a Fellow both of the Royal Society in 1778 and of the Society of Antiquaries in 1779. He wrote five papers for the Royal Institution, two on physics and three on astronomy; he was an active member of the Linnean Society; a contributor to mathematical discussions in Tilloch's Philosophical Magazine; an excellent chemist and was awarded the gold medal of the Society of Arts for his Discovery of a Lake from Madder.

His antiquarian output was no less impressive as a regular contributor to Archaeologia. These included articles on the Abbeys of Reading and of Romsey, Gothic architecture in Italy and Sicily, Lincoln Castle, Roman remains at Cirencester and ancient buildings in York.

It was this Sir Henry Englefield who, as a staunch Roman Catholic, had become so disgusted with the offensive prejudices of the neighbouring gentry, sold the estate in 1783 to William Byam Martin and so terminated the Englefield's long association of 170 years with Whiteknights. The title died out in the early 19th century as neither Sir Henry nor his brother left any male heirs.

Francis Michael in fee-tail successively, the remainder to his daughter, Teresa Ann, wife of Francis Cholmeley of Brandsby Hall, Yorkshire. Francis Michael died childless. In 1783 Henry Charles being unmarried conveyed the estate to William Byam Martin. Having left Whiteknights, Sir Henry Charles Englefield moved to London where he died on 21st March 1822. With his death the baronetcy passed into history (Soames, 1987).

A drawing of Sir Henry Englefield's house and its immediate surroundings dated 1776 and attributed to Governor Thomas Pownall shows Whiteknights at the time to be a very beautiful place. However, Horace Walpole, who visited in 1753, appears to have been rather unimpressed. He described the house as being *very insignificant* and *far from good.*

In 1798 William Byam Martin sold the property to the Marlborough Family Trustees. At the behest of the 4th Duke of Marlborough the Trustees leased the property to the Marquis of Blandford.

There are differing accounts as to when Henry Englefield conveyed the property to William Byam Martin; Dormer (1944) and Smith (1957) both say that the property was conveyed to Byam Martin in 1798 and that he in turn conveyed it to the Trustees that same year. Soames (1987), however, states that: *in 1783, the seventh and last Baron, Sir Henry Englefield, had become so disgusted at the offensive prejudices of the neighbouring gentry that he broke the family's long connection with Whiteknights and sold it to William Byam Martin who fifteen years later sold it to the Marlborough family.* Soames (1987) also refers to the fact that the architect Samuel Pepys Cockerell was employed by Byam Martin to do work on the house, he also did some work at a later date for Blandford. A survey of the bounds dated 1785, refers to William Byam Martin as the Lord of the Manor of Whiteknights (D/EDO E23). Although Sir Henry Englefield sold the Whiteknights Estate he retained land in the surrounding area; in 1801 his name appears on a list of landowners and farmers being assessed for tax (4/6d in the pound) for the upkeep of the poor in the workhouse (D/P113/12/15).

Blandford was keen to find a large estate that he could landscape to his own taste. The previous properties, Kimbolton Castle, Culham Court and Bill Hill were all leased and did not give him the freedom to make any great changes to their grounds. Bill Hill is on the outskirts of Wokingham near the Forest Road (close to the M4/A329M interchange). As it is quite close to Earley it is likely that Blandford would have known about the Whiteknights estate. Whiteknights probably appealed to him because in the mid 1700s Anthony Englefield had had the grounds laid out in the fashionable manner of a *ferme ornée* (Soames, 1987). Blandford probably saw this as a base from which to start.

Dormer (1944) and Darter (Phillips, 1985) both state that the Marquis of Blandford bought the adjoining land called Redlands and planted a belt of trees all around the combined estates and by leaving an avenue he had a private drive for nearly three miles. However VCH (1923) states that Englefield bought the adjoining estate.

Whiteknights Estate/Park

The Marquis of Blandford, George Spencer-Churchill, who was to become 5th Duke of Marlborough, acquired the estate in 1798, leasing

Grade II listed building North Lodge and South Lodge, Whiteknights Park

These lodges were built in the early 19th century from stuccoed brick and have a slate gabled roof.

The Lodges, Whiteknights Park
© Dann/Lewis 625 Rural History Centre The University of Reading

it from the Marlborough Family Trustees.

Little is known of the house and its grounds when it was occupied by the Englefields but they had begun to lay their garden out in a more Arcadian fashion (Soames 1987). When the Blandfords came to live at Whiteknights the Marquis moved the large botanical collection that he had already accumulated from his rented property at Bill Hill to Whiteknights and so the work went on and a virtually new landscape was created. Whiteknights was filled with gardens of a rustic flavour, temples, arbours, grottoes, pavilions, fountains, rustic bridges, clumps of trees and so on – expense was no object. It was at this time that the Wilderness area of the garden was designed and planted. He was influenced by the work of William Kent, 'Capability' Brown, Humphrey Repton and their school. This school of garden designers sought to promote the English landscape rather than the more formal gardens that had existed in the

Grade II listed feature
Landscaped Garden Feature
Whiteknights Park

This landscape feature which is now part of the University of Reading campus was originally part of the grounds of the former Whiteknights Estate. The main feature is an outcrop of large rocks laid out in a semi-circle at the head of the lake.

earlier part of the 18th Century (Soames, 1987).

A contemporary description of Whiteknights published in the Rusher's Reading Guide and Berkshire Directory for 1807 (No. VII) described the property thus:

> *Earley-White-Knights, a mansion not far distant from Early Court, is the agreeable seat of the Marquis of Blandford, by whom it was purchased of Sir Henry Charles Englefield, a name well known to the lovers of topographical literature. History records but few circumstances relative to this desirable manor. Its name appears, in part, derived from the antient family of the ERLES, one of whom was Knight of the Shire, in the reign of Edward I. In the 16th century there was a free chapel in this demesne, which was dissolved about the year 1540, without the previous permission of the Sovereign. This house enjoys rich and variegated prospects over Berkshire and its neighbouring county. Its present noble possessor is making considerable additions to the building. A spacious library is preparing, and a music-room, from the windows of which the views are peculiarly fine. The gardens are laid out at much expence, and in a style of superior elegance. Here is to be seen a large and curious assortment of Heaths, together with an extensive collection of Exotics. Horticulture appears to be the reigning pursuit of the Marquis, and it must be confessed the gardens do high credit to his taste and perseverance.*

The fame of these magnificent gardens was widespread and many people came to admire their splendour, Miss Mitford is known to have visited these gardens. One contemporary visitor wrote that the gardens *had few rivals in the Kingdom* and a traveller writing to his friend in London described the gardens:

> *At the distance of something more than one mile, on the south side of the town, is Whiteknights, the seat of the Most Noble the Marquis of Blandford. The house was built by the late Sir H Englefield, whose agricultural pursuits induced him to lay out the grounds about it as a ferme orneé, the general features of which it still retains, except in the park and gardens, which have been much improved by the present possessor, both by planting and ornamental buildings, but particularly by the number and variety of exotic plants, covering several acres of ground, and divided into distinct compartments according to the countries from whence they came, as the American, South Sea, Botany Bay etc gardens; but these by their great value cannot be seen by strangers without permission of the Marquis – however the park is at all times open to the public, who claim a prescriptive right of passing thro' it unmolested; this is not only a great convenience to those who have occasion to go that way, but a high gratification to every one who can enjoy the luxuries of rural scenery, presented in one of the most charming spots in England (*Man 1810*).*

View of White Knights from the New Gardens, Hofland
© The University of Reading

The extravagant, flamboyant and somewhat eccentric nature of the Marquis also saw many wondrous additions to the inside of the house. An avid book collector, Blandford soon amassed a superb collection of books such as early illuminated missals, including the Valdarfer edition of Boccaccio of 1471, The Bedford Missal, a collection of poetry from around Europe and rare fifteenth and early sixteenth century editions from both English and foreign printers, including sixteen from Caxton's press. The Whiteknights library soon came to be considered among the most famous private collections of its day (Soames 1987).

As if all this extravagance was not enough, Lord Blandford also collected works of art by such distinguished artists as Titian, Tintoretto, Holbein, Rubens, Vandyke, Kneller, Gainsborough and Romney to add further pictures to the walls of his 18th century mansion.

Sadly these splendours were short-lived. A series of scandals and some ill-conceived ventures left Blandford with serious debts and in 1812 the property was mortgaged (*via* the Trustees) to pay these off. The mortgagees were Archibald Traill, Sir Charles Cockerell and Henry Traill.

The fourth Duke died in January 1819 and Blandford succeeded his father to the Dukedom. He continued to live at Whiteknights, but his debts mounted and everything had to be sold, beginning in June 1819 with the books from his library. In September and October of the same year virtually all the rest of the contents of Whiteknights were sold at auction. Finally, in 1820/21 the mortgagees seized the property against the un-repaid debt.

The financial affairs of the 'reckless Duke' left a legal quagmire with

Marquis of Blandford (Fifth Duke of Marlborough) 1766–1840

George Spencer Churchill was born in 1766, probably in Marlborough House, London. He was the son of George Spencer, 4th Duke of Marlborough, and Caroline Russell, daughter of the 4th Duke of Bedford. As he was the eldest son of the Duke he carried the title of the Marquis of Blandford. The seat of the Marlborough family was Blenheim Palace in Oxfordshire, the estate had been given to John Churchill, the first Duke, by the nation in the reign of Queen Anne in gratitude for his military service.

George Spencer Churchill led a sheltered life because his parents were both reluctant guests and hosts preferring to spend their time either at Marlborough House or Blenheim Palace. At Blenheim the Duke carried out much work on the gardens and grounds and both Repton and 'Capability' Brown worked there.

Lord Blandford was educated at home and then from the age of ten at Eton, he was well thought of and was a gifted artist and musician, a botanist and plant collector and bibliophile. He was sent to Paris to continue his education, then entered Oxford as an undergraduate of Christ Church in 1784. He was awarded an honorary MA in 1786. Blandford became MP for Wheatfield (Oxfordshire) in 1790.

At about the time of his coming of age his extravagant nature began to surface: financially he was foolish and irresponsible, though his parents kept his money on a tight reign he borrowed from money lenders.

Blandford married Lady Susan Stewart, daughter of Lord and Lady Galloway, in September 1791, they lived first in Kimbolton Castle (Huntingdonshire) then moved to Culham Court near Henley which they rented for three years. After this they rented Bill Hill near Wokingham which was owned by Rear Admiral Leveson Gower.

It is probable that, from the time he married, the Marquis was looking for a suitable country property where he could practise his passion for gardening and botanical interests, he probably carried out some work at both Culham Court and Bill Hill. It is recorded that whilst he was at Bill Hill he had begun to collect novelties and rarities and that he corresponded with the superintendent at Kew Gardens, but he did not carry out anything long-term. His passion for gardening may have been influenced by his father's work at Blenheim. In 1798 the Whiteknights estate was bought by the family trustees. Blandford leased the property from the Trustees

A series of scandals and some ill-conceived ventures left Blandford with serious debts, and in 1812 the property was mortgaged to pay these off.

The fourth Duke died in January 1819 and Blandford succeeded his father to the Dukedom, becoming the fifth Duke of Marlborough. He continued to live at Whiteknights, but his debts mounted and everything had to be sold.

After the collapse of his estate at Whiteknights, the Duke withdrew to the old family seat at Blenheim. Fortunately for the Duke, the Blenheim estate had been entailed, so he had been unable to fritter and waste the assets tied up in this property.

Sadly the Duke and his wife were semi-estranged because of his illicit affair with Lady Mary Anne Sturt. Later, he became infatuated with the young Matilda Glover, and by the end of his life she was living with him at Blenheim, having had six children by him. The Duke died in 1840. The Duchess outlived the Duke by one year.

many creditors able to make a claim on what was left of the estate after the sale of the contents of the house and the gardens.

As if the Duke had not left behind a financial state of affairs that was complex enough, further complications arose when Francis Cholmely advanced a claim to the Whiteknights Estate. Francis was the son of Teresa Anne and Francis Cholmely of Brandsby, Yorkshire. Teresa Anne was the daughter of Sir Henry Englefield, the sixth Baronet. Sir Henry's will stated that the Manor of Erlegh Whiteknights should pass to his sons Henry Charles and Francis Michael in fee-tail successively, the remainder to his daughter, Teresa Anne, who had married Francis Cholmely in 1782. Francis Michael Englefield had died childless and Henry Charles, the seventh baronet, had sold the estate. After prolonged litigation, which continued until 1823, Francis Cholmely's claim was upheld (Smith, 1957).

In 1839 Francis Cholmely and his wife Barbara sold the house and manor to James Wright Nokes for £24,600. The terms of the conveyance were as follows:

> *The reputed manor of Earley Regis or Whiteknights all the rights and appurtenances associated with courts leet, courts baron, together with perquisites and profits of the courts, view of frankpledge, heriots, fines and amerciaments, as well as goods and chattels of felons and fugitives, felons of themselves, outlawed persons, deodands, waifs and strays.*

The house was demolished in the 1840s and only a vestige of the gardens remain but luckily a record was made; Blandford had commissioned Thomas and Barbara Hofland to make a descriptive account of the house and gardens, but by the time they had finished he could not pay them for their work (Butts, 1981), (Soames, 1987). Luckily only fifty copies had been made and they sold these to realise their expenses.

James Wright Nokes is significant, in that he was the first owner of the Whiteknights estate to purchase the property not primarily as a private residence but as a speculative investment. He was the first of a number of speculators who over the next decade tried and failed to persuade local investors to put money into property development within Whiteknights Park.

The following editorial advertisement that appeared in the 1847 edition of Snare's *Berkshire Directory* is typical of these attempts:

> *Among many projected improvements which will contribute largely to the benefit of the town, we are gratified to observe the flattering prospects of the company formed for the creation of villas on the White Knights Estate which bids fair to rival, if not excel, anything of the kind in the kingdom. The shares have been eagerly bought up, chiefly by residents in the metropolis, to whom the celebrity and*

permanent attraction of its Gardens and ornamental Lake are alone sufficient inducements for the investment of capital; and we hail, with anticipation of increased prosperity to the town and neighbourhood, the commencement of an undertaking which is as praiseworthy to the projectors as it must be ultimately beneficial to the shareholders and the public.

Despite the loss of the house and of many of the plants that had been sold in the auctions, the parkland still continued to attract a great deal of interest in the period. In 1840 the Great Western Railway Companion directed people to the garden as: *one of the most perfect specimens of landscape gardening.*

Also an account of a visit to Whiteknights Park in June 1843 records that it was still a splendid place to visit:

> *I never spent two hours with greater pleasure than I did in this earthly paradise and so it may truly be called even now although its moveable plants had been taken away under an auction of them which produced £10,000.* (Benham, 1843).

Wilderness Bridge, Whiteknights Park
© Dann/Lewis 619, Rural History Centre, The University of Reading

It was during James Wright Nokes's time that Whiteknights saw the last meeting of its manorial court. The formal notice proclaiming this event read thus:

MANOR OF EARLEY REGIS
otherwise EARLEY WHITEKNIGHTS in the
County of Berks

I George Kennet Pollock, Gentleman, the Steward of the Manor of Earley Regis, otherwise Earley Whiteknights in the County of Berks, under the authority given to me by virtue of a certain Indenture bearing date the fifteenth day of June in the Year of our Lord One thousand Eight hundred and thirty nine, made between James Wright Nokes, Esquire, Lord of the said Manor of the first part, John Beardmore, Esquire, of the second part, and myself George Kennet Pollock, of the third part, do hereby appoint you John Ward to be the Bailiff of the said Manor, and require you to give notice within the said Manor, that the Court Leet and Court Baron of the Lord of the said Manor, will be this day holden at the House known by the name of the Three Tuns Public House within the said Manor, and to warn all Residants and Tenants of the said Manor personally to be and appear and to do and perform their Suit and Service, and pay their Quit Rents, Fines and other duties as of right they ought to perform and render at such courts respectively, and then and there to make and return their several presentments and to perambulate the boundaries of the said Manor according to the ancient Custom thereof, and present the same to be duly entered upon the said Manor. And be you here also personally with the names and persons you have so summoned bringing with you also this precept. Dated this Eleventh day of May 1840.

To John Ward, Gardener — *G. K. Pollock*
Whiteknights Steward

As this was to be the last manorial court and beating of the bounds to be held in Earley, we have included the full write-up of the day's proceedings (Berkshire Archaeological Society Journal 1911–12).

The Court Leet and Court Baron of James Wright Nokes, Esquire, Lord of the said Manor holden at the House of Ann Mitchell, Widow, called the Three Tuns Public House within and for the said Manor on Monday the Eleventh day of May in the year of our Lord One thousand eight hundred and forty, Before George Kennet Pollock, Gentleman Steward of the said Manor.

Present: James Wright Nokes, Esquire, Lord of the Manor.

The following Persons as the Jury and Homage of the said Court (that is to say):

William Shackel	*Joseph Goddard, Senr.*
John Shackel	*Robert Goddard*
Thomas Chapman	*John Chapman*
Joseph Goddard, Junr.	*Henry Elliott*
Nathan Tubb	*William Elliott*
John Benjamin Tubb	*William Flower and*
Jonathan Elliott	*Abraham Pether*

Who being sworn and charged upon their Oaths touching Articles of the said Court Leet, as well as the Court Baron present and say as follows:

That having met on this Eleventh day of May now Instant at the place above mentioned, they did with a great many other persons perambulate the whole bounds or extent of the said Manor and present the same to be as follows: First: Beginning at the House called the Marquis of Granby Public House standing in the London Road opposite to where the thirty-eighth milestone stands from thence southwards along on the east or inside of the hedge next the lands within the jurisdiction of the Corporation of Reading in the parish of Saint Giles in Reading, through the Plantation and part of the Park called Foxhills to a point in the Park and thence diverging westwards about one hundred and forty eight yards and then southward to the brick wall, which crossing, they went through the Botanical Garden to another point at the opposite wall of the Kitchen Garden thence turning on the outside to the right to a mark upon a Pillar of the brick wall of the said garden thence returning northwards along the said wall to a point in the Plantation thence westward through the Kitchen garden to another mark upon the wall, thence across the Orchard Close (formerly Butchers Close) noticing that the fence erected by Sir Charles Cockerell is on the south side of the old Ditch and is therefore an encroachment upon the Manor, thence in a straight line up to the Plantation at Doles Green, now planted, keeping on the outside of the Pond to the North West Corner where Knapps Barn formerly stood, (John Flower states that many years ago Mr. Martin exchanged a piece of land in Whitley Parish for the piece of waste land called Doles Green where the Barn formerly stood) and thence again turning southward up to the Outer Avenue where a large elm tree formerly stood, and where a Post is now directed to be put down, then returning along the south side of the said Avenue on the north edge of the Close called Swing Swang (which is in the Parish of Saint Giles) up to the West Lodge, all the old elm and oak trees having been lately felled by the present Lord of the Manor, thence south-wards to the road or lane leading to Pepper Farm, thence to a point eastwards in Whiteknights Park, continuing through the park bounded by the lands belonging to Pepper Farm, in an irregular line down to the ancient lane on the west side of the park, and there we found an encroachment by Sir Charles Cockerell's agent, the new fence having been carried to the east side of the ancient lane instead of being carried up to the west side thereof and from thence turning to the right or southwards, crossing the said lane and taking in or including all the lane there up to the lane leading to Pepper Farm House – then onwards up to the place called No Man's Land, and up to and including the Pond to the extremity of the said Farm, there being a ditch on the west side of the lane next to the Parish of Saint Giles then in a parallel line with the fence on the left, about a pole from the same to the place called Noman's Land marked with a cross to another cross, and from thence inclining to the left down to the hedge of the garden of Mr Cobham and so on continuing southward taking in Elisha's cottage and crossing over Bishop's cottage down the hedge between Shinfield and Earley on the east side of the lane called Pigwash Lane, allowing that lane to belong to Shinfield, and from thence down to the lane which leads from Loddon Bridge to Shinfield and crossing that lane at the post marked S.M. – and crossing a Close, formerly the Earl of Fingal's and now Mr Cobham's, formerly called Breach Piddle, but from the said post to a point at a Willow Pollard where the fence formerly stood and thence eastward about six poles to the lane and so down on the west side thereof including the whole lane into the moors, and from thence on the west side of the moors down to the Brook called Icy Lake, and crossing that brook and taking in a meadow, late the said Earl of Fingal's and now belonging to Mr Cobham, called Pantons Eyott Mead, now forming part of a larger mead called Ducks Mead, crossing the River Loddon taking in all the river and two Eyotts on the south side of the river against Broad Mead down as far as opposite to the Boat Plot at a farm called Boswell's Farm, now Pether's Farm, and there crossing the River Loddon again at a small Eyott on the south side, and from thence up the hedge on the west side of the lane leading from Pether's Farm to Armshatch Gate and from that gate across Armshatch Lane to the Graffage, (though appearing by the printed map to lead off to the right to some distance, respecting which some future enquiry is to be made and compared with former perambulations) then into a field called Deans Pightle and thence up the Watercourse and hedge until you come to Sand Pightle, then along the west side of Sand Pightle nearly up to Mr Golding's Fish Ponds and there turning to the right along a ditch adjoining to Mr Golding's Wood at the north end of Spring Pightle and down by a small stream as far as the north east corner of Mr Golding's Close called the Gore Ground – and from thence turning northward through the Plantation about two hundred feet, then again eastward in an indirect line about one chain to the site of the Old Green Lane, and then including all the eastern side of the Lane which divides the Manor from Woodley Parish up to Earley Heath and then crossing the road by a place called Hungerford, and so up by Hungerford and crossing part of a Garden there, formerly in the possession of Francis Cooper and since of Richard Bransden, Senior, and so down by the hedge and across Mrs Newell's garden and orchard, taking in her cottage and cutting a cross x on the outside of the garden there, thence through an ancient short lane or passage leading into Bullmarsh Heath (now inclosed) and thence turning to the left up the hedge including a Close adjoining to Earley Heath called the Hungerford Pightle, in the occupation of Mr William Shackell, and on to the hedge beyond the Cottages in the occupation of the poor of the Parish of Earley, and then turning to the right by the hedge where a cross was cut and so on by Mr Wheble's Wood, called South Lands Coppice, down to the scite of Old Town Lane on the right hand – the boundary there turns up that Lane to Mr Wheble's Park about ten poles and then to the left at which place a cross was cut, taking in a small close (now part of Mr Wheble's Park) on the left hand (up to an ash tree in the Park which we marked) adjoining to the lane leading into the London Road, and so on in that lane about six poles and then turning to the right hand hedge behind the house and garden and Pightle, called Christians or the Worlds End, about twenty-four poles to the corner of the scite of the hedge – and then turn short to the left hand into the lane and taking in or including all the lane to the London Road, and there crossing the London Road at the east end of a land called Crumps, and turning to the left in a picked close, and then turning to the right down the hedge across the Great Western Railway to the opposite hedge, and thence following the same inclining hedge to Park Field and then to Earley Mead, taking in all the said mead round to the gate at Lock Corner, and then taking in half the stream or river with the whole of a very small eyott at the bottom of the mead and so up the half stream as far as the place called Kennet Mouth, and likewise half the stream of the Kennet including the mead called Shoulder of Mutton Mead, and so on to the hedge by the thirty acres and then turn up that hedge to the London Road at the place where the thirty-eighth milestone stands, near the house called the Marquis of Granby, being the place where they began.

They present that John Flower shall be and he is hereby appointed Constable for the said Manor until the next Court, and he is sworn in accordingly.

They present that the said John Flower shall be and he is hereby appointed Hayward, and that he shall impound all Cattle and Swine found straying within this Manor and that he shall be paid for so doing by the respective Owners thereof being Resiants or Parishioners, one shilling per head for every Cow, Ass or Horse, one penny per head for Sheep, and threepence per head for Swine, and that all persons who shall not be Resiants or Parishioners shall pay double fees for the same. And the said John Flower is sworn in as Hayward accordingly.

And they present that all Resiants within this Manor who have not appeared at this Court pursuant to the warning for that purpose given shall be and they are hereby fined one shilling each.

C. K. POLLOCK, *Steward.*

By the time its last meeting was held, the manorial court of Earley Whiteknights had already outlived many of its contemporary manorial courts that had been gradually going out of existence, as they were superseded by the more effective Justices of the Peace.

Smith (1957) sums up the ending of an era when he says that *Its last meeting in 1840 signalised the end of its functions, judicial, economic and governmental and marked the virtual disappearance of what still remained of the medieval organisation of the community whose interests it had served.*

Whilst many others had tried to develop Whiteknights, the inevitable breakthrough did not come until the property came into the possession of the Goldsmid family in 1849. Both Sir Isaac Lyon Goldsmid and his son Francis Henry did much to advance the cause of Jews in Britain and were also highly influential in the foundation and funding of the University of London.

Sir Isaac Lyon Goldsmid's association with Earley began in 1849 when, already over sixty years of age, he purchased the Manor and lands of Whiteknights. The Goldsmid family continued to hold the land for nearly a century, but it was Isaac, and Francis in particular, who had both a large impact on national affairs and on Whiteknights by subdividing it into six leaseholds.

The main influence of Sir Francis Goldsmid on Earley was to divide Whiteknights Park into six leaseholds in 1867. With the original house having already been demolished in 1840, the building of six new houses meant that Whiteknights once again sprang to life.

The Bridge across Whiteknights Lake
© Dann/Lewis 622, Rural History Centre, The University of Reading

Whiteknights Park House, Whiteknights Park
postcard

Sir Isaac Lyon Goldsmid 1778–1859

Sir Isaac Lyon Goldsmid was over sixty when he acquired Whiteknights. His claim to fame lay mostly in his interests and achievements in his London projects rather than locally around Earley.

His main interests lay in finance, Jewish affairs and public education. He had made his fortune as a prominent member of a London firm of bullion brokers. His growing reputation in both national and international finance led him to work closely with a number of governments. He was created a baronet in 1841, in recognition of his public service. He was the first ever Jew to have been granted this honour.

He was instrumental in introducing the Jewish Disabilities Bill in the House of Commons in 1830, and again, more successfully, three years later. Despite initially being rejected by the House of Lords, he did eventually see the Bill successfully pass into law.

Sir Isaac was also one of the main instigators in the setting up of the University of London which later became known as University College, London. He was pivotal in the birth of this great seat of learning in a number of ways. Firstly, he was able to introduce the poet, Thomas Campbell, who conceived the original idea to Henry (later Lord) Brougham. Then, when the Provisional Committee was unable to raise the capital necessary to purchase the Gower Street site, Goldsmid, in association with Campbell and Brougham, bought the site until London University had the finances to take if off his hands.

In 1867 Whiteknights was divided into six leaseholds and six large houses were built. These were: Whiteknights House, Whiteknights Park House (built on the site of the original house), Blandford Lodge, The Wilderness, Foxhill and Erlegh Park (also known as Erlegh Park Lodge, Earley Park and Erlegh Whiteknights). Access to Whiteknights House and Blandford Lodge was from the Shinfield Road, access to Whiteknights Park House, Foxhill and Erlegh Park was from the Wokingham Road (and Whiteknights Road) and access to the Wilderness was from Wilderness Road. A number of the lodges, originally on the drives to the houses, may still be seen on the estate. Whiteknights House, The

Francis Henry Goldsmid 1808–1878

Sir Francis Goldsmid was the son of Sir Isaac Goldsmid. He inherited the Whiteknights estate when his father died in 1859. Like his father he was able to break down some of the political barriers that Jews faced. In 1833, be became the first Jew to be called to the bar and later he became the first Jewish Queen's Counsel. Like his father, he worked for Jewish rights and was a benefactor of University College, London.

Sir Francis also had strong London connections, but, unlike his father he was also very active locally. He was a magistrate and deputy lieutenant for Berkshire and from 1860 until he died in 1878, he was Member of Parliament for Reading.

It was he who finally managed to develop Whiteknights in a way that so many others had tried to do but failed.

Sadly, Sir Francis met a premature death in 1878 as the result of an accident whilst stepping off a train at Waterloo Station.

This page: Erlegh Park
© Dann/Lewis 640, Rural History Centre, The University of Reading

Opposite page:
top: The Wilderness
© Dann/Lewis 609, Rural History Centre, The University of Reading

bottom: Foxhill
© Sales catalogue 1890, Martin & Pole, Nicholas

Wilderness, Erlegh Park and Foxhill were designed by the well known architect Alfred Waterhouse. The Wilderness (the house, not the woodland) did not survive for long after the Second World War.

Whiteknights remained in the Goldsmid family until it was acquired by its current owner, the University of Reading, in 1947. The story of Whiteknights is continued, later in the book when the history of the University is recounted.

THE WILDERNESS, EARLEY. 609.

Alfred Waterhouse, 1813–1905

Alfred Waterhouse was born in Manchester the son of wealthy Quaker parents who owned a mill. He was educated at Grove House, Tottenham, a Quaker school. He married in 1860, Elizabeth (Bessie) Hodgkin whose father, John, was a historian and became the first chairman of governors of Leighton Park School. Bessie (Hodgkin) Waterhouse was the sister of Jonathan Hodgkin whose son, J. Edward Hodgkin, was the first pupil at Leighton Park School when it opened on 22nd January 1890. Jonathan Hodgkin also became the chairman of governors at the school. Monica, the eldest daughter of Alfred and Bessie, married Robert Bridges the poet.

Alfred Waterhouse became an architect and designed many buildings. Probably the best known of all the buildings he designed are the Natural History Museum in London and Manchester Town Hall. On the Whiteknights estate he designed Whiteknights House for his father and Foxhill for himself. Locally, he designed both Reading and Wokingham Town Halls, Reading School and the extension to the original house, with the adjoining arch, which formed the first part of Leighton Park School. Later, he designed the first boarding house at the school, Grove House, named after the school in Tottenham. The nave of St Bartholomew's Church, London Road was designed by him as was part of the alterations of St Mary's Church Twyford and the Caversham Baptist Church in Gosbrook Road. Other buildings include: the main buildings for the Universities of Manchester, Leeds and Liverpool, college buildings of Balliol (Oxford), Girton, Gonville and Caius, Jesus, and Pembroke (Cambridge), and the Prudential Assurance Buildings in many parts of the country.

Alfred Waterhouse built three houses for himself, Barcombe Cottage, Fallowfield, Manchester in 1864, Foxhill on the Whiteknights Estate (1868), and Yattendon Court (1877/78).

Whilst living at Foxhill Alfred Waterhouse became an Anglican and he and his wife and eldest son were baptised at Earley St Peter's Church on 24th February 1877, his other children were baptised a year later (23rd February 1878). He became churchwarden of Yattendon Church when he lived there.

Grade II listed building
Foxhill, Whiteknights Park

This large house was formerly a student hall of residence. It was built in 1868 by and for, Alfred Waterhouse. Externally it is made of red brick with diaper patterning and a plain and fish scale tiled roof. Internally it has a three-flight staircase in the entrance hall with arched balustrades, carved panels and moulded handrails, a stained and traceried window to the staircase and a large hooded fireplace on clustered columns with carved capitals.

Grade II listed building
The Gate Lodge,
Whiteknights Road

This was the lodge to Foxhill and was probably built at the same time as Foxhill by Waterhouse. The walls are of red brick with dark brick bands and stone dressings. The roof comprises fish scale slates.

By Order of the Executors of the late ARTHUR EDWARD PHILLIPS, Esq.

BERKSHIRE,
NEAR READING.

PARTICULARS, WITH PLAN, VIEWS AND CONDITIONS OF SALE,
OF A HIGHLY VALUABLE AND
CHARMING RESIDENTIAL PROPERTY,
KNOWN AS

Within 2 miles of Reading Railway Station, whence London is reached in less than an hour, and comprising a
MODERATE-SIZED GOTHIC MANSION,
Erected about 20 years ago, in the most costly manner, by an eminent Architect for his own occupation, approached by a winding Carriage Drive with
ORNAMENTAL STONE-BUILT ENTRANCE LODGE,
And seated in
MAGNIFICENTLY-TIMBERED AND UNDULATING PARK-LIKE LANDS,
DELIGHTFUL PLEASURE GROUNDS,
Tastefully laid out, abounding in rare specimen Trees and Shrubs, and extending to an
ORNAMENTAL LAKE OF ABOUT 15 ACRES.
PRODUCTIVE WALLED KITCHEN GARDENS,
Vineries, Greenhouse, Forcing Pits, &c., and
A HANDSOME CONSERVATORY;
FIRST-CLASS STABLING;
COACHMAN'S AND GARDENER'S COTTAGES
AND A SMALL FARMERY,
THE WHOLE EMBRACING AN AREA OF ABOUT
22A. 3R. 9P.,
AND FORMING
A MOST COMPLETE AND PERFECT COUNTRY PROPERTY:
TO BE SOLD BY AUCTION, BY

Messrs. OSBORN & MERCER,

AT THE MART, TOKENHOUSE YARD, BANK OF ENGLAND, E.C.,
On TUESDAY, the 29th day of JULY, 1890,
AT TWELVE FOR ONE O'CLOCK
(UNLESS PREVIOUSLY SOLD BY PRIVATE TREATY).

Particulars, with Plan, Views and Conditions of Sale, and orders to view, may be obtained of Messrs. CUNLIFFES & DAVENPORT, Solicitors, 43, Chancery Lane, London, W.C.; of Messrs. HASLAM & SONS, Auctioneers, 17, Friar Street, Reading; and of Messrs. OSBORN & MERCER, 28B, Albemarle Street, Piccadilly, London, W.

VACHER & SONS, Printers, Westminster.

9 F

Previous page: Old Whiteknights House, Whiteknights Park, 2000

This page: Sale of Foxhill

Baron Hirst 1863–1943

Baron Hugo Hirst lived in Foxhill on the Whiteknights Estate. Hugo Hirsch (Hirst) was born in Munich (Germany) on 26th November 1863. he was educated in Munich at first studying chemistry and intending to go into his father's business. Instead he came to Britain and entered the electrical industry. He took the name Hirst when he became a naturalised Briton in 1883. Three years later he joined Gustav Byng who had founded a firm selling electrical appliances which were at this time newly invented thus the business was in its fledgling stage. Through Hirst's vision this company was transformed into the General Electrical Company (GEC) in1889. Hirst became Managing Director of G.E.C in 1900 and chairman in 1910 – he then held both appointments until his death in 1943. By the time of his death the company had 40 factories in Britain as well as subsidiary organisations in the Commonwealth and other countries, manufacturing and supplying every kind of electrical equipment.

Hirst was one of the first people to realise the importance of research and founded research laboratories at Wembley. Staff relations were good and ahead of their time.

Hugo Hirst served on many committees and promoted British Industry abroad, he was created a Baronet in 1923 and raised to the peerage in 1934 as Baron Hirst of Witton in Warwickshire. He married his cousin, Leontine, in 1892 and had two daughters and two sons. One son died in 1919 as the result of injuries sustained in the war, the second son, Hugh, was born four months after the death of the first son. Sadly Hugh was killed in 1941 on pilot's activities in the war, his name is recorded on a plaque in Earley St Peter's Church. Leontine Hirst died in 1938, a plaque in the Lady Chapel of Earley St Peter's Church records that the choir stalls and chancel pavement are dedicated to her memory. Baron Hirst died at his home at Foxhill in Earley on 22nd January 1943. (*Electrician*, 1943).

Blandford Lodge, Whiteknights Park, 2000

Maiden Erlegh Estate and Manor

The origin of the name Maiden Erlegh is not clear but it was first applied to part of the Whiteknights estate. The name Erley Maydens is attested to this land from 1502 and the name Maiden Early from 1761. There is no evidence available for these names being used before these dates. Names are not generally coined for documents, rather documents reflect common usage of names; it is therefore reasonable to suppose that these names were in use before the documents that record them. Whether the estate formed from the Whiteknights lands in the 14th century was called Erley Maydens from the very beginning is impossible to say.

There are several possibilities for the origin of the Maiden part of the name. The two most likely possibilities are: (a) maiden as the common noun young, unmarried women and by extension occasionally nun and hence an estate belonging to a maiden or occupied by maidens; or (b) a surname or nickname Maiden, of which some are attested from the 12th and 13th centuries in Norfolk and Cambridgeshire.

Maiden Erlegh was formed out of the Manor of Erlegh St Nicholas in 1362 when John de Earley had licence to grant two messuages (dwellings) and 19 acres of land to Robert de Earley and Joan his wife (VCH, 1923). When the estate was attested in 1502 the owner was Richard Earley who passed it on to his sister Margaret, wife of Thomas Chafyn, on his death. The manor descended to William Chafyn, who died around 1539 and the estate passed to his son Thomas who sold it to Oliver Hyde in 1545. The estate remained in the hands of the Hyde family until 1673 when it was sold to Valentine Crome. In 1685 Valentine and Philliden Crome conveyed it to Theophilus Earl of Huntingdon and John Holles. The estate was being dealt with by Edward le Grand and other members of the le Grand family in 1744 (VCH, 1923).

It is believed to have been in the possession of William Mathew Birt, governor-general of the Leeward Islands at the end of the 18th Century. This is confirmed by documents held at the Berkshire Record Office (Tithe Apportionment in the Survey of Sonning, 1773 and 1783). The next owner was the Right Hon. Edward Golding, MP for Downton, Wiltshire, Lord of the Treasury during the administration of Lord Sidmouth.

> *At a short distance from Whiteknights is the pleasant seat of E Golding Esq. This a large brick building, having nothing particular to recommend it, except the grounds about it, which if not laid out in so ornamental a style as the last, are I believe, more extensive, and better calculated to correspond with the surrounding scenes (*Man, 1810*).*

On his death in 1818, he was succeeded by his son Edward, JP, DL, who passed the estate to his son and heir, the Rev. Edward Golding, on his death in 1844. Captain William Golding came into possession of the estate on Edward's death in 1857. After leasing the estate from the Golding family for 14 years, John Hargreaves, master of the South Berkshire Hunt, eventually purchased it in 1878 (VCH, 1923).

It is believed that Hargreaves rebuilt the Georgian mansion embodying the remnants of the then existent 17th and 18th century building (Cunningham, 1960). By comparing the Berkshire Sheet dated 1877 with that of 1899 it can be seen that the house had been extended and that a boathouse and icehouse had been added. A map held by Earley Town Council clearly shows that the mansion stood between Silverdale Road and Crawford Close. One of the original trees which grew close to the house and thought to be a holm oak, stands in the middle of Crawford Close today. To get to the mansion one travelled from Wokingham Road down Maiden Erlegh Drive, most of which still exists complete with sections of Victorian fencing and the lodge.

Mr Hargreaves was a popular man in the parish of Earley. He generously supported all Parish institutions and, along with two other local men, Mr Thomas Porter and Mr Charles Stephens, he would provide any funds needed in connection with the church (Howlett, 1937).

In 1886 The Royal Berkshire Yeomanry Cavalry trained at Maiden Erlegh and in 1890 their summer camp was held there.

Mr Hargreaves died in 1895 and the estate was leased to Mrs Nichol who remained there until it was sold to Solomon Barnato Joel in 1903 (*Berkshire Chronicle*, 1903). Sol Joel or Solly, as he became known, became the most famous and remembered owner of Maiden Erlegh and was the last person to own the whole estate and use it as a family home. His generosity and lavish lifestyle have been written into the folklore of Earley.

During Joel's time at Maiden Erlegh the mansion and estate were one of England's show places. The mansion boasted seventy rooms, fifty of which were bedchambers. At a cost of £12,000, he installed a Pompeiian swimming pool built of Italian marble with a fine painted fresco of nude figures of adults and children on one wall. He also commissioned the famous Palm Court, a room with a Cupola fountain in the centre and marble pillars in the corners with palms growing up the walls. The drawing-room was furnished with a massive gilt collection that had come from the palace of a Belgian King. Rich oriental rugs of immense value covered the floors while on the walls hung landscapes and portraits by the great masters like John Constable and Thomas Gainsborough. On the shelves of the luxuriously furnished library were sets of classics in beautiful bindings. The entire contents of the house went up for auction after Joel's death and the catalogue gives an insight into just how luxurious the inside of the mansion house was.

Solly Joel – Ace of Diamonds – *1865–1931*

When Solly bought the Maiden Erlegh Estate in 1903 he was already a well-known figure in Britain. From his humble start in life in 1865, as the son of a poor publican, brought up in the tough East End of London, to millionaire diamond dealer, is a story in itself. Soly or Solly Joel had many business interests including diamond and gold mining in South Africa, brewing, the City & South London Railway and the Drury Lane Theatre in London.

His uncle on his mother's side was Barnett Isaacs, later to be known as Barney Barnato The Diamond King, who has recently been named as an ancestor of the actress Esther Rantzen (Daily Mail, 2000). It was through this uncle and a need to make a living that Sol Joel found himself, along with his brother Woolf Joel, in South Africa in the early 1880's. This was to prove to be the stepping-stone to his fortune.

The following entry in the 1922 edition of *Who's Who* shows just how successful Joel was:

> Joel, Lieut.-Col Solomon Barnato, JP Member of firm Barnato Bros.; Director: de Beers Consolidated Mines, New Jagers Fontein Mining Company, Premier Diamond Company, Standard Bank of South Africa, South African Breweries, Knights, Spring Mines; Chairman: Johannesburg Consolidated Investment Company, Randfontein Estate Ltd, Randfont Central Gold Mining Company Ltd, Langlaagte Estates and Gold Mining Company Ltd, New Primrose, Glen Cairn, New State Areas, Government Gold Mining Areas, Van Ryn Deep, Consolidated Langaagte Mines etc.
>
> Son of late Joel Joel & nephew of late B.J. Banarto m. (d.1919), three sons and two daughters.
>
> Recreations, yachting, racing, motoring.
>
> Address. Maiden Erlegh, Reading; Sefton Lodge, Newmarket; 2 Great Stanhope Street.W.1.T: Mayfair 7015.
>
> Clubs: Royal Automobile, Royal London Yacht, principal racing clubs.

Events at Maiden Erlegh while it was under Joel's ownership have always attracted a lot of attention and these have been written into the folklore of Earley. Stories of his lavish parties and famous visitors have been passed down from one generation to the next. Even the current spelling of Maiden Erlegh is attributed to him. Apparently Mr Joel was very superstitious and realising that the spelling of Maiden Erleigh had 13 letters, dropped the 'i', thus giving us Erlegh. However, an Ordnance Survey map of the area surveyed in 1881/2 reveals that the spelling was already in existence before Solly Joel purchased the estate. He is also believed by some to have had the lake created, again maps of 1756 show it to be already in existence. The large island within the lake can probably be attributed to him, along with the thatched summer house which stood on the north side of the island until the late 1960s.

Lavish parties took place at the Mansion and many people living in Earley at the time remember his famous Ascot Sunday parties. Each year for a quarter of a century Solly hosted his Sunday-before-Ascot luncheons, one of the great events of the racing season (Mayer, 1958). Around three hundred guests attended each year and local people would wait at the lodge gates to see them arrive in their motor cars, a rare sight in those days. Guests were all male and included the elite of the turf as well as many who were prominent in the political, literary and artistic circles (Mayer, 1958).

Audax who wrote a column in the magazine *Horse and Hound* wrote the following about the Ascot Sunday luncheons after Joel's death in 1931.

> Although somewhat inclined to be domineering, Solly was brimful of kindness and an excellent host, as all those can attest who have attended the luncheon he gave annually at Maiden Erlegh with its lavish laid-out grounds on the Sunday before Ascot. I attended these for years, and all were very enjoyable, especially when Lord Dewar was present and delivered one of his droll speeches (Mayer, 1958).

Joel invested heavily in the estate which created many jobs for local tradesmen. The estate was everything a millionaire could want in a country home – including a deer park and shoot, trout streams, bridle paths, wooded glades, cricket and football grounds, hard and grass tennis courts and a polo field. Joel had an aviary constructed for birds he collected from all parts of the world. He is also reported to have imported zebras and monkeys from Africa to his country estate, as well as two enormous white donkeys from Egypt and a mongoose. Whether these animals ever lived at Maiden Erlegh is unclear, although when his children tired of them, the zebras and the mongoose were presented to Whipsnade Zoo (Mayer, 1958). To the south of the house were terraces and lawns with ornamental fountains, statues and classic temples (Howlett, 1937).

As well as the additions Joel made to the outside of the

house he made many inside. He commissioned the famous Palm Court, a replica of this, believed to be Joel's favourite room, was used as a set in the 1920s for *Good Luck*, a show at Joel's Drury Lane Theatre (Mayer, 1958). He also installed a Pompeiian swimming pool and it was there that the famous party was held which many old residents of Reading still talk about today. Solly is reported to have been having one of his lavish parties at his Maiden Erlegh home attended by chorus girls from his Drury Lane Theatre. He invited the girls to join him for an evening swim, however the girls had not brought their swimming costumes. Solly is reported to have provided them with chic-looking bathing suits made of a new material. To their horror once in the water their costumes disintegrated to nothing, Joel explained that it was a new 'waterproof' material he was trying out! Friends of Joel thought it was more likely to have been one of his humorous pranks, something many had been victims of themselves. Solly delighted in playing practical jokes on his friends when they were guests at his town house or country seats they were often treated to bizarre experiences (Mayer, 1958). One of his favourite tricks was to hide an old rooster in a basket in a guest's bedroom. One can imagine how startled the poor guest would have been at daybreak!

Although Joel's relationships with his immediate family were not always amicable, when his five children were small Christmas was usually spent at Maiden Erlegh when he would dress up as Father Christmas and hand out presents (Mayer, 1958).

Joel was a very generous man and donated large sums of money to many organisations and individuals who found themselves in difficulties. He never spoke of these loans and many were never repaid. Many were to people in the slums where he had been reared and the number was not clear until they turned out in their hundreds to mourn his death in 1931 (Mayer, 1958).

The gift that Joel is most famous for in Earley was that of £10,000 and twenty acres of land in Earley to the National Playing Fields Association in 1927. The Duke of York (later King George VI) was president of the association and in July 1927 lunched at Maiden Erlegh with Solly and his distinguished guests, before officially opening the playing fields. The park was named *Sol Joel* after Solly. The pavilion where the Duke was photographed and the playing fields remain today. The Borough of Reading initially refused to allow the park to be open on Sundays. The Star newspaper ran a series of editorials in indignant protest and sought Solly's support. At an interview he said: *Go ahead and rub it in until the kiddies of Reading are in their playground on the one day of the week when they'll enjoy it most* (Mayer, 1958).

Other institutions in the local area to benefit from Joel's generosity were: Reading University; Reading Football Club, the Earley Volunteers (Earley was the first parish in the district to form a volunteer detachment during the 1st World War and Joel provided them with a rifle range and trophy (Howlett, 1937)), the Royal Berkshire Hospital, which gained a fully equipped motor ambulance to replace an old horse-drawn one, and Wokingham Town who were given a piece of land called The Holt for the public to use as a recreation ground (Mayer, 1958).

When Sol Joel died on 22nd May 1931 it was the end of an era for Maiden Erlegh and Earley the likes of which were never to be seen again.

The luxurious contents of the mansion were sold by auction. The mansion itself was eventually purchased in February 1932 by Captain T. S. Waterlow Fox of Courtenay Lodge, Berks, who transferred his

Above: Maiden Erlegh House

© Collier Collection Maiden Erlegh 16, Rural History Centre, The University of Reading

Below: The gardens, Maiden Erlegh House

© Collier Collection Maiden Erlegh 11, Rural History Centre, The University of Reading

Above: Maiden Erlegh House with Maiden Erlegh Lake in the foreground

© Dann/Lewis 637, Rural History Centre, The University of Reading

Below: The swimming pool, Maiden Erlegh House

© Sales catalogue, 1931, Martin & Pole, Nicholas

Above: The drawing room, Maiden Erlegh House

© Sales catalogue, 1931, Martin & Pole, Nicholas

Below: Palm Court, Maiden Erlegh House

© Sales catalogue, 1931, Martin & Pole, Nicholas

South Berks hounds in front of Maiden Erlegh House

Postcard, 1907

Courtenay Lodge Boys School there renaming it Maiden Erlegh School for Boys. (Harris, 1977). During the summer a punt was used to take pupils onto the large island on Maiden Erlegh Lake and lessons were held in the thatched building which stood there until the 1960s. All that remains on the island today is a brick from the summerhouse and the original iron steps.

The school remained at the house until 1945 when Captain Waterlow Fox retired and the Mansion was sold to the Church Army who used it as a training college. In 1952 it was decided that the building was too expensive to maintain and inconveniently remote from their Headquarters in London. The college was moved to Cosway Street, Marylebone and Maiden Erlegh was put up for sale (Lynch, 1989)

ICI purchased the Mansion and grounds for use as a conference centre and offices. During this time the Forest Boys School used the stable accommodation as an annexe because they had outgrown their building – Woodley Hill House. They later moved to a new school building at Winnersh, the present site of Forest Boys School today (Pettit, 1998).

Cooper Estates Ltd. purchased the site in 1954. In 1956 they allowed Hungarian refugees escaping the Soviet invasion of their country to live in the mansion. The refugees were its last residents, the bulldozers started their destruction in March 1960. The County Council had considered purchasing the site from ICI and establishing their offices there. They opted for the site at Shinfield instead, Shire Hall, now occupied by Foster Wheeler. In 1965 due to pressure from local residents, Earley Parish Council held an open meeting followed by a referendum on the option to purchase the lake and the surrounding woodland (6¼ acres). In exchange Cooper Estates were allowed to develop an equivalent area south of the lake. Initially Wokingham Rural District Council was opposed to this development as it was outside the defined Earley Town Map but pressure from Berkshire County Council and the Parish Council persuaded them to change their mind. The lake and surrounding woodland (including woodland ceded from Wokingham District Council in 1991) became known as Maiden Erlegh Park and in 1997 it was granted Local Nature Reserve status by English Nature. It is now known as Maiden Erlegh Nature Reserve.

GREAT WESTERN RAILWAY.

Maiden Erlegh Steeplechases,

WEDNESDAY and THURSDAY,

November 15th & 16th, 1905.

ON THE ABOVE DATES

Cheap Tickets

WILL BE ISSUED TO

READING

From	By Trains as under (A.M.)	(A.M.)	Return Fares 1st Class s.	d.	2nd Class s.	d.	3rd Class s.	d.
Swindon ...	9 15	10 50	8	9	5	5	4	4
Shrivenham ...	9 25	Noon 12 0	7	6	4	6	3	9
Faringdon ...	9 22	12 0	7	3	4	7	3	8
Uffington ...	9 38	12 13	6	3	4	1	3	3
Challow ...	9 46	12 21	5	10	3	9	2	11
Wantage Road	9 56	12 31	5	0	3	2	2	7
Steventon ...	10 8	12 42	4	5	2	9	2	2
Oxford ...	9 35	A.M. 11 35	5	8	3	9	2	11
Abingdon ...	9 30	11 12	5	3	3	4	2	8
Radley ...	9 46	11 46	4	9	3	2	2	5

From.	By Trains as under (A.M.)	(Noon)	Return Fares 1st Class s.	d.	2nd Class s.	d.	3rd Class s.	d.
Culham ...	9 53	11 53	4	2	2	6	2	1
Didcot	10 24	12 5	3	7	2	4	1	10
Wallingford ...	10 20	12 2	3	2	2	0	1	7
Cholsey & Moulsf'd	10 34	12 16	2	6	1	8	1	4
Goring & Streatley	10 43	12 26	1	11	1	3	1	0
Newbury ...	10 33	11 39	3	7	2	4	1	10
Thatcham ...	9 25	11 57	2	10	1	10	1	5
Midgham ...	9 31	12 5	2	3	1	6	1	2
Aldermaston ...	9 37	12 9	1	11	1	3	1	0
Basingstoke ...	10 5	11 45	3	2	2	1	1	8
Bramley ...	10 15	11 56	2	3	1	6	1	2
Mortimer ...	10 23	12 3	1	6	1	2	1	0

The Tickets will be available for return from Reading by any train after 6.0 p.m. on the day of issue only

Children under Three years of age, Free; Three and under Twelve, Half-Price.

THE TICKETS ARE NOT TRANSFERABLE.

NO LUGGAGE ALLOWED.

Should an Excursion or Cheap Ticket be used for any other Station than those named upon it, or by any other Train than as above specified, it will be rendered void, and therefore the Fare paid will be liable to forfeiture, and the full Ordinary Fare will become chargeable.

PADDINGTON, November, 1905. JAMES C. INGLIS, General Manager.

Wyman & Sons, Ltd, Printers, Fetter Lane, London, E.C., and Reading.

Above: Advertisement for a steeplechase at Maiden Erlegh, 1905

Below: Syndrian (1915), bred from Polkerris and Sunder

Maiden Erlegh Racecourse

During the 19th century horse racing in Berkshire became very popular and many major meetings were held annually. In the 1880s point-to-point racing effectively got underway and the owner of Maiden Erlegh Estate at the time, Mr J Hargreaves, founded a course for hunt and yeomanry races, (similar to the modern hunter chases today) at his Berkshire home (Boyd, 1978). The course extended over the area now covered by Hillside Road, Sutcliffe Avenue and Mill Lane. The Grand-stand stood on an area which is to the back of the houses in Hillside Road, opposite Loddon Junior School. The main gate was roughly by what is now a newsagents on the Wokingham Road.

The racecourse remained open after Mr Hargreaves's death in 1895 and the following advertisement appeared in the Berkshire Chronicle on Saturday 7th February and Saturday 7th March 1903.

> *Maiden Erlegh Spring Steeple Chases will take place at Reading on Wednesday and Thursday 8th and 9th of April 1903*

After Sol Joel bought the estate racing continued there until the First World War. In 1905 the Great Western Railway advertised cheap tickets to the Maiden Erlegh Steeple Chase on the 15th and 16th November. When the racecourse was demolished the grandstand was re-erected at Newbury racecourse.

Maiden Erlegh Stud Farm

Maiden Erlegh stud farm was established by Solly Joel and went on to become one of the most famous racehorse stud farms in England. Joel renamed New Farm, which had been created during the 1820 enclosures, Home Stud Farm and successfully bred horses like *Maiden Erlegh* and *Syndrian* there. Joel's first big success on the turf came in 1906 when his horse *Bachelor's Button* beat the celebrated *Pretty Polly* in the Ascot Gold Cup. Joel bought a horse called *Polymelus* which won for him many races; and a statue of this horse is believed to have stood outside his Maiden Erlegh home. In 1915, *Pommern* a son of *Polymelus*, won the *Two Thousand Guineas*, the *New Derby Stakes* (the first war-time Derby ever held) and the *St. Ledger*. Joel also won many important handicaps, the *Royal Hunt Cup* at Ascot, *the Cambridgeshire* (twice) and the *Doncaster Cup* to name a few. Such was Joel's success on the turf that in 1921 he headed the list of winning owners.

> *In the early years of the twentieth century, Joel had a racemare named Doris. When she broke down in training, he decided to sell her, believing she would have no value as a broodmare. Solly Joel's brother, J.B Joel, told him he should not sell her as she had won races and was also named after one of his daughters. Solly Joel retorted that if his brother thought so well of the mare, he could have her. It was a remark S. B. Joel lived to regret: Doris became the dam of his brother's Derby winner of 1911 Sunstar, as well as the 1914 dual fillies Classic winner, Princess Dorrie* (Mayer, 1958)

The Stud Farm was situated near what is now Marefield, off Rushey way, which runs straight through fields where horses once grazed. Laurel Park is all that remains of those fields today.

At one time there were 14 men employed at Home Farm and as many as 70 horses being looked after. Joel also purchased Bearwood Stud which is on the outskirts of the main Estate. Here six men were employed and horses were sent there for grazing and primary training before being sent to Home Stud Farm.

In 1932 the Stud Farm was purchased and continued to operate as a stud farm until the 1980s when its last owner, Lady Sybil Beatty, sold it for the development of Lower Earley.

In the 1940s R Black owned and ran the Maiden Erlegh Stud as well as running a riding school. His brother, James Black, ran another riding school from buildings on the other side of the Maiden Erlegh estate (*Kelly's Directory*, 1940).

4 Earley's Development

From Hamlet to Town

The story of Earley is one of great change and transformation. Whilst every village in Britain has seen change and growth, Earley's lack of an original centre and explosive growth sets it apart from the norm.

There is no Anglo-Saxon Charter for Earley. The *Domesday Book* (1087) records that there were two manors, Earley Regis and Earley St Bartholomew both held by King Edward the Confessor. The boundaries of Earley were not defined. The main occupations of this time were farming and fishing.

The next 800 years saw little change. Earley during this time was dominated by the large estates of Whiteknights, Erleigh Court, Bulmershe and Maiden Erlegh and a number of large farms. The vast majority of the then small population were agricultural peasants or worked in the agricultural support industries as blacksmiths, wheelwrights, millers, hurdle makers and eel trap weavers.

Until around 1850 the population remained fairly constant. Then Reading began to get land hungry and began to make its presence felt. Earley's first big expansion took place between 1850 and 1880, as houses began to be built at an ever-quickening pace between Cemetery Junction and the Three Tuns. The massive population explosion that occurred during this time was entirely comparable with the growth that was to occur one hundred years later in Lower Earley.

In 1887 the Corporation of Reading made a successful bid for this area of houses, and with Newtown and Earley Rise absorbed into Reading, Earley's population reverted to its former size.

The next big building phase occurred during the 1930s when the sale of Erleigh Court released land for building more houses. At the same time linear development began to occur along and around Wokingham Road and Wilderness Road (see Map 18, page 246).

The war and the post-war shortage of building materials slowed up Earley's development, but the expansion was given a boost when a large amount of development land was released with the sale of the Maiden Erlegh estate to Cooper Estates in 1954. The Maiden Erlegh estate is essentially a sixties development and filled in most of the remaining high ground between the 1930s developments along the Wokingham Road to just south of Maiden Erlegh lake.

The biggest change came with the development in Lower Earley. This was mostly a 1980s development and led to the trebling of Earley's already large population in just a decade. The Lower Earley development was until recently the largest private housing development in Europe. Today Lower Earley is generally recognised as the area to the east of Mill Lane, to the south of Rushey Way and to the west of Radstock Lane.

Final touches to the Lower Earley development during the 1990s, such as around the Police Station and Marsh Farm, have brought Earley's structural development to an end: Earley can expand no more. The boundaries with Woodley and Reading, the rivers Thames and Loddon and the M4 motorway prevent any further major residential development.

At the end of the year 2000 two burning issues in the Lower Earley community were at very different stages of development. The swimming pool at the Loddon Valley Leisure Centre at the District Centre was nearing completion. Whereas the secondary school was still a dream and the remaining land at Marsh Farm was being considered for such a school.

Land Use

The land use of any area is dependent on the topography (*see* Topography, Chapter 1) and soil types. It is very instructive to look at a map with contours and then walk over the area and gain a feel for the land and try and see it as our ancestors would have done, stripped of roads, modern developments etc. Such an examination helps to give us an idea of how Earley developed. Earley rises from the banks of the Kennet and Thames to a high point which is now a main east-west route onto the Reading and Shinfield borders and drains through what is now Whiteknights lake to the Thames in the north and through what is now Maiden Erlegh lake to the Loddon; alluvial soils are found around the rivers. River Gravels and Reading Beds rise from the valley gravels in the north to the London Clays and Plateau Gravels. The alluvial soils were developed as meadows, these were (and are) lands that flood regularly; the river gravels became the open fields; the plateau gravels were heathland, trees, bushes, gorse, broom and some open land for grazing. The London Clays were woodland and meadows until they were drained in the nineteenth and twentieth centuries.

The *Domesday Book* gives us an indication of the type of agriculture and its prosperity before and after the Norman Conquest. The two manors, containing arable land as well as meadows, woodlands and fisheries are recorded as supporting a population of about 100 people (18 families). The value of the manors decreased after the Norman Conquest (*see* chapter 3).

It is not known whether or not it was part of Windsor Forest or whether the boundary of the forest was the Loddon. But in Berkshire there was extensive deafforestation in 1227 (Hatherly and Cantor, 1979–80). During the reign of Richard I stump-hoppers, sent around Berkshire to thwart the removal of trees, visited Earley. Earley was one of a group of villages that was fined half a mark each for assarting the woods (assarts or clearings were defined as any place where a man standing on a stump of a tree could see five other stumps around him, Scott, MacLaughlin, 1984).

In 1276 Richard de Earley's manor included *a park of 40 acres* (Hatherly and Cantor, 1979–80) A park was a common feature of medieval landscapes. It was part of the desmesne lands of the lord of the manor and typically consisted of unimproved lands generally poor and less adaptable to cultivation and was usually wooded to provide cover for deer. It was normally situated on the edge of the manor and the park boundary often coincided with the manorial or parish boundaries.
It was there to provide red meat and game for the lord of the manor and was stocked with red, fallow or roe deer. The park had to be securely enclosed to contain the deer usually by a substantial earth bank, topped with wooden gates into the park and a deer-leap where deer could jump in but not out. Many medieval parks were adapted to serve as amenity grounds. Was this the embryonic Whiteknights Park? Or was it associated with Park field in north Earley and so part of the Manor of Earley St Bartholomew?

A further land use change is recorded in the reign of Henry VII when William Trewe was fined forty shillings for turning 40 acres of arable land into pasture on land that was previously occupied by 8 people.
He was ordered to convert the pasture back to tillage (Leadman, 1897).

The Earley Meads by the Thames flooded regularly, and still floods, and have always been meadows. They were probably worked as Lammas meadows, i.e. the cattle were removed between Candlemas (1st February) and Lammas (1st August) to allow for a hay harvest.

In 1657 nine open fields are recorded (BRO EN 1/2/12), six in 1669 and seven in 1742 (BRO D/EDO E33).The six open fields of Earley are shown in the map of *A topographical descrn of Earligh Comon Fields and Comon Mead, scitterate in ye Countre of Berks by Edward Blagrave, pract. Mathe 1669* the map is not drawn to scale and tantalisingly only shows the area of the alluvial soils, Valley Gravels and Reading Beds, the best agricultural land in the area which is now covered by Earley Rise, Newtown and north Earley. Wharf field bordered on the Kennet and contained wharves for the boats coming to and from the main highway of the Thames. The wharves were present into the nineteenth century. This field was bordered to the east by Lynch field which in turn was bordered by the Thames and Earley Meads (meadows), to the north and by Park

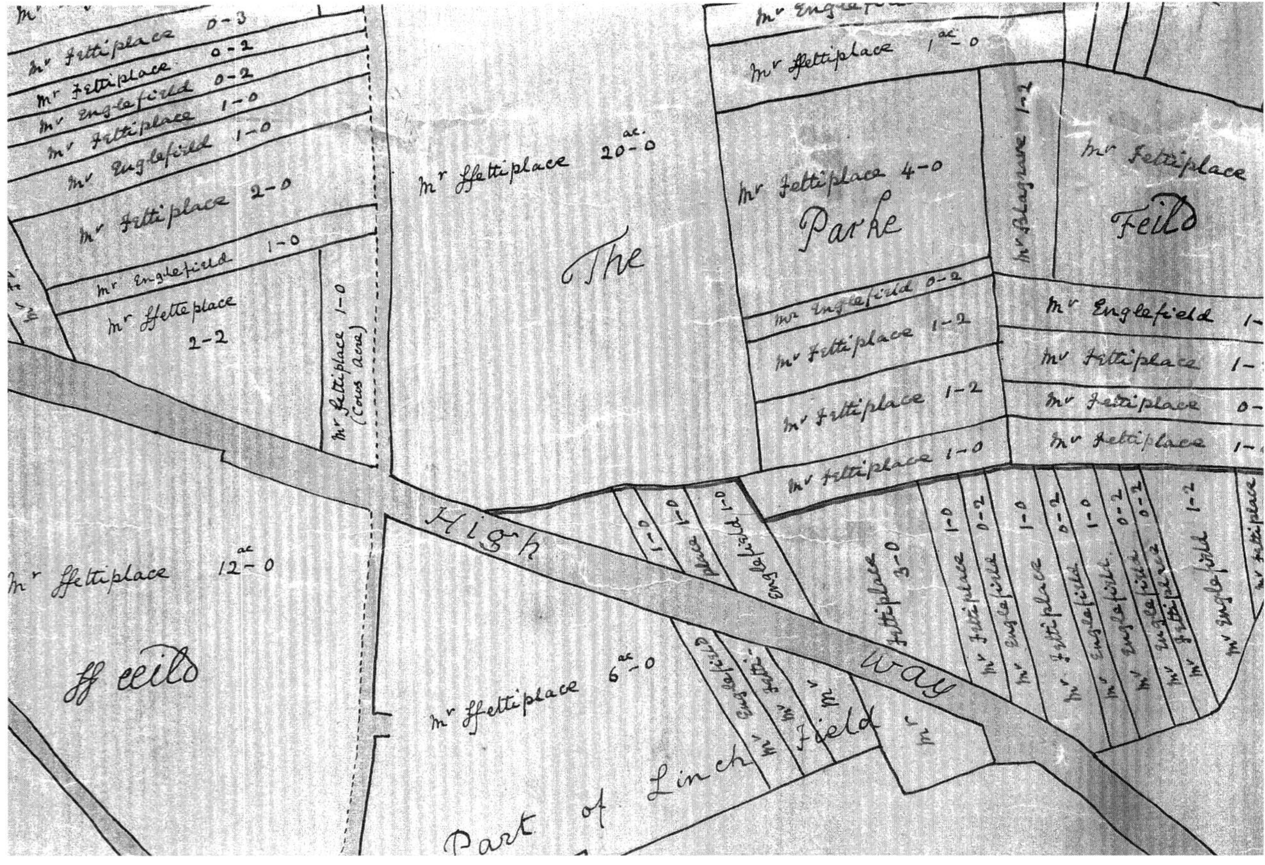

Map 6: The new Bath Road cutting through strips of the open fields of North Earley.
Copy of the Blagrave Map, 1669, Earl of Macclesfield, RLSL

field to the east. The present A4 was the approximate southern edge of these three fields. In 1669 the Bath Road is shown as cutting diagonally through certain strips in the common fields (*see* map 6 above).

The other three fields to the south of the A4 were Hawthorn (Long field in the eighteenth century), Earley or Mace and Symons fields moving from west to east, respectively. The southern edges of these fields abutted on to Earley Heath and Hawthorn field ranged into what is now Whiteknights Park. The western boundary between Reading and Earley was delineated by a hedge and ditch from the Kennet to Whiteknights. Wharf field is now part of Newtown, Lynch field Suttons Business park, Mace field is occupied by Reading Cemetery and Palmer Park and Symons Field was later occupied by the park of Erleigh Court, now North Earley. In Earley or Mace (Mase) field were pits called mace holes. They were 15 to 20 feet in depth, contiguous with each other and covered nearly an acre of ground. They became filled with brushwood and young trees growing

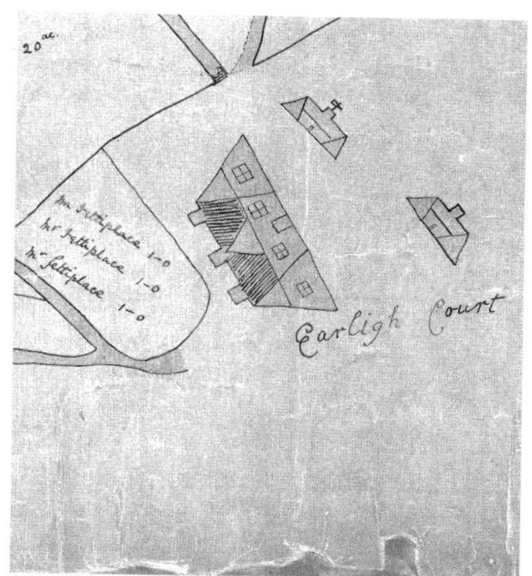

Above: Erleigh Court
Copy of the Blagrave Map 1669, Earl of Macclesfield, RLSL

Below: Map 7, Open fields, Earley Heath and Earley Lower Wood and Upperwood Commons, 1742

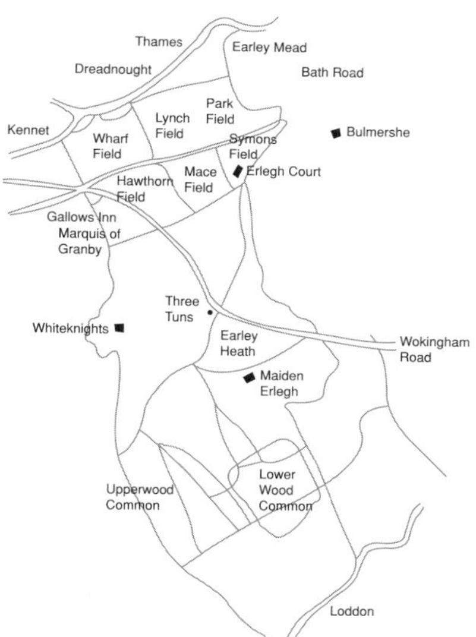

to some height. They may have been mediaeval in origin and dug to extract flint or chalk for building or agricultural purposes (Coates, 1802; Underhill, 1981).

The common fields and mead were divided into strips of about one acre each, ranging from half a rood to 20 acres (Dormer, 1927). The biggest landowners were the Hydes, Fettiplaces of Erleigh Court, Blagraves of Bulmershe and Englefield who was lord of the manor and lived at Whiteknights. Two freeholders, John Greenaway and George Thorne, owned a few acres; and the Provost and Scholars of Queen's College, Oxford had land, which had been given to them by the Fettiplaces. We learn who the landowners were but not who tilled the soil and where those people lived. Only one house is shown – Erleigh Court.

We do know that other houses had been built by this date but all were on the edges of Earley Heath and Upper and Lower Wood Commons or on the boundaries with Reading (Noman's land in the Elm Road area) or with Woodley (Worlds End, Pitts Lane area). These substantial houses belonged to yeomen. But where did the labourers live? No village has been recorded. Their homes were certainly expendable as it was recorded that a number of hovels were pulled down when the Wokingham Road/Forest Road was improved and straightened in 1759 when it became a turnpike road.

We surmise that the six open fields were ideal for growing wheat, barley and legumes. There were wharves alongside the Kennet for moving grain by barge to London and a ready market in Reading, as well as mills to grind the wheat and brew houses to use the barley for beer. The sandy acid soils of Earley Heath would have been a source of timber as well as being used for grazing. The thick glutinous soils formed over the London Clay would have been pasture and woodland.

Maps were drawn to show land holdings and claim taxes of some sort. Dormer (1927) states that the 1669 map was drawn up to determine which lands were tithable to the Rectory of Sonning. This argument continued over the next two centuries. Joe Pettitt (unpublished) suggests that there may have been a seventh field, Randalls. A few pieces survived in 1742 a total of 5 acres 1 rod 23 perches and included land around Heath Close and Tovey's Piddle (around Talfourd Avenue). All were enclosed for Sir Henry Englefield.

In 1742 the main landowners brought a private bill to enclose the six open fields (423 acres in total) (Tate, 1943).

Another landowner was Queen's College, Oxford whose lands were consolidated into pieces near Solly Joel Field and the junction of College Road and Wokingham Road.

The land was consolidated around the big houses in the three manors as it was fashionable at the time to have landscaped parks. Areas of arable

Enclosure of the open fields, 1742

Act for Confirming, Establishing and make effective certain Articles of Agreement made and entered into for inclosing and dividing the several Common fields lying in the Township or Hamlet of Earley in the Parish of Sonning in the County of Berkshire for exchanging several ancient Inclosures with the said Township or Hamlet of Earley aforesaid. The several Common Fields: Hawthorn, Mace, Simonds, Warfe, Lynch, Park and Randalls – 423 ac and upwards.

Owners: Sir Henry Englefield, Edward le Strand, George Blagrave seized divers lands in the Common Fields, Elizabeth Manley widow and William Soley Esquire are seized in equal moieties, as Tenants in Common of divers lands and grounds in the said Common Fields (BRO D/EDO E33).

land became parks and brought about changes in the employment of local people. Labour was needed to prepare and maintain the gardens and parks. The land was lost to agriculture, but the parks created employment for gardeners.

The enclosure of the open fields allowed for the consolidation of holdings into farms. One of the main reasons for enclosing was given as the improvement in farming efficiency. A farmer could now work a block of land instead of strips of land in the open fields. The fashion for enclosing spread all over England. More than 35% of England was enclosed in the1720s and more than 25% was carried out by private Acts, as was the one in Earley which was brought by agreement of the landowners. The landowners had to meet the cost of the formal agreement, pay the parliamentary commissioners and plant and maintain hedges around the fields.

The area was then divided into the three estates and the following farms: New Farm (later London Road Farm), Erleigh Court Farm (later Grange and Sidmouth Grange Farm), Earley Heath Farm, Mockbeggar Farm, Lodge Farm, Elm Farm, Coppice Farm, Upper Wood Farm, Lower Wood Farm and Home Farm,

The 1756 map of Earley Whiteknights (BRO D/EB/PI) showing the land holdings of Sir Henry Englefield gives a clear picture of the rectangular fields of inclosure in North Earley. The fields around the Heath and two commons were sub-rectangular in shape. Joe Pettitt (unpublished) suspected that they may have been enclosures from the waste at some unknown date before any statutory enclosure.

In 1761, seven acres 3 roods of Earley common were enclosed by formal agreement (Tate, 1943) and 4 acres 30 perches for Sir Henry Englefield. Mavor (1809) states that this agreement was made between the commoners and Sir Henry Englefield before the bill for inclosing was procured. In 1798 a further two roods 30 perches of Earley Common were enclosed for growing timber.

The Earley Meads were divided into 100 fragments and covered 59 acres 1 rood and 20 perches in 1752 but by the late 18th century they were composed of 110 strips covering 85 acres. This land was enclosed in the early 19th century, probably about 1810 but there is no record of their enclosure. The area that the meads covered is bird-shaped and is still recognisable on modern maps. Earley Meads were divided between the following landowners:

Sir Henry Englefield	Whiteknights	52 pieces 33ac 0r 17p
Sir William Scott	Earley Court	22 pieces 22ac 3r 8p
E. Golding	Maiden Earley	18 pieces 11ac 3r 37p
J. Wheble	Bulmershe Court	15 pieces 11ac 0r 0p

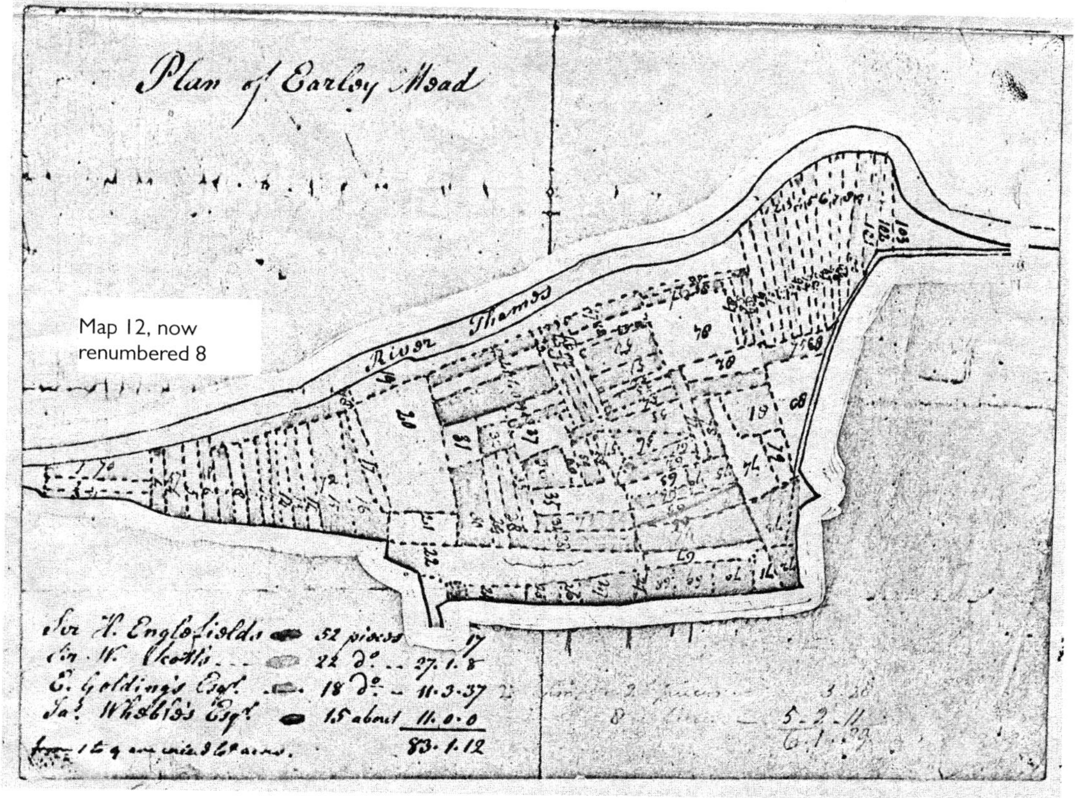

Map 8, Earley Meads, late 18th century
BRO D/EDO/P3

A total of 78 acres was enclosed. By 1873 George Palmer owned the meads and rented them to Colebrook and they became known as Colebrook Meadows by generations of people growing up in Newtown and Earley Rise. Cattle grazed the meads until the Thames Valley Park development began. The shape of meads would still be recognisable to Earley residents of centuries ago. But it is no longer used for agriculture. It is now the largest open space in Earley and is used by walkers and cyclists travelling between Reading and Sonning and the footpath is part of the Thames cycleway and footpath.

In 1816 Earley Heath and Earley Upper and Lower Wood Commons and the remaining roadside wastes, were enclosed and divided between the main landowners who are identified as Sir Henry Englefield, Edward Golding of Maiden Erlegh, James Wheble of Bulmershe Court and William Scott of Erleigh Court (D/P/113/26A).

Provision was made for the poor of Earley in compensation for their loss of rights on the commons. Initially the land was advertised for use as allotments but it was said that it was too far away from where people

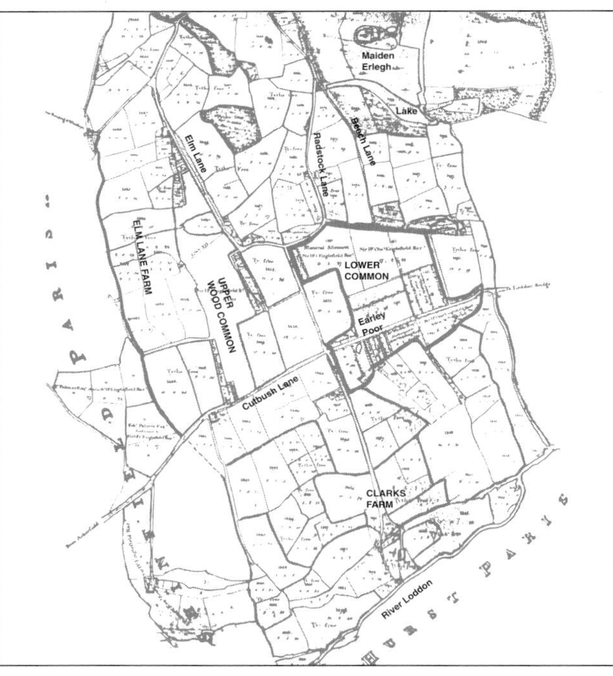

Left: Map 9, 1820 Enclosure of Earley Heath in the Liberty of Earley BRO D/R113/26C

Right: Map 10, 1820 Enclosure of Earley Upperwood and Lowerwood Commons in the Liberty of Earley BRO D/R113/26C

were living. We have no record of the effect of the final enclosure on the non-landowning people of Earley. But William Silver Darter in his reminiscences wrote that he was part of the yeomanry that met on Bulmershe Heath (enclosed 1816) in 1821:

> *Many cottagers used to cut the heather turf on the common which they dried in the summer and it served them for fire and to heat their ovens. An old servant of ours married and occupied one of the small houses on the edge of the heath in which two or three generations of the family had lived and who had always been accustomed to rear geese and poultry on the common, but when the late Mr Wheble's father enclosed the heath all of these privileges were swept away.* (Phillips, 1985).

Bulmershe Heath abutted onto Earley Heath so maybe the cottagers who lived in Earley suffered the same loss of privileges, although they would have received some compensation from the Poor's Charity if they were one of the deserving poor.

Up until the mid 19th century Earley was completely agricultural. There was a market for its grain in Reading and for its cattle at Loddon Bridge (Reading Mercury, 1840) and access to London from its own wharves. The fisheries mentioned in the *Domesday Book* were present and eel traps would have been made from locally grown withies. The fields were ploughed by Black Berkshire horses (Mavor 1809) which were strong and powerful with legs somewhat short, bodies thick and remarkable for strength rather than activity. Oxen were rarely used, although there is evidence for such at Barkham (VCH, 1923). In the arable fields rotations of wheat/beans (*Vicia faba*) and a fallow of turnips and clover were grown. The fields were manured with stable manure, which later in the century was brought from London.

During the agricultural riots of 1830 the local MP, Robert Palmer of Holme Park, Sonning, kept the troubles in the area to a minimum. The repeal of the Corn Laws had a drastic affect on local farmers. The laws had given farmers a protected price for their wheat which kept the price of a loaf of bread very high. Robert Palmer voted against the repeal of the Corn Laws (Berkshire Chronicle, 1855). Local farmers must have felt very threatened as in 1843 the Berkshire Association for the Protection of British Agriculture and Other Branches of Native Industry was formed by Mr W Mount (President) and Mr G Shackel (secretary). They wanted the maintenance of a protection system for agriculture to offset the high taxes that they paid, competition from foreign countries and the heavy cost of labour (costs were 40% higher than in other countries). This association did not last long (VCH,1923).

An example of a 19th century farmer is Joseph Goddard. He farmed the 160 acres of Elm Farm. He lived on the farm with his children and employed 6 men and 3 boys.

The average wage for agricultural labourers was 10/6d per week and 15s 6½d per week (plus the help of his wife) during harvest. In comparison carters and shepherds earned 11–12s/week and brick layers and labourers £90/year (Caird,1851) Out of that the agricultural labourer would have had to pay 2/6d per week for rent of the cottage. He would have grown all his own vegetables and fruit and probably had hens as well as catching rabbits. The agricultural labourer was dependent on the Poor Law in times of hardship such as bad weather, illness or old age.

The coming of the railways affected farming in Earley. The farms in north Earley were bisected by the railway lines and cheaper food from other parts of Britain and other countries could now be transported easily. The increase in manufacturing in Reading led to the loss of land for housing and for a new type of agriculture, flower and vegetable seed production for Suttons (who rented 33 acres 0 rods 4 perches in Mace field from George Palmer). The farms then turned their production to supporting the burgeoning population of Reading – cattle from Colebrooks for their many shops in the area, barley for Simonds brewery, wheat for the mills and milk from the new dairy farms for Huntley and Palmer's as well as for local people and horse breeding on the Maiden Erlegh estate.

The lands in Lower Earley were wet and difficult to manage until they were drained. Even now springs open out during wet weather. Draining started in the nineteenth century and continued into the twentieth century. In the 1860s 2inch drains were put in at a depth of four feet and 24 feet apart. Mr Bunce, the last farmer at Radstock Farm, said that the land was unworkable for arable crops until deep drains were put in.

The wet lands were grazed and coppiced. In the Loddon flood plain withies (willows) were grown and harvested. they were used for basket weaving, eel traps, fish baskets and hurdle making.

During the World Wars allotments became very important as sources of fresh vegetables and fruit for the many people who now did not work on the land.

Reading's *land hunger* and the proximity of Earley to Reading has led to a progressive loss of agricultural land to housing, industry and transport routes. House building started alongside the Kennet and alongside the eastern border of Reading as far as Whiteknights Park, continued across north Earley to central Earley and along Wokingham Road. The building continued along the eastern Reading border on the other side of Whiteknights Park, the Maiden Erlegh estate and finally the remaining fields of Lower Earley.

Suttons with their fields of flowers and bulbs have long since moved to Torquay. The names of the farms, a few farmhouses and the shape of the fields still exist but the only food being grown is in our gardens and the allotments at Culver Lane and Bulmershe.

The Spinney

The Spinney is a thatched cottage with black beams and a well in the garden tucked away behind modern housing off Elm Lane.

The house was probably built in the early sixteen hundreds. Remains of wattle and daub, using cow manure, was found when the house was renovated 40 or 50 years ago. It was originally two farm cottages and was situated on the edge of Upper Wood common. The common was enclosed in 1816. There were a number of houses in the area making a little settlement. The Spinney is the only one that remains from that era.

In the early 20th century it was owned by the Allsebrooks, who made water pumps in Reading, and a builder called Goodall. The Colebrooks owned the farmland around the house before they bought the house in the early 1940s. It was the home of Peter Colebrook and his family until the University bought Elm Farm in the 1960s.

Peter Colebrook said that various people commented that they had seen a ghost in the form of a lady wearing diaphanous night-clothes. Jenny Cuff, a recent occupant, said that a neighbour's brother-in-law, who is psychic, said that he had seen a little girl dressed in a green dress going into the house (*Bricks and Mortals*, 1994).

Grade II listed building
No. 1 Radstock Cottage,
Radstock Lane

This cottage was originally built in the early 17th century. Externally the cottage has a timber frame encased in painted roughcast and a tiled-gabled roof. Internally it has a complete, visible timber frame. The beams and joists are chamfered with lambs tongue stops. It also boasts a queen post roof, an inglenook chimney and a bread oven. No. 2 (Radstock Farm Cottage) adjoining was formally part of No. 1.

Grade II listed building
Rushy Mead, Cutbush Close

This is a late 16th century cottage with 19th and 20th century alterations. Externally it is timber framed with painted brick infilling and an old tiled, gabled roof.

Internally, it has a complete exposed timber frame and queen post roof trusses and windbraces.

Top: Radstock Cottages, 2000

Centre: Lowerwood Farm (Rushy Mead)
1930s, Ruth Coles

Bottom: Lowerwood Farm (Rushy Mead)
1930s, Ruth Coles

Transport

Earley is bounded by three rivers: the Loddon, Kennet and Thames, the latter two being major routeways which carried much of the traffic into and out of the area. In mediaeval times the Thames would have been a more reliable route than the roads; in 1220 the Dean of Sarum came on a visitation to Sonning along this river. At this period and later, goods were carried to and from London by barge up to Reading, where wharves extended into Earley giving the name to Wharf field which abutted onto the Kennet. In 1733 Peter Breach, fisherman of Sonning, was granted a 99-year lease of The Dreadnought, a pub near Kennet Mouth which was well used by boatmen (Dormer, 1944). Later, a Peter Breach built an eel buck (barrier) which caused an obstruction for barges which had great difficulties sailing through the fast flowing Thames. Breach was ordered to remove the buck. With the canalisation of the Thames and Kennet in the eighteenth and early nineteenth centuries, traffic on the river increased. Barges took wheat, barley, flour and malt from Berkshire and Oxfordshire to London (Mavor 1809) and coal in the reverse direction (VCH 1923). In 1813 the first steam boat sailed from Bath to London. The wharves were still in use in the early Victorian period (Dormer, 1944) until competition from the railways destroyed the river trade.

In the nineteenth century a ferry was used to carry people across Kennet Mouth; the Ferry House is included in the Census returns for 1891. In 1999 a ferry was again used when the Horseshoe Bridge was refurbished.

The most important road through Earley was the Great West Road (now the A4) between London and Bristol/Bath. The Marquis of Granby (formerly the Gallows Inn) on the Reading/Earley boundary was an important stopping place for travellers. The Bath Road ran between some of the open fields and across strips of unenclosed land as shown in the 1669 map (Blagrave Map 1669). The whole road, often called the Road to Bath, was turnpiked in the early eighteenth century, the stretch of road from Sonning Lane end to the Bear Inn, Reading becoming a turnpike road by Act of Parliament in 1736, with a tollgate at the Marquis of Granby. The maintenance of the road passed to a Turnpike Trust which used the income from tolls for repairs; formerly this was the responsibility of the parish. The road was heavily used until the coming of the railway. When the mail coaches ceased to use the road, income from the tolls declined from a maximum of £1415 in 1825 to £234 in 1842 (Rudd and Rudd, 1990). By 1846 all coach services along the Bath Road had ceased. The growing use of the motor car in the twentieth century restored the importance of the road.

In the 1930s the road, now called the A4, was upgraded. By the late 1960s Reading was clogged with traffic. The opening of the M4 in 1972 relieved the congestion in the centre of Reading but its effects on Earley were dramatic as its route through Lower Earley and along the Loddon valley cut Earley off from most of the River Loddon. Local government responsibility for this part of Earley was transferred to Arborfield and Newlands, Shinfield and Sindlesham. The A329M, the most intrusive of motorways, was built in 1975. During its construction three men were killed and ten were injured when a 120 foot section of partly built bridge crashed into the Loddon 30 feet below (*Berkshire Mercury*, 1977). It cuts a swathe through the heart of Earley from the M4 to the Thames Valley Park. Large tracts of land were lost at the Bulmershe Allotments and north of Culver Lane; houses and gardens were lost along the west side of Anderson Avenue. Mays Lane whose route had been changed by the railway was now cut in two. The A329M was known as the motorway that went nowhere until it was extended into the Thames Valley Business Park.

Until the enclosure of the large open fields in 1746, travellers from Reading had an alternative route to London via a lane which ran across Mace field (now Reading Cemetery and Palmer Park) to the narrow tree-lined Culver Lane (also known as Lovers Lane, Water Lane or Clover Lane), round the back of Erleigh Court to Pitts Lane and so onto the Great West Road. This route might still have been used by local people but by the 17th century through traffic used the Great West Road direct from Reading.

Another east-west route through Earley was Three Tuns Lane, later called Wokingham Road. It formed the beginning of the Forest Road. It ran, as it does today, from the Marquis of Granby past the Three Tuns to Loddon Bridge, Wokingham and eastwards. It was an important route and is shown on all maps of Berkshire from that of Saxton in the sixteenth century onwards. In 1759 Wokingham Road became part of the Windsor Forest Turnpike whose Trust was founded under an Act of that year . The preamble to the Act states that: *the Road leading from a place called The Old Gallows* (later an inn called the Marquis of Granby*) in the parish of Sunning (Berks), through the town of Wokingham, new Bracknowl and Sunning Hill to a stream of water or rivulet called Virginia Water in the parish of Egham, Surrey, is in a ruinous condition, narrow in many places and dangerous to Travellers, and the same cannot be effectually repaired and widened without the aid of Parliament* (BRO D/EGL/O1). Many houses were lost when the Trust improved and straightened the road across Earley Heath. However for travellers the changes were a distinct improvement. In 1822 William Cobbett said of his road from Binfield to Reading that it was *as smooth as a die, a real stockjobber's road.*

The bridge over the Loddon has been rebuilt many times; as early as 1617 there are records of its repair, at this time it was built with two arches (BRO D/EZ 38/1). It was one of the main points of entry into Windsor Forest from the west. In 1754 the bridge was rebuilt by David Rich Esq., Olivia Barker widow and Sarah Biggs widow and others, whose responsibility it was to maintain it. As a result there was *much greater traffic over the said bridge than otherwise would have been*. For this maintenance work, the Turnpike Trustees paid them a special commission of £7 per year. After the Turnpike Trust took over this responsibility a toll was extracted from each vehicle to cross it. Those drawn by six animals were charged one shilling with a decreasing scale of charges as the number of animals reduced. The tollgate was on the Winnersh side of the Loddon, approximately where the Loddon Bridge roundabout is now. Another tollgate was built at the Marquis of Granby (Farrar, 1984). Coach services continued along the Forest Road to London *via* Wokingham until the 1850s. The William's Windsor Park coach from King Street, Reading called at the Rose Inn Wokingham daily except Sundays to and from London. The journey took 5 hours.

The profits from tolls declined between 1844 and 1850 making it increasingly difficult to find investors. Direct competition from the railways began in the mid-19th century and in the 1860s the Turnpike Trust was dissolved. The present, very utilitarian bridge, was put in place in the 1950s, unfortunately for the current residents of Earley, as it lacks most of the aesthetic qualities of its predecessors.

Carters used the Forest Turnpike and other roads though many were dangerous; highwaymen, footpads and rogues being a constant threat. Some Post Office employees walked from Reading to Wokingham and

Loddon Bridge and The George
Postcard, 1930s

back daily between 1816 when the foot post started until 1857 after which time all post was sent by rail (Homer Wooff and Jones 1981, 1982). Travellers to the area described their impressions of the scene:

> *About two miles to the eastwards of this place is the pleasant and extensive village of Sonning, affording a delightful walk by the verdant side of the Thames, which is nearly as wide as at London Bridge. If you go by the turnpike road the distance is something greater, but on your way you pass the seat of Sir William Scott (Erleigh Court) in front of which is a small park laid out with taste. The house is neat, and affords a bird's eye view of the Oxfordshire Hills ranging alone in front of it.*

They also said that there were three routes into Reading. In summer time he recommended the route through Windsor Forest but in winter the main Bath Road (Man, 1810).

The internal lanes of Earley were largely in place by the early nineteenth century; Mary Mitford who lived at Three Mile Cross often walked across to Erleigh Court a distance of three miles accompanied by her dog and with her long crook-handled staff for hooking flowers out of the hedge. In 1816 the enclosure of Earley and Bulmershe Heaths eliminated the tracks across them. The map shows the other lanes which existed then but with different names from today; they reflected the names of the farmers who lived and farmed the areas. Maiden Early Lane, which ran to the east of the walled garden (now occupied by Maiden Erlegh Bowling Club) on the Maiden Erlegh estate, was closed by the Enclosure Act, and a new route, the present Beech Lane, was built. Whiteknights Road was an estate road and the Shinfield/Sonning Road was directed south of the Duke of Marlborough's park. This part of the road was later renamed Wilderness Road. Another lane, Englefield Lane, is shown on the 1742 Enclosure Map. It ran from the Forest Road (Wokingham Road) near to modern Green Road and appeared to take a south-west direction across Earley Heath. The internal lanes are largely in place to this day. The decision to leave the lanes and build a network of new roads during the development of Lower Earley has left the old lane network in place and parts of them are footpaths/cycleways.

A lane called Gallows Lane which led to the corner of Elm Road and Elm Lane possibly has a sinister history. This corner was a large piece of open land referred to as Gallows Common (part of which is now the roundabout). Until the late 1930s a huge elm tree stood there (Doble, 1961). In 1818 William Norris owned an allotment near the Great Elm on Elm Lane called Gallows Commons (BRO D/R113/26c) and W. S. Darter (Philips, 1985) called the area Gallows Tree Common. It was said that prisoners were taken there from Reading Gaol to be hanged. Darter remembered talking to a farmer, Mr Goddard, living in Lower Earley who pointed out the spot where the executions had taken place and stated that the culprits were dragged up out of the cart. Darter remembers his father telling him about the hangings and that:

> *it was no uncommon thing for the culprit and attendant to stop at the Oxford Arms, Silver Street on their way from the gaol to Gallows Tree Common, and there partake of liquor of some kind.*

The last hanging was in 1793. The elm tree was chopped down in the 1930s (William Breadmore). Doble suggested that the name might have been given to the tree to warn highwaymen not to molest travellers on the nearby turnpike road (now Shinfield Road). The turnpike gate was between Elm Lane and Whitley Wood lane.

There are now only six rights of way in Earley:

- Shepherds House Lane, the lane to the Meads
- the path that runs from Mill Lane alongside the stream, across Toseland Way to the Loddon
- the remnants of the path that was formerly the boundary between Earley and Shinfield and ran down to and across the Loddon, it now runs from Elm Road to Rushey Way; formerly called Pigwash Lane
- the right of way across Whiteknights Park from Whiteknights Road to Shinfield Road
- the route between Pepper Lane and Elm Road running behind Trelawney
- Town Lane running from Pitts Lane to Grays Crescent in Woodley

The coming of the railways (Great Western Railway in 1840 and London and South East Railway in 1849) effectively sandwiched a large parcel of Earley between the two lines and cut off the Thames and Earley Meads from the rest of Earley. These two lines following the line of the two major roads through Earley had a dramatic effect on the movement of people as old routes were cut through and lost. The Great Western Railway from London Paddington to Bristol was begun in the mid-1830s; from Twyford it runs through the north of Earley. The line between Twyford Station, which opened in July 1839, and Reading Station was plagued with delays and disasters mainly due to the construction of the Sonning Cutting, the western end of which is in Earley. The cutting is nearly two miles long and 60 feet deep in places. The hill, Scotsman's Knob, is said to be formed from the spoil. It took three years to construct and at one time 1,220 men and 196 horses were employed. Many lost their lives during the construction of the line. The route through to Reading station was completed in 1840 and ran through water meadows and farmland close to the Thames in Earley, crossing the river Kennet near its junction with the Thames. Later the land south of the line became the trial ground for Suttons Seeds, the row after row of blooms were always a splendid sight from the train and a reminder for commuters that Reading station was only five or six minutes away!

The Reading, Guildford and Reigate Company was incorporated by Act of Parliament in July 1846. The company was authorised to build a line from the GWR at or near Reading Station to join the London, Brighton and SE Railway in the parish of Reigate. On 15 October 1849 the double line, nearly 46 miles long was completed to its junction at Reigate. The South Railway Company leased the line at an annual rent of £41 000. The line through to Waterloo was built later. The development of the line through Wokingham was excluded from more lucrative connections with the rest of the country since no junction could be made without the consent of the GWR which understandably was reluctant to give it.

Above: Front of Earley Station
© Collier collection Earley 6, Rural History Centre, The University of Reading

Below: Earley Station platform
Postcard

Above: Tram terminus at the junction of St Peter's Road and Wokingham Road
Lent by P. Little

Below: Tram terminus at the junction of St Peter's Road and Wokingham Road

Earley station was formerly in Woodley! It was opened in 1863. Insufficient land was available for a normal type of station so the upper floor above the station offices on the down platform was given an iron spiral staircase. This upper floor, which had typical board cladding doubles as a platform canopy. When the station was closed to goods on 6th January 1969, an oil depot sidings was opened for BP Petrol Depot. Houses were built on this land in 1999.

Prior to electrification a concrete footbridge (replaced by a steel footbridge in 1990) was put over the line. The level crossing was used for access to a dwelling, the goods yard and the up platform. The signal box and hand-operated gates were closed on 4th February 1973.

The first electric train service started on 1st January 1959 when 36 electric trains from Reading to Waterloo replaced the 20 steam trains. Steam continued on the line to Sandhurst; the last scheduled steam-hauled passenger train to leave Reading South was the 10.40 pm to Guildford on 3rd January 1965 (Maggs, 1993). The Stagecoach Company now runs South Eastern Trains.

Woodley Airport was developed in the 1920s and was in use until the 1950s; older residents were used to aircraft flying overhead. Travel by aeroplane is now commonplace and the close proximity of Earley to Heathrow Airport means that the area is overflown regularly.

Populace

The population of Earley had always been small until the nineteenth century but exactly how small it is not possible to say. Until the first national census of 1801 we can only make estimates using tax and church records, though even these do not always survive for Earley.

The Domesday Survey of 1086 records 18 peasant families and three slaves living in the two manors of Earley, probably less than 100 people. By the early fourteenth century the population of Earley was possibly larger if it was experiencing the same growth as the rest of England. In the Lay Subsidy of 1334, a tax on all non-churchmen, Earley paid £7 6s 8d, more than Sonning or Wokingham; how many taxpayers there were is not recorded. There were certainly fewer by 1400 after the Black Death of 1348–9 and other plagues which reduced the population of England by 30 or 40%. The poll tax returns of 1381 do not survive for the Sonning Hundred making it impossible to estimate the effects of these epidemics on this locality. The population would not have started to grow until about 1500, if it did even then; the Lay Subsidy of 1524/5 shows Earley with only 19 taxpayers making it the smallest and poorest community in the Hundred of Sonning (PRO E/179/73/141).

All parishes were ordered to keep records of baptisms, marriages and burials from 1538 onwards. Earley was in the parish of Sonning whose register does not survive before the 1550s. The next 100 years nationally were a period of population growth in which Earley may have shared but since addresses are rarely given in the register, it is not possible to judge the changes in Earley. However the community could not have been insulated from the effects of the Civil War which raged across Berkshire between the headquarters of Parliament at Windsor and that of the King at Oxford in 1642–6. Soldiers would have been scouring the countryside looking for food, fodder and horses and the open fields would have provided easy pickings for them. During the great siege of Reading in April 1643 there was a huge outbreak of typhus (camp fever) which spread into the surrounding area. Sonning parish register records 88 burials for 1643 and 69 the following year, nearly three times more than was normal. Some of the dead would have been from Earley.

In the later seventeenth century a few Earley people are named in the register. *John, son of John Simmons of Earligh Heath* was the first in 1659 (RLSL Sonning Parish Records). Simmons is spelt in many ways throughout the registers. Other references to Simmons in Earley about this date include Symons Hedge on the 1669 map and a John Symons an appraiser of the goods and chattels of Richard Smith the elder, yeoman in 1704 (BRO D/A1/122/129). Between 1665 and 1681 the children of Anthony Engelfield of Whiteknights were baptised at Sonning Church even though they were known to be Roman Catholics.

In 1699 Elizabeth daughter of Joseph Pither of Earley was baptised. The name Pither survives in Earley until the early twentieth century; they were farmers and a Miss Pither was living at Woodbine cottage, Cutbush Lane in 1936 (*Kelly's Directory*).

Since 1801 a national population census has been held every ten years giving a more or less accurate figure for the population. The table shows what happened in Earley though the figures are deceptive since the area covered is not always the same. Until 1881 it included that part of Earley absorbed by Reading in 1887 and other boundary changes have occurred to Earley-outside-Reading in recent years.

Population of Earley

1801	**1811**	**1821**	**1831**	**1841**	**1851**	**1861**	**1871**	**1881**	**1891**
436	440	447	441	471	487	566	1534	4663	496
1901	**1911**	**1921**	**1931**	**1941**	**1951**	**1961**	**1971**	**1981**	**1991**
438	456	584	847	*war*	4,583	8,493	10,811	11,957	28,605
	1998								
	29,558 (estimated)								

Until 1841 only the statistics survive but after that the forms used by the enumerators who collected the information house by house give us a glimpse of individuals, their ages and occupations as well as the household unit in which they lived. In 1841 the population was largely agrarian; farmers, their families and agricultural labourers are recorded as well as innkeepers, beer sellers, blacksmith. In 1851 the first biscuit and railway workers appeared. The inhabitants were born mainly in Earley or locally. Between 1861–1881 a huge increase in population was recorded in Newtown, the area adjoining Reading. The houses accommodated workers including those at Simonds and Huntley and Palmer's and those from around the Marquis of Granby up to the Three Tuns the burgeoning middle classes: lodging houses, small schools, retired soldiers from the Empire, bankers, shopkeepers and clerks. In fact everyone needed to support the growing commercial centre of Reading and its industries. The vast majority of these residents came from outside Earley and Berkshire. The great houses like Maiden Erlegh House had their wealthy families (the Hargreaves in 1881) plus a hierarchy of staff needed to support the family and the estate.

After the absorption of Newtown and Earley Rise into Reading the population reverted to its former size, although now the area of Earley had decreased from 2280 to 1917 acres. The next big increase came between 1931 and 1951. The sale of Erleigh Court released land for building houses for the workers employed in the industries on the north side of the A4 (Suttons, Earley Power Station and later Ideal Windows) as well as in Reading. At the same time land was released around Wilderness Road and ribbon development continued around the Maiden Erlegh estate along Wokingham Road. The next big release of land came with the sale of the remnants of the Maiden Erlegh estate to Cooper Estates. Wokingham Rural District Council refused the application but this was overturned by Government Inspectors hence the local planning authority lost control of the development and little open land was left for the residents. This shortfall was finally made up with the acquisition of land now known as Laurel Park.

Another explosion in population came with the development of Lower Earley. Unless building is allowed in the Loddon flood plain our township is now full except for small amounts of infilling. No longer are homes occupied by people who live and work in the area alone but those who work all over the country as well occupy them

The census data tell us very little about the condition of Earley people. For a short time in the early nineteenth century the parish registers give the occupation of some of the fathers of those being baptised: the vast majority were agricultural labourers with just a few others – a carpenter, shoemaker, smith. Most lived hand to mouth with no reserves for times of sickness, unemployment or the loss of a breadwinner. Centuries earlier the government of Elizabeth I had introduced a system for dealing with the problem of poverty and vagrancy which had become serious during her reign, the Poor Law Act of 1601. Each parish was to levy a rate to pay for poor relief and to provide work for the able-bodied, punishments for the indolent and relief for the sick and the aged and apprenticeships for poor children. Unpaid officials called overseers of the poor were elected every year by the parishioners to collect and distribute the poor rate (BRO D/P113/18/4). By the 18th century the parish of Sonning was divided into liberties, each with its own overseers of the poor.

In the 1660s several Settlement Acts modified the law to clarify which parish was responsible for relieving a poor person; this was where he or she had settlement. Initially it was the parish where a person was born but he or she could acquire a new settlement by, for example, contracting to work in another parish for a year or, in the case of a woman, by marrying. A person leaving his or her settlement parish was often given a settlement certificate guaranteeing that the parish would take him/her back when poor relief was needed. On 30 July 1746 William Webb with his wife Mary and son William were given a certificate when they moved from Earley to Burghfield (BRO D/P29/13/4/39).

If a person or a family without rights of settlement fell on hard times, the parish where they lived would try to force them to move by applying to the magistrates for a removal order. Between 21 July 1812 and 22 March 1850 14 removal orders were issued sending people back to Earley (BRO D/P/113/1&2) and three between 3rd November 1818 and 7th October 1828 sending people out of Earley: William Norris, labourer to Tilehurst, Ann Brunsden, singlewoman, to St Mary's Reading and William Betteridge, Elizabeth his wife and their five children aged 8 months to 10 years old to Bray (BRO D/P113/12/1).

Fathers were responsible for the maintenance of their children, whether or not they were legitimate. If an unmarried mother named the father of her child and he could be traced, he would be served with a bastardy order. Elizabeth Kislingbury of Earley, formally questioned by Richard Marlborough, JP, admitted giving birth to an illegitimate son on 30 April 1821. The Earley overseer, Joseph Goddard, applied for a warrant ordering the constable of Earley to arrest the father, James Prosser, a servant or former servant of the Duke of Marlborough. Susan Fulker had a baby at the home of Lucy Easton in the Liberty of Earley on 10 May 1831. By the 25 June 1832 a bastardy order was brought against her and the father, George Exall of Earley, a labourer. He was ordered to pay forty shillings for charges at the birth (the cost of the midwife) and ten shillings for the affiliation order. Susan Fulker had to pay one shilling weekly if she did not nurse or care for the child herself. These were harsh penalties for people earning ten shillings and sixpence a week.

Earley had its own Poor House, but its position is uncertain. It may have been situated on the eastern side of Beech lane near the modern Dene Close; an area called Poors Land now occupied by Radstock House is shown on a map of 1756. In 1689 John Treadwell of Reading leased Brickneys House consisting of a messuage, orchard and garden with two closes, five and a half acres in total, for the Poor in Upper Earley (BRO D/EZ 7/21). We have been unable to identify this site.

The cost of poor relief began to escalate nationally at the end of the eighteenth century, the consequence of a fast-growing population, a run of bad harvests and the French Wars. Even small parishes were affected; between 1778 and 1803 the amount paid by Earley rate payers each year for poor relief rose from £244 1s 7d to £669 8s 9d, reaching 6s 6d in the pound. By 1819 the cost, though high, was falling. In that year £422 was collected in Earley; two individuals paid more than fifty percent of this tax (the Duke of Marlborough paid £143 and Mr Golding £72).

After a nationwide inquiry by a Royal Commission, the old poor law was amended in 1834 to group parishes into Poor Law Unions administered by a locally elected Board of Guardians with a national Poor Law Board in London. Each union was to have a workhouse to which all able-bodied poor would be sent; in theory there would be no more payments to the poor in their homes. Earley became part of the Wokingham Union, an amalgamation of ten parishes and five liberties. The guardians tried to keep down the cost of poor relief by using four existing parish workhouses at Wargrave, Hurst, Shinfield and Wokingham instead of building one which complied with the specifications laid down centrally. But the Poor Law Commissioners insisted and eventually the guardians purchased land on Barkham Road and the new workhouse was opened 2 October 1849 (BRO G/WO1/1&4).

The new red brick building with its spacious day rooms,working areas and sick wards was designed by Mr John Billing and cost £6,600. Inmates were set to work stone breaking and bone crushing; the women also cooked, cleaned and did the laundry.

The board which met every fortnight included guardians from each parish elected by the ratepayers; Mr William Shackel, Joseph Goddard and Mr May were at various times elected from Earley. The business of the meetings included the appointment of salaried officials; they employed the master of the workhouse, a medical officer, a chaplain and two relieving officers who paid out poor relief or sent paupers to the workhouse as the guardians directed. Since the union was large, it was divided into two with one relieving officer for the north and another for the south. Earley was in the north. The guardians also discussed the purchase of items such as bedding, clothing and food for the workhouse inmates, putting out tenders to get the best bargains. In the 1850s in the northern district up to £50 a week was spent in handing out small sums of money, plus bread, to keep people in their homes rather than in the workhouse. Often the only place for paupers to wait for their relief was the local public house. The accounts show that in April 1851 about 240 paupers were on out relief, far more than were in the workhouse. They received about 4 shillings a week and about 11 pounds of bread which seems quite generous (BRO G/WO1/5).

In the 1851 census 17 paupers are recorded of whom only four had been born in Earley; one came from Ireland and the rest from surrounding parishes and towns and all except one infirm 27 year-old were in their sixties or older. Many were living with their grown-up children who presumably were unable to support them from their wages. The majority were agricultural labourers or single or widowed. The Poor Law Guardians were abolished in 1929 and their powers were transferred to Wokingham Rural District Council and Berkshire County Council.

Early Centres

Earley has the reputation of being the town (and before that the village) without a centre. Even today the so called District Centre, Silverdale shops and Maiden Place, all fall far short of being true community focal points for Earley.

This is not to say that Earley did not have fledgling centres in the past. The most prominent of these were Little Hungerford and the Three Tuns crossroads.

The Hamlet of Little Hungerford was documented, by name, as early as 1747 (Pettitt, 1985) and there are many theories as to how it got its name. However to date no conclusive evidence is available to validate them and the origins of the name remain a mystery. The hamlet is shown on maps as a piece of land sandwiched between the manors of Maiden Erlegh and Bulmershe. It has often been described as a parcel of Sonning Manor. It covered an area along the north side of the Wokingham Road between Earley Station and Loddon Bridge (*see* map 11).

It has been estimated that in 1761 around five cottages were in the Hamlet increasing to seventeen by 1872 and, of these, thirteen remained in 1984 (Pettitt, pers comm). They were small owner-occupier tenements and described by the early 18th century as in Little Hungerford Hamlet. Between 1805 and 1843 James Wheble purchased these cottages and built some new cottages to let out to the labourers on his estate (Lloyd, 1977). Evidence of this can be found in 1848 when J. J. Wheble, owner

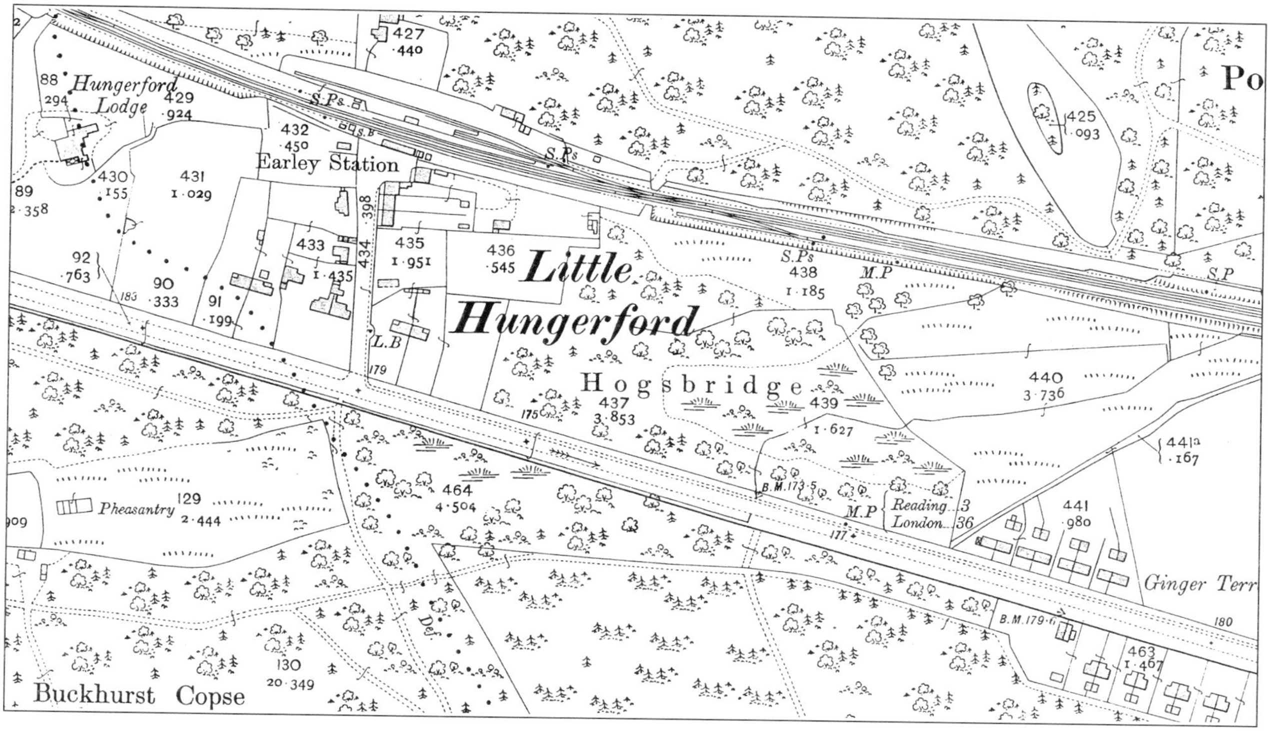

Above: Map 11, Little Hungerford

Reproduced from 1st edition 1891, 1:2500 Ordnance Survey map with permission of Her Majesty's Stationery Office © Crown Copyright, NC/00/1037

Right: Audley House adjoining Earley Station

© 1926 Sales Catalogue, Martin & Pole, Nicholas

of the Bulmershe Estate claimed compensation of £2900 for the loss of land, especially the grounds of Earley Cottage, danger to a third thatched roofed cottage and general loss of amenities from the Reading, Guilford and Reigate Railway. Railway Minutes recorded an arbitration award of £2,100; they also show that J. Wheble was a director of the company (Pettitt, pers comm).

With the building of the railway came Earley Station, a terrace in Station Road and Ginger Terrace on the Wokingham Road, opposite Maiden Erlegh Terrace. Local tradition says that they were built to house Irish railway labourers and as ginger is the colour of an Irishman's hair they were named Ginger Terrace.

One of the more prominent buildings in Little Hungerford was Hungerford Lodge or Earley Cottage as it was known up until 1890. This house is believed to have been built in 1803 or 1804 on the site of a former cottage. It stood about 650 feet back from the Wokingham Road, and occupied the land which is now Stanton Close. The house stood half in Earley and half in Woodley with the boundary running through it. When Captain James St L Wheble either sold or leased Bulmershe Court to Mr Rushbrooke, in 1908, he moved into Hungerford Lodge where he remained until his death in 1925. The lodge was sold by auction in 1926 after the death of his brother Major Tristram Wheble (Lloyd, 1977).

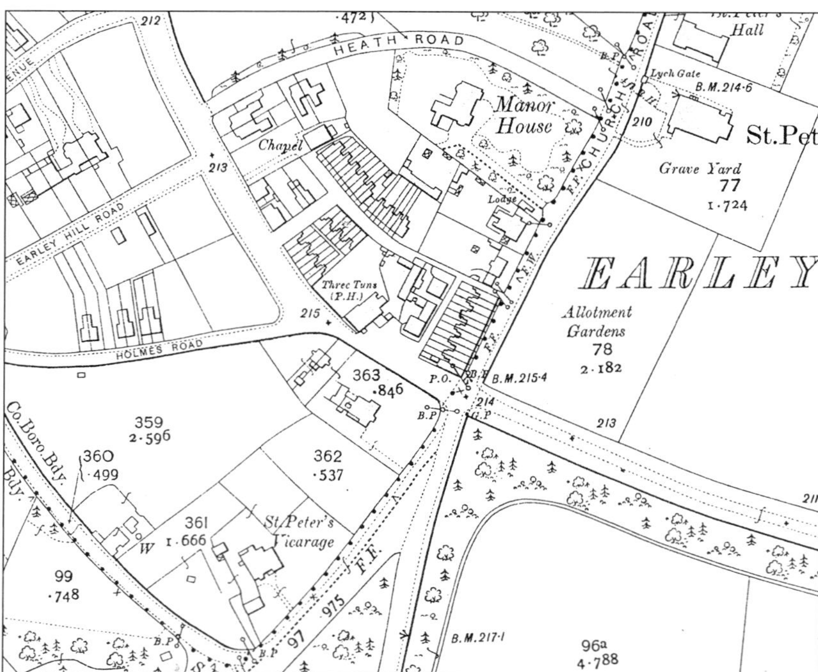

Map 12, Three Tuns Crossroads
Reproduced from 1st edition 1891, 1:2500 Ordnance Survey map with permission of Her Majesty's Stationery Office
© Crown Copyright, NC/00/1037

A Summary of Bulmershe Estate in 1908 lists Bulmershe Court and vast amounts of land and cottages in Woodley as well as Hungerford Lodge and land and cottages in Little Hungerford. Whether these were sold in 1908 is unclear. However, Hungerford Lodge appeared in the same sales catalogue as Bulmershe Court in 1926, suggesting that the Whebles may have still owned both of these properties until this date. The catalogue situates the property as *in the Parishes of Woodley and Earley, practically adjoining Earley Station on the Southern Railway possessing a frontage of about 650 feet to the main Wokingham Road.* The property is described as a *Farmhouse-style Residence, which has been modernised, stands well back from the main road, being approached by a Carriage Drive about 300 feet in length, is of pleasing elevation, being built of brick with tiled roof.*

The property contained 3 reception rooms, conservatory, 7 bed and dressing rooms, bathroom, servants' offices, garage and stabling, grounds and paddock extending to about 5 acres.

The house was demolished in the 1950s to make way for the development of Stanton Close. The name Little Hungerford was revived in 1978 as a name of the electoral ward comprising of South Woodley and part of Maiden Erlegh in Earley.

Having the Three Tuns public house, Earley St Peter's School and the Porter Institute built around it, gave the junction between the Wokingham Road and Church Road a prominent place in Earley's development.

A contributor to the Reading Mercury in 1936 captured the essence of the Three Tuns crossroads when he wrote:

> *With the passage of years, old landmarks disappear with little comment or ceremony; but occasionally they are recalled by a chance observation of aged folk impressed by the rapid urban development of the fields and woods of their childhood days. Some years ago, when delving into the history of the Manor of Bulmershe, in the parish of Sonning, I had occasion to devote some attention to a group of buildings which centred about the old Three Tuns Inn at Earley. I was struck by the fact that it appeared to be the focal point of four ancient manors; Erlegh St Nicholas, Earley St Bartholomew, Bulmershe and Maiden Erlegh, the last-named being a sub-manor probably of Erlegh St Nicholas. The economic lay-out at this spot included the inn, the forge, the pound, the farm (now enlarged and called the Manor House in Church Road), a pond and an early 18th century cottage near to the forge. Later, on the opposite side of the road, came the Victorian Post Office, and there may be one or two, even today, who can recall the postmistress, Martha Kislingbury. The ancient mills of Earley would have been on the Loddon at Lower Earley. They have vanished. The road which ran from Reading to Wokingham past the inn door, led across Earley*

Above: Culhams Stores, corner of Wokingham Road and Church Road
postcard, 1934

Below: Three Tuns public house
Collier Collection Early 5 Rural History Centre, The Uversity of Reading

Above: Three Tuns crossroads from Church Road
Dann/Lewis 626 Rural History Centre, The University of Reading

Below: Jarvis garage (formerly Erleigh Hill) the Three Tuns crossroads
Jarvis collection 1940s–1950s

Heath or Common to the Loddon Bridge. Between the inn and the brow of Loddon Hill a stream meandered across the road to form Hog Moor Pond, now built over. The length of highway from The Marquis of Granby at Reading to Wokingham was piked by an Act of Parliament considerably over a century ago; before that it was little more than a trackway across the heath.

For centuries the rural scene persisted about the neighbourhood of The Three Tuns, The Woodley Cavalry, formed during the Napoleonic menace, used to meet at the inn and periodically regale themselves when news came filtering through of the success of British arms in the Peninsular War. But things are very different now, and the borough of Reading, in its sturdy growth, is thrusting itself on to the manor lands to the east and the south. One has to go farther afield for the somnolent plough team. The Three Tuns has been rebuilt, the pond has gone and there is now no shower of sparks leaping, in the autumn dusk from the flaming, cobwebbed forge.

Joe Pettit

The late Joe Pettitt spent many years studying the history of Earley and area from documents and on the ground.

He tried to determine if there had ever been a centre or village settlement in the Liberty. He determined that there was an open field called Dean Field which was lost when Whiteknights Park was made, or extended in the eighteenth century. A dean or dene is a valley; there are two in Earley one in Whiteknights Park and one at Maiden Erlegh Lake/Old Pond Copse. He considered that there might have been a settlement where Whiteknights Lake is now. The village would have been lost when the lake was created, probably after the 1742 enclosure.

He examined the settlements around Elm Lane. In this area there were several houses and a three-acre pond but no likely place for a village centre.

However, a field near the stream, formerly called Moat Coppice, east of Elm Lane and south of Redhatch Copse appears on a map of 1754 which shows fragments of a moat and the field is littered with tilesherds and bricks; none of these can be dated earlier than the sixteenth century.

Industry

For the last thousand years the land that now lies within the boundaries of modern Earley was used almost entirely for agriculture. The late 18th century through to the early 20th saw some of this land taken out of agriculture to form parkland for the big estates, but generally very little changed. The big change came during the second half of the twentieth century when almost all of this agricultural land disappeared under large-scale housing developments.

It is obvious from the above that Earley has never been a major commercial or industrial centre. The reasons for this are largely geographical. Initially the housing development in Earley was to provide accommodation for the workers of Reading's growing industrial sector, i.e. Huntley and Palmer's, Sutton's, etc. Then to provide homes for the growing numbers of office workers in Reading's service-centred industries, such as Prudential Insurance; and finally with the building of the M4 to provide houses for commuters working in Swindon, Newbury, Basingstoke, Maidenhead, Windsor, Slough and London.

Many of the newly built houses were occupied by people who moved into the Thames Valley to take up positions they had been offered in all of these neighbouring urban towns that already had established industries. This has meant that Earley has not had to establish its own industrial sector.

This is not to say that Earley has been, or indeed is, totally devoid of its own industrial development. Some of Earley's industries have been based on agricultural production, e.g. Sindlesham Mill and Sutton's, others have been to supply raw materials to the growing population, e.g. Earley Power Station and Ideal Casements, whilst the most recent developments such as Sutton's Business Park, Thames Valley Business Park, Cutbush Lane Industrial Area (and the neighbouring Winnersh Triangle Industrial Estate) have been attracted to the Earley area by the town's high skills base.

The following gives the history behind some of Earley's most significant commercial/industrial employers:

Sindlesham Mill, 2000

Sindlesham Mill

A mill at Sindlesham (Synnel's Ham) was recorded in the *Domesday Book* as belonging to the Bishop of Salisbury's Manor at Sonning. The present building dates from the mid-nineteenth century with alterations in the twentieth century. It was in use, grinding corn into the late 1960's when it was bought by the Weston Family. It is now a hotel, restaurant and club. The mid-nineteenth century bridge at the side of the Mill goes over the millstream.

Alder was grown and coppiced along the Loddon. The rods were used to weave eel traps, baskets and hurdles.

Sutton's

Of all the local companies, Sutton's is the one most closely associated with the Earley and Reading area; and probably the one most fondly remembered.

The company started in 1806 when John Sutton established a small corn business in King Street, Reading. The company started to develop when John Sutton's son, Martin Hope Sutton, joined the company in 1836. In this year the company switched emphasis and moved into the flower and vegetable seed trade. It also physically moved in that year into new premises in Market Place, Reading.

Sutton's has always been a leader in its field. It pioneered many developments such as developing special lawn seed mixes for the domestic market and putting their seeds in foil packets. Amongst all of these developments, two in particular led to its becoming a household name. First, with the railway network, Sutton's became one of the first mail order companies in the world. This idea was further developed when in 1856 Sutton's first Amateur Seed Catalogue was published. Second, Sutton's pinned its reputation on being the first seed company to guarantee the quality of its seeds. Martin Hope Sutton was closely involved in the war against seed adulteration (which at that time was the industry norm), and was instrumental in the Adulteration of Seeds Act becoming law. Sutton's pioneered the testing of seeds and was one of the first to have its own seed testing laboratory.

In 1873, the original premises were replaced by extensive new offices and warehouses, covering over six acres. Part of the site was the garden of the old Reading Abbey. The business continued to grow fast, and by the turn of the century Sutton's employed about 1,000 people.

Sutton's long association with Earley began when 60 acres of land was bought in the parish to be used as a trial ground. Much of this land was purchased from George Palmer and from the Erleigh Court estate.

This site was advantageous. First it was close to the area of Newtown where Sutton's built four streets of terraced houses and grander villas for

Below left: Front cover from Sutton's booklet

Below right: Bulb fields, Sutton's

its employees; and second, it was a great advertisement. When people travelled on either the old Great Western line from Reading to Paddington, or on the Southern line to Waterloo and Guildford, they could see the trial grounds and the areas of sweet peas and other flowers. For many years, the railway bridge by the Sutton's Industrial Estate had a sign on it saying Sutton's Seeds from Reading, no agents – best in the World. In the early 1960's, the Ministry of Transport decided to put an inner ring road through part of the Forbury. This would have gone right through the back of Sutton's warehouse and across Kings Road. Under pressure to move, Sutton's exchanged their freehold site for a new building at their trial grounds in Earley in 1962.

Below left: Main pavillion and range of glasshouses, Sutton's

Below right: Sutton's experimental grounds

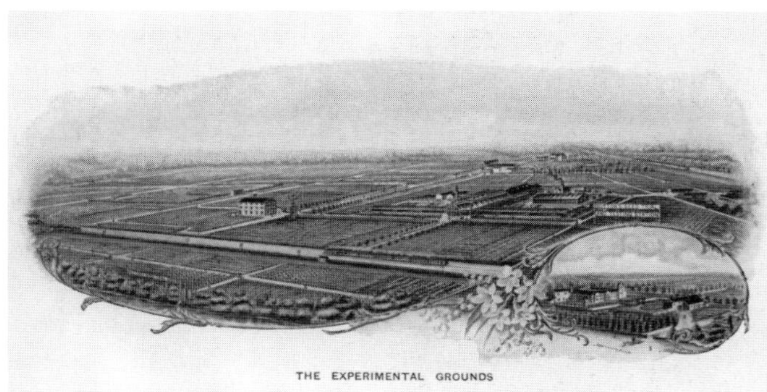

One the most famous landmarks of the Earley site was a superb range of glasshouses, built at the end of the last century. These greenhouses were entered by going through a truly stunning centrepiece conservatory built out of teak and cast iron. Sadly this magnificent building was demolished to make way for the Sutton's Industrial Estate when Sutton's moved from Earley to Torquay in 1976.

Ironically one of Sutton's employees who chose not to move with the company received a telephone call from a man in London who said: *I've got a client who's interested in buying your old greenhouse pavillion, facing the railway on the old trial ground site*. Unfortunately he was too late – it had been bulldozed and removed only a couple of days before!

Sutton's was a typical family business of the Victorian era. It looked after its workforce in a paternal manner, offering many perks aside from the usual. These included an employee's pension fund, a sick fund, a burial fund, company outings and paid holidays. At its peak, Sutton's was a household name. It is now part of a conglomerate of European companies. There are no Sutton's left in the business. The days of it being a family run benevolent local company have long gone. It was a world in itself, and a world that has now passed away.

Earley Power Station

In late 1941, on once peaceful Colebrooks Meadows alongside the river, the war came to North Earley. Railway sidings were built, and work started on the construction of a generating plant, to provide power for weapons production and subsequently American air and military bases, since within weeks the United States were to enter the war.

In the north-east an electrical engineering company, Parsons, was completing work on a generator and turbine, and in the Midlands, the International Boiler Company, on five boilers ordered in 1939 for a power station to be built in South Africa. Two of the boilers were actually shipped to South Africa but were lost when the ship carrying them was sunk. The South African project was then abandoned and the three remaining boilers were sent to Earley as Britain's need was now greater and the race was on to construct a building to house them. As soon as McAlpines had the foundations laid, steel erectors from Dorman Longs were constructing the framework of girders. Cranes lifted these into position and, working from scaffolding, men heated rivets in portable furnaces, plucked them out with tongs and threw them to the riveters who hammered them home, their only protective clothing being leather gloves and aprons, no hard hats. These men were unworried by height, walking along narrow girders as easily as they would on the ground.

Within a brick shell around this framework the boilers were installed, surrounded by iron grating, walkways and stairs. A gang of laggers had the job of encasing the boilers and the pipe work in a fireproof insulation made from asbestos powder and water, slapped on like plaster and held in place with chicken wire. For weeks the building was full of asbestos dust, how many of those men survived to a ripe old age?

The station was the first to include precipitators, an environmentally friendly innovation. Before the smoke reached the great chimneys, a high voltage electric current was passed across the smoke between two electrodes, causing the heavy soot particles to fall out.

A huge concrete base to carry the weight of the turbine and generator had to be poured into shuttering, the dimensions being of a good sized detached house, a continuous process, taking two days and nights to complete.

The station was commissioned in 1943, but work which had already started on an extension was slowed down when labourers were taken off to work on a top secret project that was to make D-Day possible. That was the construction of the Mulberry Harbour. Earley provided one of a series of small power stations built at this time that served as standby stations in the event of bomb damage to Battersea. To give extra capacity, a new gas turbine-powered generator was constructed and commissioned in 1964.

Earley Power Station
© *Trust for Wessex Archaeology*

Earley Power Station was served by four exchange sidings constructed by GWR in June 1941. They were controlled from the nearby Sonning box which was enlarged at the same time. The internal lines were worked by a Robert Stephenson and Hawthorn 0–4 OST (Works No 7058) (1) and was joined by a second RSH 0–4 OST (Works No 7306) (2) in 1946. During the 1960s the two steam locomotives were joined by a pair of diesel mechanical shunters. The first was a Motor Rail Limited 0–4 ODM No 3966 (3) which was joined for a short time by an Andrew Barclay 0–6 ODM No 422 (4). No 2 was broken up on site, No 3 was transferred to East Yelland Power Station, Devon in 1970 and the two remaining engines were sold (No 1 to Gwini Railway and No 4 to Farthingstone Silos Ltd (Waters, 1990)).

Earley Power Station was small in comparison with more modern stations and it became uneconomical to run. When Didcot Power Station was built Earley became surplus to requirements and was closed in March 1976. It lay derelict for a number of years before being partially demolished in 1983. The whole site was finally cleared in July 1986. The site is now part of the Thames Valley Business Park.

286,000m^3 of pulverised fuel ash – material deposited by the Central Electricity Generating Board over a period of 50 years at the power station needed to be excavated and removed before the site could be used as a Business Park. The ash was deposited in pits lined with clay alluvial material from the site and geotextiles were used to contain the fine ash particles (*Evening Post*, 1988).

Mr Percy Colebrook

The Colebrook family were well known in Earley and Reading. The farm at the end of Shepherds House Lane was owned by them; this was sold to Mr Sidney Cook when he wanted land to build the Ideal Casements factory. The family lived in the Manor House, but exchanged it, with the Cooks, for Hungerford Lodge.

Mr Colebrook ran ten butcher shops in Reading which he supplied from his three farms Elm Farm, Home Farm and Hillside Farm. In 1935 he had sixteen farm workers and five pairs of plough horses. He grew his own animal feed and the Hillside field was the workers' vegetable plot. His son Peter was the last of the family to live in the newly built Hillside Farm.

The recreation field beyond Hillside's school field looks out over the Loddon Valley and a battery of guns was sited there for shooting at aircraft during the war.

The only doodlebug to fall on Earley fell on his land at the top of Redhatch and killed a cow.

Ideal Casements

The company Ideal Casements was started in 1948 by Sidney Cook, who owned the builders J T Cook and lived at the Manor House, Church Road, Earley. He started the company in order to supply steel windows to his various housing schemes.

Initially he set up the company in the yard of a small business that he had bought from Toogoods. The business was *Bellevue Works* a smithy and general ironworks on the corner of Belle Avenue and Whiteknights Road. By the early 1950s he needed more space so he bought Colebrook's farm at the end of Shepherds House Lane and built a factory there to make steel windows. Subsequently he added a galvanising plant.

In the early 1960s, the factory was extended and another galvanising plant was added. Ten years later tube mills and a paint plant were added and the company began to manufacture aluminium windows and doors.

Ideal Casements' factory, north of the GWR railway line

By the early 1980s UPVC windows and doors were being manufactured. At this time the name of the company name was changed to *Ideal Windows* and was composed of 12 different companies. At its peak it employed 950 people.

By the end of the 1980s, the company was scaled down by its then owners, McKecknie Engineering, until only the UPVC and the aluminium windows were being manufactured. Finally, the much smaller company moved to Commercial Road, Reading and the owners sold the land to Speyhawk who developed it for the Thames Valley Business Park.

Sidney Cook

Sidney Cook was a well known builder, who made a lasting contribution to Earley as many of the houses built between the 1940s and 1960s were built by him. Even today houses are advertised as Cook-built homes as the firm had a reputation for good work and value. Though the last home Mr Cook and his wife, Mollie, lived in was the Manor House, which technically is now in Reading, his associations are most definitely with Earley.

Sidney Cook was the youngest of six children. His father was a builder and when he died Sidney carried on the family business. The family had a builder's yard in Holmes Road, from where building work in the locality was directed. The houses in Redhatch Drive, Salcombe Drive, Aldbourne Avenue, Ramsbury Drive and Wilderness Road were all built by Sidney Cook. His widow, Mollie, now Mrs Marsh, remembers that when they built the houses along Wilderness Road they were priced at just over one thousand pounds, but they still had some difficulty in finding buyers for them, so they offered £5 to any one making an introduction which led to a sale.

Mr and Mrs Cook lived first in The Homestead on Wilderness Road, from there they moved to Hungerford Lodge on the Wokingham Road, which they bought from Mrs Heelas. The Cooks lived in this house during the war, and indeed, looked after some evacuee children there. In 1946, they moved to the Manor House in Heath Road at the instigation of Mr and Mrs Colebrook, the then owners, who asked them to swap homes as Mrs Colebrook wanted to live in something smaller. From an experiment with a metal framed window he installed in his own home Sidney Cook founded a business to make metal window frames for the windows in the houses he built. The company began in Whiteknights Road.

It was when Mr Cook was living in the Manor House that it was decided to renovate the tower of St Peter's Church (opposite the Manor House) as it had become unsafe, and it was decided to replace the original pinnacles which had become dislodged in a gale in 1930. Mr Cook generously offered to fund all the work. For various reasons the work took almost two years to complete. Finally, on 11th September 1964, all the work had been completed and the scaffolding was taken down. Sadly Mr Cook died the following day.

Sutton's Business Park and Thames Valley Business Park

Residents on Shepherds House Lane protested about Wokingham District Council's decision to allow Slough Industrial Estates to build a factory on Sutton's trial grounds for Collins Radio. The deputy planning officer said that the light industrial use would be preferable to warehousing (*Berkshire Mercury*, 1977). This land is now owned by Standard Life Investment and contains many business units. The Bowling Club was given replacement land at Chalfont Park for a new bowling green and pavilion.

In 1987 the land north of the Great Western Railway line covering McKecknie's Engineering Works, Earley Power Station and the floodplain of the Thames was given planning permission for a business park. The former power station and the pulverised fuel ash were removed. The offices have been built above the flood plain, which has been left as open meadows, a country park and a towpath along the river for cyclists and walkers. The business park covers 31.9ha, strategic highways 4.6ha and the country park 32.8ha. Access is along the extension of the A329M into the park, Shepherds House Lane under the railway line was too narrow. In the planning permission given in 1987, an Information Age project, a watersports centre and a railway station were to be built.

The Development of Lower Earley

Although the name of Lower Earley is very old and applied to low lying land that lay between the old Maiden Erlegh Estate and the River Loddon, the name as it is used today applies to a large area of modern houses built in a 25 year period from 1975 to 2000. At one time this development had the honour of being the largest private housing development in Europe!

The story of Lower Earley starts in May 1953 when the Minister of Housing & Local Government approved the Woodley/Earley Town Map. Lower Earley at this time was shown as an area of unannotated white land.

Wokingham Rural District Council became concerned about the direction of future development in this area when in June 1969 the Secretary of State decided to release land for residential development off Beech Lane, Earley, and off Colemansmoor Road in Woodley.

In August 1969 the District Council's Planning Committee and Finance & General Purposes Committee resolved:

> *That it was imperative that an overall plan illustrating how this area could be developed should be prepared and that consultants should be engaged for this task, the brief to include the road systems related to such development.*

By October 1970 the Berkshire County Council and the Wokingham Rural District Council had jointly appointed the Shankland Cox Partnership to prepare a Master Plan for Woodley and Earley.

This was followed in October 1971 by the setting up of a joint Steering Committee composed of members of the Berkshire County Council, Wokingham Rural District Council and Reading Borough Council.

In November 1971, the *Woodley and Earley Interim Report* and the *Woodley and Earley Survey* were presented by the Shankland Cox Partnership. These interim reports concluded that residential development was acceptable in the area. A number of options were put forward ranging from a minimum development involving 12,500 people to a maximum development involving 22,000 people for Woodley and Earley.

After a period of intensive public consultation, a final report, *the Woodley and Earley Master Plan* was submitted to the Steering Committee by the Shankland Cox Partnership in June 1972. This Master Plan was approved by the Wokingham Rural District Council in December 1972 as a basis for planning in the area.

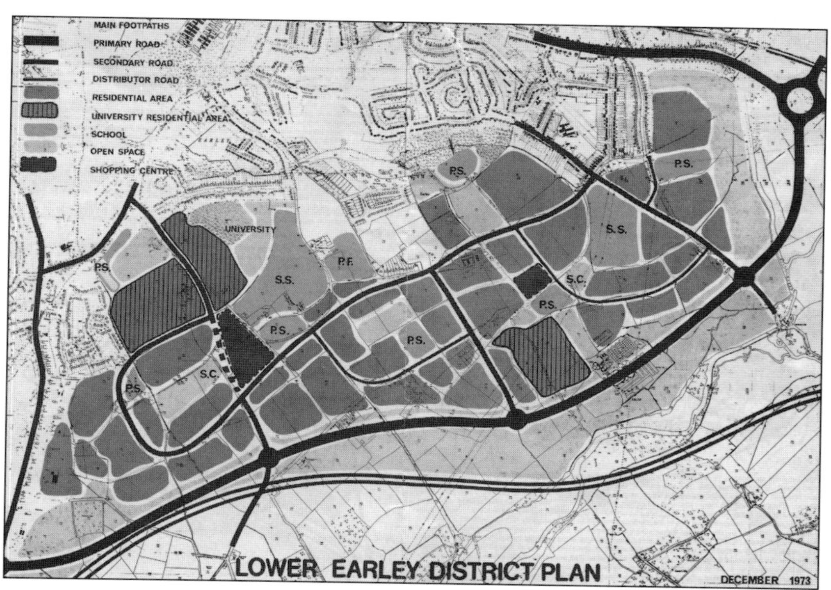

Map 13: Lower Earley Proposed District Plan for a consortium of owners.
Barton Willmore and Partners, December 1973

At about this time, a group of landowners joined together and appointed consultants to act on their behalf. This led to a number of meetings taking place between representatives of the landowners, their consultants, officers of the local authorities and the Woodley and Earley Steering Committee.

Arising from these discussions, Barton Wilmore & Partners submitted a report entitled *A Plan for the Comprehensive Development of Lower Earley*. The most important difference between this report and the Shankland Cox proposals was that a much greater area of land was proposed for residential development.

In October 1973 Barton Wilmore & Partners, on behalf of their clients, submitted 7 applications for residential and associated development at Lower Earley.

A public consultation exercise was carried out on the Barton Wilmore proposals in November and December 1973. This involved a number of public meetings and the distribution of 10,000 leaflets. Following an evaluation of both the Barton Wilmore proposals and the public comments they generated, a new District Plan was adopted by both the District and the County Councils.

The adopted District Plan for Lower Earley, and the phasing proposals of Barton Wilmore, and the road proposals of the County Surveyor formed the basis of a public exhibition held in Lower Earley on 29th/30th November 1974.

On 24th December 1974 an application (No. 01945) for proposed developed at Lower Earley was submitted by the University of Reading, Bovis Homes (Southern) Limited, J.A. Pye (Oxford) Limited, Madrey Properties Limited and North British New Homes Limited for residential and associated development. This application alone covered about 880 acres of a total of 1,000 acres covered by the District Plan.

On 10th September 1975, an Extraordinary Meeting of the Wokingham District Council adopted the development and road phasing plans that formed the basis of application No. 01945 and the development of Lower Earley was officially under way.

Map 14, Key

1 Wiltshire
2 Herbs & Spices
3 Essex
4 Yorkshire
5 Norfolk
6 Buckinghamshire
7 Vicars of Earley St Peter's Church
8 Somerset
9 Cornwall
10 Nottinghamshire
11 Bedfordshire
12 Sussex
13 Kent
14 Birds
15 Local Houses
16 London
17 Councillors
18 Cambridgeshire
19 Leicestershire
20 Staffordshire
21 Oxfordshire
22 Cumbria
23 Dorset
24 Lincolnshire
25 Suffolk
26 Lancashire
27 Devon
28 Huntingdonshire
29 Leicestershire
30 Yorkshire
31 Trees
32 Hampshire

Map 14: The distribution of the names of the estates throughout Lower Earley

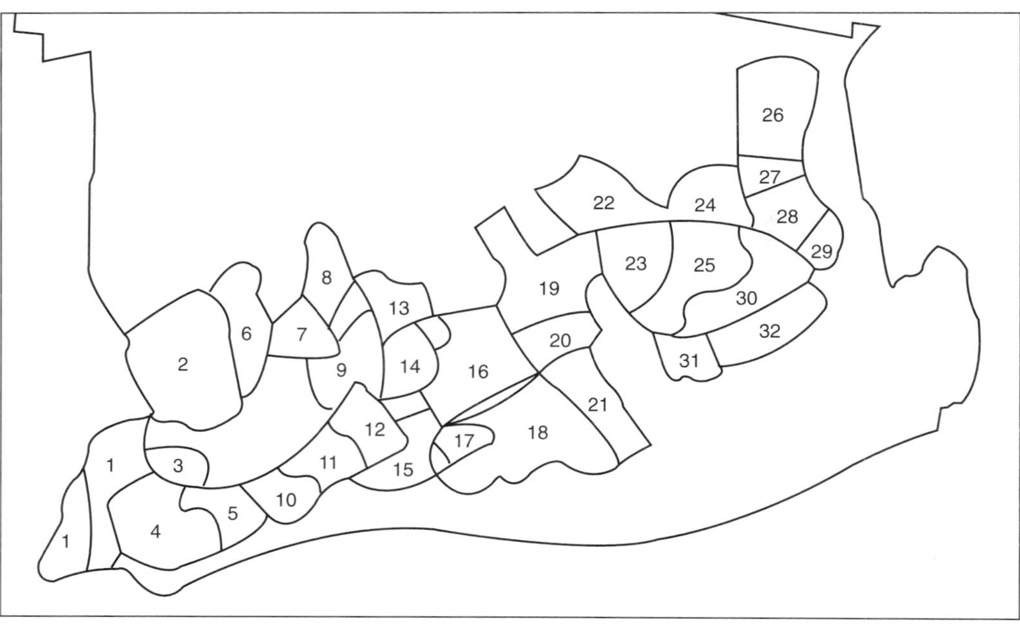

5 Community Buildings and Institutions

Local Government

Although Earley has been a civil parish since the middle of the last century, perhaps the two really significant dates in local government terms have been quite recent; April 1974 and April 1998. In 1974, there was extensive reorganisation of local government in Britain. Primarily, principal authorities were affected and the previous Wokingham Rural District Council became Wokingham District Council. At the same time, the Town Council as we know it today was formed. In those early years it was organised on a much smaller scale than the present day. A part-time Clerk to the Council, Mr Marchant, was appointed. He also worked as a Local Government Officer for Reading Borough Council. There was no Council Office as such and indeed the Council's records, such as they were, were kept at an address in All Hallows Road, Caversham. Later in the first year of its existence, the Town Council appointed a Mrs Walker of Anderson Avenue at the princely rate of 60p per hour to give assistance to the Clerk.

One particularly interesting feature of the first meeting of the newly elected Council in 1976 was that the newly elected Councillor, Adrian Paddick, attending his first meeting and in the absence of anyone else willing to accept the post, was thrust into the role of Chairman of Council. He was to continue in this role for some years, and by the time of his death in 1997, had become the elder statesman of the Town Council, highly respected by his colleagues and by the local residents for his wisdom and calming effect on proceedings.

Adrian Paddick, 1921–1997

At the time of its formation the Town Council looked after an area with some 12,000 inhabitants. At this stage, the development of Lower Earley had yet to commence, so no substantial administration was required.

Little is known of the early years of the predecessor Parish Council. Parish Clerks worked from their homes and although records were kept in the parish chest, its continual movement from home to home led to its eventual loss.

Despite there having been a civil parish since the middle of the 19th century, it was not until the middle of the 20th century that Earley Parish Council made its first known land acquisition. In response to pressure from local residents and the Planning Authorities, Cooper Estates agreed to sell Maiden Erlegh Lake and its associated surrounding woodlands to

Earley Parish Council in exchange for being able to build on another greenfield site. The land consisted of the Lake itself, plus Oakwood, Old Pond Copse and a small part of Moor Copse.

As the purchase would lead to an increase in the rates, the Parish Council of the time held a public meeting and a referendum. With the backing of the people of Earley, the Council purchased the site for £8,500 in 1965. The Reserve, as we know it today, dates from 1991 when Old Lane Wood was purchased from Wokingham District Council for £1.00.

Early meetings of the newly formed Earley Town Council were held in St Peter's Church Hall on Church Road. At first the part-time Clerk of the Council worked from home but the Council shortly afterwards rented office space in the Porter Institute near to the Church.

The Council tried to buy the Porter Institute as office and meeting space, but was unsuccessful. So in 1978, it struck a deal with Maiden Erlegh School, and began to hold meetings in the staff dining room and set up an office in a converted storeroom. The Council took on its first full time Town Clerk in January 1979 when Mr Leslie Norton became clerk to the Council.

Following a review of parish boundaries held in 1980 by Wokingham District Council, the boundaries of Earley were modified. The original proposal by the District had been to divide the local area into six small parishes. This plan was resisted by Earley Town Council and the plan eventually implemented involved transferring the triangle south of the M4 to Shinfield Parish Council and the south Woodley area from Woodley Town Council to Earley Town Council. As part of these land changes, Earley Town Council took over the management of Meadow Park. In lieu of the loss of Meadow Park, residents of Woodley were given preferential burial rates in Mays Lane Cemetery, which had been previously owned and managed by St Peter's Church until its transfer to the Town Council.

Despite its comparatively small size, the Town Council responded positively to the challenges with which it was being faced with the impending Lower Earley development. The Radstock Lane Community Centre was opened in 1983 and included a small suite of offices which became the Council's administrative home until its final move to Radstock House, on the opposite side of the road, in 1987. The new offices had previously been the old farm house to Radstock Farm and both it and its cottages had a fairly interesting history which included a three-day gun siege between the police and one of its previous owners as recently as 1982.

In 1986 the Council took over responsibility for the Culver Lane Allotments. These were provided on land which had been previously the responsibility of the Huntley & Palmer Trust. Initially, the land had been put up for sale and the Council had made an unsuccessful bid. In the end a compromise deal was struck whereby the two ends of the site were sold for development and the Council purchased the middle section.

1986 also saw the building of the Maiden Place Community Centre by Pye Development. Initially it included a small room plus kitchen and toilets. However, having taken over the management of the building, Earley Town Council decided in 1987 to add a main hall, bar and upstairs room. The improvements were completed around 1989.

The two Community Centres proved to be much needed facilities. With over 6,000 houses being built on the Lower Earley development and a population expansion from c.11,000 in 1974 to some 28,500 in 1990 and 34,500 in 2000 the new facilities were essential additions to the Town's infrastructure. There was also significant activity by the Town Council during this period to try to improve facilities at Maiden Erlegh Reserve.

As the population of the Town grew, the Town Council had to adapt to various new roles. During the 1970's and early 1980s, many functions both administrative and practical were undertaken by Town Councillors themselves. As an example, at that stage in its life, the Town Council did not possess any computers, and sometimes reports, notices and financial information were prepared by elected representatives. On the practical side, much of the conservation work now undertaken by the Town Council's Park Ranger Service is based on initial work undertaken entirely by volunteers who included several councillors who had a particular interest in that field.

At the same time, the structure of the Council was gradually changing to meet the new demands. Despite the fact that the Town Council was a third tier authority, political parties were gradually becoming interested in winning seats on the Town Council. In the days of the Parish Council and immediately after 1974, the Town Council had members who were not politically labelled. Gradually their numbers had dwindled and by the mid-1980s, all elected representatives were members of one of the three main political parties.

As the responsibilities of the Town Council increased, so the respective roles of councillors and their staff similarly changed. Mr Leslie Norton had steered the Town Council through the difficult period during the development of Lower Earley. By the time of his retirement in 1991, the Town Council recognised the need for improved administrative systems to consolidate its earlier achievements.

In 1991, the brief of the appointment panel was to find a replacement with experience of a much larger authority who would have the ability to put into place the administrative systems now needed to handle the ever increasing amount of work. When advertised, the post attracted a large number of applicants but eventually Mr Richard Raymond was chosen primarily because of his central administrative experiences with a larger Borough Council. Following his appointment, the councillors themselves felt able to concentrate more on the Council's policies and able to leave the development of the Town Council's administrative structure in experienced hands.

The Town Council is re-elected every four years and, through the efforts of the succeeding three Councils, an efficient administrative structure was put in place with the capability to deal with all the additional facilities now provided by the Council and to meet the increasing demands of Central Government. For many functions, Town Councils of the size of Earley, Woodley and Wokingham are now regarded as principal authorities, and have to bear the cost and responsibility of the greater Central Government scrutiny now required.

It has been during this period that the role of the Town Council as it is today had evolved. Working in partnership with the then Berkshire County Council and Wokingham District Council, the Earley Help Shop was established. This increased the number of residents being helped monthly at the Radstock Lane Offices from a figure of around 200 to some 1,500 in 1999–2000. The Town Council can now be regarded as being fully into the 21st Century. It is completely computerised and was one of the first third tier authorities to provide its own web site from which even the Town Council's minutes and Committee reports can be accessed by local residents.

During the course of this latter period, a Park Ranger Service was established which through its work, eventually led to Maiden Erlegh Reserve being designated as a Local Nature Reserve in 1997. The Town Council Offices were properly renovated and provided with a Council Chamber which doubles as an Information Centre for local residents during the day with support from staff of the Mobile Information Centre and the Citizens Advice Bureau. Meadow Park was transformed from a field to a formal Park with flower beds and play equipment, part of Sol Joel Park was leased from Reading Borough on which the Town Council has provided an innovative Sports and Skate Park. The Cemetery at Mays Lane has been extended and transformed, and an Interpretation Centre has been provided in the Local Nature Reserve for the use of local school children and students.

That the various improvements mentioned were attained and also that many other innovations were achieved gives some indication as to the extent of the efforts of both councillors and staff in the short life of Earley Town Council since 1974. During this period the debts incurred by the earlier Councils to provide the Community Centres, purchase the Council Offices and improve the Local Nature Reserve were paid off without any further debt being incurred and with a *pro rata* 14% reduction in the Council Tax burden to local rate payers.

A list of the Chairmen of Earley Town Council to date is set out below:

1974–1976	R E Boulton
1976–1981	A C Paddick
1981–1983	A W Spratling
1983–1987	J Busby
1987–1988	A W Spratling
1988–1989	Mrs V J Santon
1989–1990	D J Fruin
1990–1991	P Devonald
1991–1992	A W Spratling
1992–1994	Mrs F M Rolls
1994–1996	Mrs E Spratling
1996–1998	M Richman
1998–1999	Mrs E Spratling
1999–2001	A D Long

The 1998 Local Government re-organisation significantly affected Earley in that the first tier authority, Berkshire County Council, became defunct as a new system of Unitary Authorities, based on the areas of the old district councils, was put into place. The changes themselves had little impact on the Town Council's work, but local government in this area has only two tiers instead of three as previously.

Public Houses

Public houses have always been important in every community. They have served their local areas as community centres where local people could meet their friends; as communication centres where gossip and information was spread before most people could read; and as a source of safe liquid refreshment in days gone by when it was much safer to drink ale and wine than to risk drinking well or tap water.

The public houses of Earley served all of these purposes; in the 19th century Earley had nine public houses. Of these, eight have since been lost to Earley, either due to closure or to boundary changes. The one remaining old pub in Earley, The George, has in recent times been joined by four new pubs – The Maiden Over, The Culpeper, The Earley Retreat and The Seven Red Roses.

Boundary changes have moved The Shepherds House into Woodley; The College Arms, The Roebuck, The Three Tuns and Marquis of Granby into Reading. The western boundary of the old Liberty of Earley took in the old inn, now known as **The Granby** (the Marquis of

Above: The Marquis of Granby, Cemetery Junction
Postcard, 1905

Below: The Dreadnought on the Thames near Kennet mouth, 1928

Granby); it was previously known as the Gallows Tavern because a gallows once stood at the nearby crossroads.

The Shepherds House was originally a private cottage which once stood on Shepherds House Hill, a small lane leading down from the London Road to the Earley Meadows. Tradition has it that this beerhouse became the chosen place of refreshment for the gangs of workmen, or navigators ('navvies'), who were working on the construction of the Great Western Railway in 1839–40. Later, the beerhouse moved to premises further up the hill. The premises were rebuilt in about 1930.

Another public houses situated close to the river was **The Dreadnought.** This pub was originally not so remote or inaccessible as it now seems since the two railway embankments have been formed (Dormer, 1944).

Above: The old Three Tuns
postcard, 1870s

Below: The new Three Tuns
(built in the 1930s)

It is in parts an old house and is referred to in documents of the 18th century as the Broken Brow, from the place name of a portion of the old Wharf Field adjoining it. It was largely patronised by bargees and fishermen and may have obtained its later name from a strong, closely woven cloth much used in the eighteenth century by sea faring and riverside men.

If in times gone by Earley could have been said to have had a centre then this would have been the Three Tuns crossroads. The present public house which fronts onto Wokingham Road replaced a much older building which was knocked down when the formerly tree-lined road was straightened and widened in the 1930s. Over the years **The Three Tuns** has served both as an informal meeting place where locals could come to exchange gossip and as a more formal meeting place.

The Woodley Cavalry used the inn for many of its gatherings, including the annual dinners. The cavalry was established following the passing of the 1796 Act which provided for the establishment of a force of yeomanry and volunteer cavalry for home defences at a time when it seemed that Britain might be threatened by Napoleon's forces. The cavalry consisted of 3 officers and 54 men. Henry Addington who lived at Woodley Lodge (later known as Bulmershe Court) was in command. The Captain was Edward Golding, of Maiden Erlegh, the Lieutenant was Richard Palmer, of Holme Park, Sonning, the Hon Thomas Windsor was a Cornet, and the Chaplain was Dr Valpy, the Headmaster of Reading School. Many well-known local names are also recorded as privates e.g. Blagrave, Bulley, Hove, Earley, Monck, Simonds and Wheble. The barracks of the corps was near to The Three Tuns in some old cottages in Church Road, Earley.

The Inn also served as a meeting place for The Whiteknights Manorial Courts. Their last recorded meeting was in May 1840 when George Kent Pollock, Steward of the Manor summoned *all Residents and Tenants of the said Manor personally to appear and do and perform their suit and service ... and to perambulate the boundaries of the said Manor.* Although these Courts have officially ceased to function, they are occasionally revived to beat the bounds.

The George is the oldest inn within the present boundaries of Earley. It stands next to the River Loddon and the Loddon Bridge on Wokingham Road which connected Wokingham with Reading. It was one of the turnpike trustees that built the inn around the middle of the eighteenth century. This trustee was a brewer and he built The George

The George Inn, Loddon Bridge
Postcard

HOTEL
Photo Dee, Reading
A. HORSLEY, Proprietor, Loddon Bridge.
GOOD ACCOMMODATION FOR MOTORISTS, CYCLISTS, FISHING PARTIES AND BEANFEASTS

The George Inn, a meet of the South Berkshire Hunt
Postcard

in order to sell his local brew to thirsty travellers despite the fact that it was illegal for anyone associated with alcohol to be a turnpike trustee. Fortunately for him the local magistrate was partial to a glass or two of The George's ales and he therefore decided to turn a blind eye to the double occupation.

Churches and Chapels

The act of worship has long been the focal point of most communities. John Blair suggested that the Anglo-Saxon Minster at Sonning was a community of monks, nuns and priests but after the Viking attacks in the 870s it was restructured into a local mother church with a small staff of clergy. By the 950s the parochial authority over this area set it in law. Sonning was also the second seat of the Bishops of Ramsbury from the late ninth or early tenth century (Dils, 1997). Earley was one of the four liberties of Sonning. All Earley people would have had to attend Sonning Church as well as paying tithes to it. In Earley the two large manors of Whiteknights and Erleigh Court were allowed to have their own chapels which were called free chapels. Free chapels were founded by the king or by subjects authorised by him. Maybe the two chapels were in place before the Norman Conquest (Dormer, 1912).

The earliest known reference to the **Chapel of Earley St Nicholas** is in 1220 and there were close ties between this chapel and the leper hospital in Reading. In 1314 John de Erlegh transferred 7½ acres of land in Earley's open fields to Richard Kimberle, parson of the chapel, and to his successors for the celebration of divine service in the chapel for Christian

Souls. The land consisted of three pieces plus one acre of arable land in Earley Field plus tithes from the manor and lands of Whiteknights.

In 1548 the chapel, with its lands and tithes, was sold to Henry Polsted and William More (Coates, 1802). Although Robertson (1840), states that the free chapel was dissolved by Thomas Beke, without the King's licence (Henry VIII). He said that the chapel was on the highest point in the Park, near the lodge which opens onto Wokingham Road. The Marquis of Blandford...

> *...re-edified the remains of the old building in the ornamental Gothic style. It has an extremely picturesque appearance. Being covered with ground ivy and surrounded by a fine grove of trees.* (*Robertson,* 1840) (*see* page 34).

The Chapel of Earley St Bartholomew was first mentioned in 1220 during a visitation by the Dean and Chapter of Sarum (Rylands, 1907). It was founded for a priest to celebrate mass on St Bartholomew's Day. A pension of two shillings per year was paid to the Rector of Sonning. At this time the chapel was owned by Thomas de Erlegh, Knight and the Chaplain was called William.

The following description was given of the chapel which was in the process of being rebuilt:

> *The chapel was built of wood. There was, however, an area around the chapel, enclosed by a fence and partly ready for making a cemetery and heaped stones were laying about as if the construction of a new chapel of stone was about to be taken in hand. There was no font and no bells but in the grounds was a wooden cross on which was hung boughs and branches on Palm Sunday.*

In 1526 Sir William Fettiplace gave the free chapel and some other land in Earley to the Provost and Scholars of Queen's College, Oxford. In 1545 the chapel and its strips in the open fields were conveyed to the owner of the manor. Eventually the chapel became so dilapidated that it fell to pieces. The stones were used in the building of stables at Erleigh Court. The site of the chapel, in a field to the south of Erleigh Court, was marked on maps from 1820 to the 1930s (Dormer, 1912).

For many centuries the people of Earley had no public place of worship of their own (apart from the private chapels mentioned above). Instead they had to undertake the arduous journey to Sonning to worship with people coming from up to 10 miles away. Apart from seeing these people at Sunday worship they were complete strangers to them.

The decision was taken in the early 1840s to build the Church of Earley St Peter and Earley now has a number of churches of different denominations giving the inhabitants a choice of places of worship.

Grade II listed building

Earley St Peter's Church, Church Road

The Parish Church was built in 1844 by J. Turner in the Early English style. Aisles and a chancel were added in 1882–3. The exterior is constructed from grey vitreous brick stone dressing and a slate gabled and coped roof. The tower is constructed in three stages and has a clock on each of the four faces.

Earley St Peter's Church was consecrated on 14th May 1844. Originally the vast area covering Sonning, Woodley, Earley and Lower Earley from the River Thames in the north to the River Loddon in the south was all one parish, that of St Andrews Sonning. This giant ancient parish was split into four Liberties to make administration easier. These were Earley, Woodley with Sandford, Dunsden (in Oxfordshire) and Sonning itself.

The expanding population of the area in Victorian times saw a number of new churches being built. These were All Saints at Dunsden in 1842, Earley St Peter's, 1844, St John the Evangelist, Woodley, 1873 and St Bartholomew's on the London Road in 1875.

The church of Earley St Peter's was founded so that the people of the area, mainly tenant farmers and estate workers living on the scattered farms and cottages in the outlying parts of Earley and Lower Earley, did not have to make the long journey to the mother church in Sonning, especially in the winter when the fields and lanes would often be impassable.

Robert Palmer (no relation to the biscuit Palmer) of Holme Park, Sonning and his sister Caroline had funded the building of All Saints Church at Dunsden and had already thought of building a new church in Earley, when Marianne (or Maria Anne), the Viscountess Sidmouth, died and left a generous bequest of £1,000 to fund a minister. This gave impetus to the project and soon many local people had pledged money, with donations coming from many of the local gentry, including Robert and Caroline Palmer, local farmers and several schools.

Lord Sidmouth, husband of Marianne, gave land for the church to be built on and £500 towards the cost of the building in memory of his wife. Lord Sidmouth owned Erleigh Court (see chapter 3). The land and the money having been secured, building work began in April 1843. John Turner, surveyor on the Holme Park estate, was chosen as the architect for the project. The building contract was given to Biggs and Son of Queens Road, Reading.

The foundation stone was laid on Thursday, 20th April 1843 by Viscount Sidmouth's daughter, the Hon. Mary Ann Addington assisted by the Dean of Salisbury and his son. The church was consecrated just over a year later on Tuesday, 14th May 1844. The church which had been designed in the Early English style, boasted a 76 ft high tower and seating for 350 people. It also contained two stained glass windows in the south wall of the sanctuary. These two windows were made by Nixon and Ward of Soho, one depicting St Peter was donated by the architect, John Turner, and one depicting St Andrew (in recognition of the mother church in Sonning) was a gift from the building committee (Dormer, 1944) and (Hanna, 1994).

Above: St Peter's Church
© Collier Collection Rural Earley 2, Rural History Centre, The University of Reading

Below: The interior of St Peter's Church
Lent by Doris Taylor

Wall paintings

The wall paintings or frescoes in the Sanctuary of the Church depict scenes from the Life of St Peter. Susannah Stephens paid for them to be done as a memorial to her husband Charles who died in 1901 (see later for further details). The paintings were done by Ion Pace who normally designed stained glass windows (Hanna, 1994).

The decorative framework around these paintings and the border below the two paintings on either side of the altar were covered up in the 1970s. They were uncovered when the church was redecorated in 1992. Luckily only the decoration below one of the paintings was lost; it would appear that after the work on painting out the decoration began someone suddenly had the foresight to cover the remainder with paper and paint over that. This meant that the decoration could be uncovered if required.

Whilst the church was able to seat most of the local Earley residents, it was soon too small to accommodate the residents from the outskirts of Reading which by this time were within walking distance of the church. In the summer of 1881 the then Vicar, Havilland Durand, drew up plans to expand the church. This time the chosen architect was Francis Bacon, a former Earley resident then living in Burghclere; the builders were Wheeler Bros.

The estimate for the work when it started was £3,200 (less than half of which had been raised) but by the time it was completed in 1883 the cost had risen to £4,338 15s 9d. Nothing is new in this world – not even budget overruns! The building works had been very extensive with only the tower, the nave roof and the west end remaining intact from the original building and yet despite this, not a single Sunday service needed to be cancelled during the building works. The church was rededicated by the Bishop of Oxford on 29th March 1883.

In 1887 it was decided to investigate the possibility of installing a peal of bells in the church tower as a permanent memorial to Queen Victoria's Diamond Jubilee. However, on further investigation it was found that the tower was not strong enough to support the enormous weight of the bells and it was decided to install a commemorative church clock instead. An appeal was launched in the June which eventually raised £168 10s. In August the clock was ordered from Messrs Bracher and Sydenham and installed in time to be set running on the morning of Sunday, 14th November 1897, for a final cost of £175.

Although the tower was not strong enough to hold a conventional peal of bells, in 1919 a much lighter set of tubular bells, a carillon, was installed. The carillon was made by a Coventry firm in 1887 and shipped to the Roman Catholic community at the College Anglais at Douai in northern France. When the community moved to Woolhampton in west Berkshire they brought the carillon with them but decided not to use it in their new abbey church. Cannon Fowler heard about the carillon's existence and sent Edward Heelas to Woolhampton to purchase it. The carillon was installed in the tower and was first rung at St Peter's on 11th May 1919.

In 1900 John Hargreaves, son of John and Mary Hargreaves of Maiden Erlegh made a gift of 3/4 acre of land to the church, thereby doubling the size of the churchyard. The additional land was L-shaped and included 1/4 acre from the allotments which lay on the southern side of the churchyard and 1/2 acre from the church field on the eastern boundary. The churchyard extension was consecrated on 15th November 1902 by the Bishop of Oxford. On the same day the lych-gate was dedicated to the memory of Charles Stephens. The graveyard now contains about 1,000 gravestones, the oldest dating from 24th November 1845.

When the church was built it was still part of the parish of Sonning

Canon Fowler

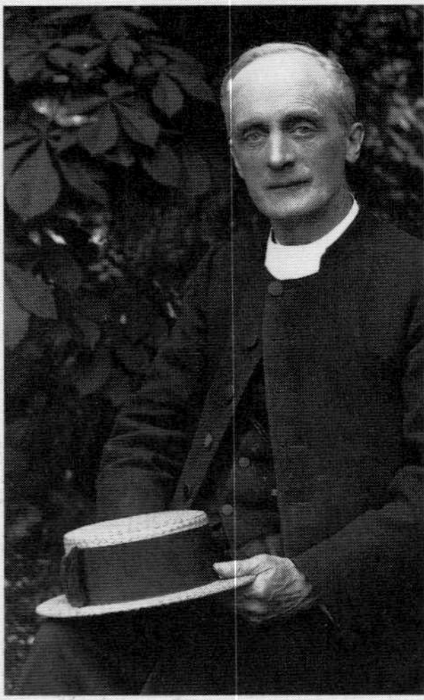

William Weekes Fowler was born in Barnwood, Gloucester in January 1849, the son of the Revd Hugh Fowler.

William Fowler was educated at Rugby School and Jesus College, Oxford and was ordained Deacon in 1873 becoming a Housemaster at Repton School in the same year. He was priested in 1875 and elected Headmaster of Lincoln School in 1880 remaining there for twenty years. During his stay at Lincoln, Bishop King appointed him to the Prebend Stall of Welton Brinkhill (in Lincoln Cathedral 1887).

Canon Fowler relinquished his post at Lincoln School to become Rector of Rotherfield Peppard from 1901 to 1904. He became vicar of Earley in 1905, remaining there until he died in June 1923.

Apart from his work in the church, and though as an undergraduate he read classics at Oxford, he was a keen and able entomologist, well known in entomological circles for his work on the Coleoptera (beetles) (*The Entomologist*, August 1923). In 1885, whilst at Lincoln School, he became sub-editor of the Entomologists' Monthly Magazine, a post he retained until his death. He was also secretary of the Entomological Society of London from 1886 to 1896 and president of the Society from 1901 to 1902. Oxford University conferred on him a Doctorate of Science in 1902 (*AES bulletin*, 1923; *Entomological News*, October 1923).

Canon Fowler was author or co-author of a number of works mainly on the Coleoptera; his best known work *Coleoptera of the British Isles* (in five volumes 1887–1891) is still regarded as the definitive work on this subject (*Entomological Monthly Magazine*, July 1923).

He also wrote books for school use on the classics. In 1907, whilst at Earley, he became President of the Headmaster's Association, he was also a member of the Reading Board of Guardians, sitting for the Victoria Ward, and on the Board of Management of the Royal Berkshire Hospital.

Canon Fowler was also a Fellow of the Linnaean Society and served on its Council as vice-president for the year 1906–1907; he was a keen gardener and a valued member of the scientific committee of the Royal Horticultural Society. He was also involved with the local Horticultural Society being well known for growing daffodils and tulips. Towards the end of his life Canon Fowler became very frail. He died suddenly on June 3rd 1923 in the Church vestry whilst preparing to take the 11am service of matins. The service was abandoned on realising that Canon Fowler had died (*Proc. Linn. Soc.* 1923–4).

Many stories concerning the death of Canon Fowler are told by the older members of the parish who were children at the time. Many of them were sent to morning Sunday School, some 'truanted', returning home at the appropriate time as if having attended Sunday School. When the news of the death of Canon Fowler and the abandoning of the service got around, they were well and truly found out!

In 1924 the Archdeacon dedicated the Epiphany window in the Lady Chapel of Earley St Peter's Church to Canon Fowler's memory. A memorial plaque was also placed on the wall of the Lady Chapel. A room in the old church hall was also dedicated to him and this has been perpetuated in the new hall. Canon Fowler was the last vicar to live in the old vicarage.

William Heelas (1867–1937)

The first reference to the Heelas family is in papers relating to the Wokingham workhouse in 1835. There are references to the family being the suppliers of blankets to the workhouse. Mr William Heelas was a member of the Board of the Wokingham Union.

A branch of the family set up a drapers shop in Reading. Edward Daniel Heelas owned the shop in Reading and lived in Hungerford Lodge on the Wokingham Road, previously owned by the Wheble family. He was a sidesman at St Peter's Church for many years and became a churchwarden in February 1914 continuing in that office for twenty-three years until his death in May 1937. In 1919 Edward Heelas bought a set of tubular bells, the carillon, from Douai Abbey, Woolhampton, and had them installed in the tower of St Peter's Church. The carillon was restored in 1939 as a tribute to Edward Heelas and the long service he gave to St Peter's Church.

St Peter's Church, Lychgate
Collier Collection Earley 1, Rural History Centre, The University of Reading

and served by a curate. It became a district church in 1854 and a parish church in 1884.

The third quarter of the nineteenth century saw an explosion of housing development spreading eastwards from the Cemetery Junction area. The main driving force for this development was the increasing need for more employees to work in Huntley and Palmer's biscuit factories.

In order to meet the needs of people living in the Newtown area, the church began holding services, firstly in the open air on Mr Oliver Dixon's meadow and then, in 1887, in a mission room on land in Cumberland Road.

It was clear that this could be only a stopgap measure and plans were quickly made to build a new church. This new church was built on a piece of land which was given to the church by its then owner, George Palmer (of Huntley and Palmer) and was endowed by Caroline Palmer of Holme Park, Sonning. Much of the adjoining land later became Palmer Park. The church was dedicated to St Bartholomew's as it was built near Erleigh Court and the ruins of the chapel of St Bartholomew.

The first Vicar of Earley St Bartholomew, the Rev. Charles Honey was, fortuitously, a friend of the famous architect Alfred Waterhouse. Owing to a shortage of funds, Waterhouse designed a simple church with the idea that it could be expanded when further finances could be found. The builders, Stephens and Bastow of Bristol, built the church in just ten months at a cost of £3,600. The church was consecrated by the Bishop of Oxford on Wednesday, 30th April 1879. In 1883 a new vicarage was built for the church and, shortly afterwards, a nearby quarter-acre of land was purchased as the site of a new church hall.

The original church had been simply a nave and in April 1897 a meeting was held to plan for the addition of a chancel and chapels. Altogether £4,000 was raised, George Bodley was selected as architect and Francis Newberry began work on the improvements in July 1902. Lack of money stopped work at the end of the year and work did not recommence until March 1904. The newly expanded church was at last consecrated by Francis Paget, Bishop of Oxford, on 17th March 1905.

Between the foundation of the church and its enlargement, boundary changes transferred it from Earley to Reading.

A Methodist Church serving Earley opened in 1887. Services were held there regularly until 1926 when it closed. The church lay on the Wokingham Road, behind a dwelling and row of shops between Heath Road and The Three Tuns Public House. Boundary changes in the late 19th century took the building out of Earley. The building is now known as Mount Zion. Ayres (1988) wrote:

Methodist Church, Wokingham Road, Earley. The outcome of work begun in the open air in Lower Earley, this church opened on 9th October 1887 and services were held regularly until June 1926 when a resolution to cease services was made. The building remains and is used by the Assembly of God Pentecostal Church.

Primitive Methodist Chapel, Beech Lane, now a private residence, 1998

Local tradition has it that a private dwelling known as the Old Chapel House in Beech Lane was once a primitive Methodist Chapel, and it may well be this building that is being referred to by Ayres (1988) as *in the open air in Lower Earley*.

Earley's Roman Catholic Church has a long history of development, but it was not until 1976 that the church of **Our Lady of Peace and Blessed Dominic Barberi** was completed.

By the early 1940s mass was being said in Earley in St Peter's Church Hall. In 1943 the mass moved to the Cricket Club Pavilion of the Reading Cricket Club (situated just past the allotments off Church Road). In 1946 St James's parish was divided to create the new parishes of St William of York in Upper Redlands Road (now a parish in its own right), St John Bosco in Woodley and Christ the King in Northumberland Avenue, South Reading.

A house in Whiteknights Road (number 53) was purchased for the priests for Woodley and Earley. Masses for the people of Earley were held in the long room there.

After a church was built on the site of the old lodge bungalow in

Woodley, attention turned to Earley and fund raising began in earnest. There was some very serious talk at the time of combining Woodley and Earley with St William of York and to this end the land at Earley Cross-roads was purchased with the view to it becoming the focal point of both parishes. In 1952 voluntary labour was used to build a church hall on this land. This became the mass centre for the area. By 1957 it had a congregation of 50 people.

In 1975 the foundations of the church were laid out and finally in June 1976 the church opened. By this time a larger hall was needed and the Community Centre was opened on 18 September 1980.

By mid-1980 the very large development of Lower Earley was proceeding rapidly and the diocese decided to split the parish into two.

Recusants in Earley

18th century Reading was unusual amongst small towns in southern England in that it had a Catholic congregation. Throughout the centuries of persecution the Catholic faith had been kept alive in this area by people of all social classes and walks of life aided by the ministry of French priests. The landed families such as the Englefields at Whiteknights, the Blounts of Mapledurham and later the Wheble family at Bulmershe were all catholics and this must have helped the cause as they often had private chapels where mass could be said and they could give shelter to priests more easily. The Englefields were notable recusants and the marriage of Anthony Englefield's daughter Teresa to Lister Blount of Mapledurham linked up the two most important Roman Catholic families in the neighbourhood (Dormer, 1944).

These families also entertained other famous catholics such as Alexander Pope who lived at Binfield.

Throughout the 18th century Reading catholics had been served by Franciscan Friars who found refuge and a base for their missionary work at Whiteknights. Sir Henry Englefield was a great friend of the catholics, his brother Charles Felix Englefield was a Franciscan Priest serving in the Reading Mission in about 1734 (Mullaney, 1987). The Englefields left the area in the 1780s, but before leaving, Sir Henry Englefield founded an Endowment for a perma, as the parishes were then known. When the Whiteknights estate passed out of the Englefield family's ownership it was quite a blow for the catholics of the area. The loss was compensated by the arrival of the Wheble family. James Wheble bought the Bulmershe estate in Woodley from Henry Addington in 1801. Catholics of the area were able to attend mass there. There was an old house on the site of Maisonette and for some years it was occupied by the émigré Abbé who served the private chapel at Bulmershe Court (Dormer, 1944). Maisonette was on Church Road, Oldfield Close now occupies the site. Abbé Pierre Louis Guy Miard de la Blardière a French priest is recorded as having lived there. He was driven into exile under the French legislation of 1792. He was in the Reading Mission in 1802 and served the private chapel at Bulmershe Court (Mullaney, 1987).

In 1829 the Catholic Emancipation Act was passed and in the same year the Irish Catholic Reformer Daniel O'Connell came to Reading to be Godfather to James Wheble's youngest child. With the passing of the Catholic Emancipation Act catholics were allowed to hold office and his son was appointed High Sheriff of Berkshire in 1854.

James Wheble had financed and took part in the excavation of Reading Abbey ruins. In 1834 he bought a piece of the Abbey land and a church was built on the site. St James's Church opened in August 1840; James Wheble died the same year. St James remained the only Catholic Church in Reading until St William of York was built in 1904. The boundaries of St James's parish at this time were the Thames to the north, the Loddon to the east, the Hampshire border to the south and the Reading to Basingstoke railway line in the west.

A house was bought in Sawtry Close to serve as a daily mass centre and presbytery while Sunday mass was celebrated in Hawkedon School. After about a year it was deemed necessary to buy a larger house; 56 Gypsy Lane was purchased and Sunday mass was transferred to Loddon County Primary School.

Before land could be obtained to build a church, it was decided in 1990 that the parishes should once more be amalgamated and the new parish of Our Lady of Peace and Blessed Dominic Barberi was created.

There was a chapel dedicated to St Nicholas in the 12th century in what is now Whiteknights Park though no one knows its exact site (see chapter 3). This was part of the ancient manor of Erlegh St Nicholas. The present day church of Earley St Nicolas takes its name from this.

St Nicolas' Church in Sutcliffe Avenue is a daughter church of St Peter's. The population of St Peter's Parish grew from about 5,000 people in 1906 to 10,000 in 1943. As the area around Sutcliffe Avenue became more populated due to housing developments on the land released by the breaking up of the Maiden Erlegh estate, it was felt that there was a need to provide a local centre for the community to meet in. In 1935, one and half acres of land was purchased on Sutcliffe Avenue to provide a church and a hall.

The Second World War intervened and despite a lot of planning little happened on the ground until May 1946 when Mr Clark, a South Lake resident, offered a small hut (40ft × 18ft) that had been used to house a school that had been evacuated from London. Work to dismantle and re-erect the building continued over the summer and autumn, and the building was finally completed by early December. The first service was held on Sunday 22nd December, but it was not until 29th June 1947 (St Peter's Day) that the building was officially opened by the Bishop of Oxford (Robinson, 1947).

In 1949 building work began on a combined church and hall. The wood from the old hut was used to build the new roof – there are painted beams hidden behind the ceiling. Curtains from the old hut were used to make new hassock covers. The church and hall had cost less than £2,000, church people had built it themselves under the supervision of a local builder; the builder's daughter still worships in the church. Twenty-five years later the new church was built next to that building. The old church and hall became the church hall.

In 1976 St Nicolas' became an independent parish and now not only serves the area around Sutcliffe Avenue but a large part of Lower Earley which has developed rapidly within the last two decades.

The story of **the King's Church in Earley** began in 1942 when a Sunday school was started in a home in Hilltop Road. The first meeting was held on 8th November 1942 with two teachers and eleven children.

From the beginning the school had aspirations of buying its own piece of land, then building a hut on it and eventually a proper brick building.

A site was acquired on 1st July 1943. A plan for a new building was then prepared but, owing to wartime difficulties, the erection of any building had to be delayed until October 1949 when Hilltop Hall was completed. It had been built using volunteer labour for the cost of £929 6s 5½d. Within the building costs a figure of £2. 13s 1½d had been spent on oil and cigarettes! A service of dedication for the hall was held on 22nd October. In November, it was agreed that a church should be formed and on Sunday 4th December, the first church service was held in Hilltop Hall.

From the beginning it was decided that the Sunday school should be undenominational. This ethos was continued with the new church and in 1952 Hilltop Free Church joined the Fellowship of Independent Free Churches.

The church continued to flourish and during the sixties new church buildings were erected. In 1975 Eric Bird became the second full-time pastor and a new charismatic style increased membership in the church from 40 to 100. In 1981 the church adopted its new name of King's Church.

In 1982 a new congregation started to hold meetings at Maiden Erlegh School. By 1984 the Brookside Christian Centre was built and quickly paid for and the Maiden Erlegh congregation moved into this new building. The church celebrated its 50th anniversary in December 1999.

Trinity Church in Chalfont Close is an Ecumenical Church made up of members from the Methodist Church, the United Reformed Church and the Church of England.

Trinity began in 1983 when members of Christ Church Woodley Methodist Church and Park United Reformed Church started to hold joint services in a house in Lower Earley. Church of England participation began in 1987 with support from Earley St Peter's Church. In June 1993 services commenced in the Radstock Community Centre, before moving to a new building in Chalfont Close on November 7th 1987.

1992 saw the establishment of a new Church of England Parish (Earley Trinity). This was celebrated on 16th January 1993 in the first *beating of the bounds* – a walk around the parish boundary.

The Lower Earley Baptist Church was started in the mid-1980s to accommodate members from Wycliffe and Sindlesham Baptist Churches who had moved into the area. The congregation first met in Loddon Primary School, but since 1990 it has met in Maiden Place Community Centre.

The Porter Institute

The idea of a Men's Club was first mooted during the time when Revd Haviland Durand was the vicar, but it was not until May 1895 that the Revd Braybrooke, the then curate, and Alderman F. A. Sergeant started the project. With Vicar Firmstone's support they convened a meeting to plan the way forward.

Fortunately for the project, one of those invited was Mr Thomas Porter who at the time resided at Erlegh Whiteknights. Mr Porter, who had already given a large sum to the church restoration fund and had borne a considerable share of the cost of enlarging St Peter's School, offered to pay for the entire cost of the building of the working men's clubroom. It had cost him £929 15s 9d.

The Porter Institute was built on the glebe land with Mr Porter laying the foundation stone. The building was formally opened on 21st July 1896, only six months before Mr Porter died on 10th January 1897. Five months after his death, his widow Charlotte gave the Institute a portrait of her husband.

Below right: The Porter Institute, now part of St Peter's School
© Dann/Lewis 636 Rural History Centre, The University of Reading

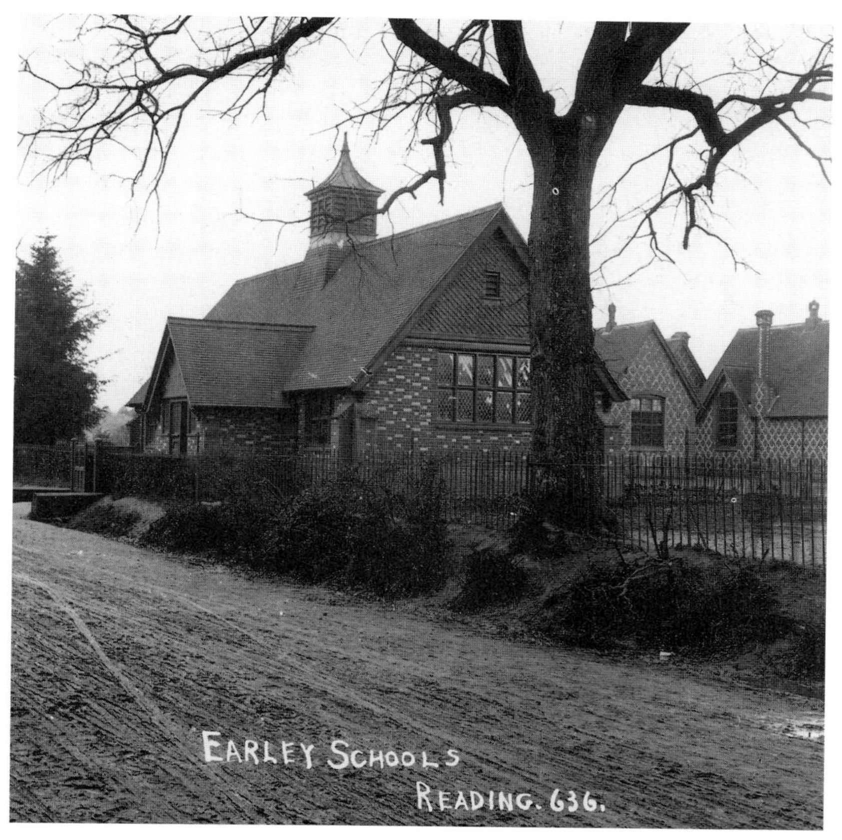

Thomas Porter (1813–1897)

Thomas Porter became very wealthy as a merchant in the West Indies. He was born in Devon, and served in the army. He married a native of Antigua and later returned to England to live in Erlegh Park House, one of the six villas on the Whiteknights Park estate, and one of the four which had been built by Alfred Waterhouse. It was demolished in the 1960s, Wessex Hall, a university hall of residence, now stands on the site.

Thomas Porter was a very generous benefactor. He gave money to Earley St Peter's school and to other good causes. He is best known for offering to pay for a Working Men's Institute, the Porter Institute, which now forms the staff room and administration block of Earley St Peter's School. The Institute was opened in 1896, sadly he died the following year.

In 1976 Earley Town Council expressed an interest in buying the Porter Institute at a time when St Peter's required money for organ restoration work. Berkshire County Council opposed the sale because of increase in demand for car parking and having adults casually on a school site. Berkshire County Council and the Oxford Church of England Diocesan School Board expressed an interest in buying the Institute to compensate for the two classrooms used by the school at Woodley Hill House. In 1977 the Institute was bought by Berkshire County Council for £8,750 and conveyed to the Oxford Diocesan Commission. Earley Men's Club was ordered to quit the Institute as the church authorities decided that it should be available to other organisations in the area. The Club complained that it flaunted the wishes of its benefactor Mr Thomas Porter. The Institute is now part of Earley St Peter's School and is used as a staff-room and for administration.

Schools

Formal learning is a recent phenomenon in Earley. The Earley School was built in 1848 followed in the 1870s by Newtown School which was owned jointly by the Reading and Earley School Board. There was then a long gap before Loddon Primary, Whiteknights Primary, Maiden Erlegh and Aldryngton Schools were built in the late 50s/early 60s. This was followed by another quiet period before a further three schools were built to service the expanding population of Lower Earley.

Earley St Peter's School was known as *the Earley School* until 1964 as it was the only one in Earley. When other schools were built in the area it officially changed its name to Earley St Peter's School.

The school which stands next to the church was founded in 1848. Several other schools in the area were founded around this period – the church school in Sonning (1839), and one in Woodley (1855). Both of these were founded with the help of Caroline Palmer of Holme Park who was interested in education, it is possible therefore that she was party to the founding of St Peter's school.

The school was built on the Vicar's glebe land and consisted of a Headmaster's house and three classrooms. The school has changed out of all recognition since the time when the children paid 1d a week for their schooling. None of the original buildings exist, these were demolished in 1961/2 when much of the present building was erected (Watts *et al*, 1998). It was a sad day for Earley when the original school building was demolished as it was a beautiful red brick Victorian building with an intricate pattern of diamonds built into the walls using lighter coloured bricks. With the breaking up of the big estates of the area and the land being sold for housing there has been a constant battle to provide accommodation for the education of the ever-increasing population. The school has been enlarged many times, including in 1860, 1887, 1891, 1937, 1951, 1963 and 1998.

Right: Old School House, Earley School

Below: Earley School Standard I, 1916–21.

© Mabel Jacobs

Three classrooms built in the 1930s remain, at present these form part of the infants' accommodation. The Porter Institute which stands on the main road and is now part of the school was built in 1896 as a Working Men's Institute. It was funded by Mr Thomas Porter of Erlegh Park Lodge on the Whiteknights Estate and was converted for administrative use (offices and staff-room) in 1998. Mr Thomas Porter was a great benefactor; he gave money for the enlargement of the church and the school as well as for building the Porter Institute.

Above: The Crowning of the May Queen
© Doris Taylor (who was at the school from 1927–31)

Below: Earley School Maypole Dance, 7 May 1935
© Betty Purcell

At the beginning of the Second World War, the ARP took over the school and books and equipment were transferred (in wheelbarrows) to St Peter's Hall. The hall was shared by Earley School and two London schools. The Porter Institute was also used to provide emergency accommodation.

A Horsa building added to the school in the 1950s was demolished in August 1997 and four new classrooms were built on this site.

The school site controller's house, 20 Church Road, stands between the school and the railway (Reading to Waterloo). It was bought by the LEA in 1981 for this purpose. Originally it was a private house called The Nook.

Whiteknights Primary School started in April 1956 with 30 infants in Shinfield Working Men's Club. The school settled on its present site, the highest point in Earley, on a field called Great Horse Close in September 1956 with 42 children in four modern classrooms. In the following year the school had grown to 88 children including 27 junior aged children. It was now a fully-fledged primary school. In 1960 an additional building comprising a hall, kitchen, staff accommodation and three infant classrooms was added to the site and in the following September there were 226 children on roll. During the building of Lower Earley the school grounds were enlarged and the school increased vastly in size to accommodate the children coming into the area until Radstock School and then Hillside School were built. The original wooden buildings were replaced in 1994. It is now a two-form entry primary school with over 400 children from Reading, Earley and Shinfield on the roll.

Aldryngton Primary School opened in 1964. A group of older children was taken in during the summer term and the school had its first official intake of five-year-olds in the autumn term of 1964.

The school takes its name from Henry de Aldryngton, a wealthy landowner in the Goring District who bought the Manor of Earley Whiteknights around 1362. He also purchased Erlegh St Bartholomew and had other possessions in Whitley, Reading, Englefield, Shinfield, Sonning, Cholsey, Tilehurst, Burghfield, Sulham, Theale and Goring. Both his wife Elizabeth Loveday and his mother have brasses dedicated to them in Goring-on-Thames Church.

Hawkedon Primary School was built in two main phases, the first in 1984 and the second in 1987–88. When the first 70 pupils started, the school was not finished so the pupils were bussed to The Hawthorns Primary School in Woosehill, Wokingham. The school now has over 450 pupils.

Loddon Junior School takes its name from the River Loddon which flows nearby. The school logo depicts the river flowing under the bridge on the Wokingham Road. The school was built in 1950 as an eight-class primary school catering for both Infant and Junior children. At that time the school was surrounded by farmland and Silverdale Road did not exist. In April 2000 it celebrated fifty years of service in the community.

The first Head of Loddon Junior School decided that a swimming pool should be built and apparently, Loddon School was the first primary school in Berkshire to have its own pool. The initial fund raising effort was a collection by parents of Queen Victoria bun pennies. At first the pool had a plastic lining and this kept splitting under constant use! At present the maintenance and upkeep of the pool is completely funded by parents through the efforts of the Loddon Schools' Swimming Pool Association.

When Russia invaded Hungary in 1956, the school admitted twenty Hungarian children who knew no English. They were housed nearby in Maiden Erlegh House and stayed for three months.

With the continued building of houses, there was an increase in the number of pupils. It became necessary to build a separate school on the same site; this became Loddon Infant School. The area has continued to expand and develop and the school's catchment contains a mix of established and new housing developments. There are now children attending the school whose parents attended it as children.

Radstock Primary School was officially opened on September 1st 1983 with 86 pupils. Radstock originated because of its location adjacent to the Lower Earley housing development; and was designated as the first new school for the area.

Initially Radstock was built for 210 pupils but it quickly became clear that this number was a rather conservative estimate and within one term plans had already been drawn up for the expansion of the school.

By 1986 building work had progressed rapidly and the school was a sprawling mixture of permanent brick buildings and several temporary classrooms. By 1986 the school had a pupil roll of 420. In the 1990s a 52 place nursery unit was built.

Hillside Primary School was built on the former site of Hillside Farm which was owned by Peter Colebrook. It opened in 1986 with a Head teacher, four teachers and 110 children. It quickly filled to twelve classes as the final areas of housing in Ryhill Way and Hilmanton were completed. In February 1987 the Ryhill Playgroup opened in the school and moved to its present premises a year later. The nursery was officially opened by the last Chief Education Officer of Berkshire in 1997. The school has been extended twice already to make room for an office, teaching area and art studio. It now has plans for a computer suite.

Until **Maiden Erlegh School** was opened in April 1962 Earley had no secondary schools of its own and even today Maiden Erlegh remains the only secondary school in the parish.

The first 90 children, who had previously attended the secondary school in Woodley, made up the first three forms in that first summer term. The school was designed to accommodate 500 pupils but it now has 1500 pupils on its roll. The school was built at a cost of £170,000.

Much of the credit for laying the foundations of the school's good reputation has been attributed to the school's first headmaster – Mr James Dunkley who guided the school through the first 21 years. A flavour of his authoritarian style can be glimpsed from his insistence on having a very high standard of school uniform a principle that was not in vogue for secondary modern schools at that time. The girls even wore straw boaters and white gloves in the summer!

Within the building programme of Maiden Erlegh School provision was made for a new branch of the County Library. The Library was built at a cost of £1,500 and officially opened on 13th June 1962.

Above: Maiden Erlegh School, the first day, May 1962

Right: Maiden Erlegh School, school trip, 1962

The 150 acre Bulmershe Court Estate was to have been a huge Education Park. The new Earley Grammar School (now Bulmershe school) was opened in about 1964. Another secondary school and two primary schools were to be built as well as a Teacher Training College. However, only one primary school William Gray (now Highwood) and the college were built.

Earley's Charities

Earley's poor have over the centuries benefitted from monies distributed by a number of land-rich charities. In 1987 two of these charities, the Englefield Charity and the Earley Poor Charity were combined to form the Earley Charity.

Englefield Charity

The origins of the Englefield charity are shrouded in mystery and may have been the source of the 'mystery benefactor' when this charity was amalgamated with the Earley Poors' Charity in 1987

An ancestor of the Englefields left by will a rent-charge of £6 charged on 6 acres 3 roods 28 perches of land and property on Elm Lane and Elm Road (Great Elm Tree Piddle, frontage Allotment, Charity Tree Acres and a cottage and a garden). The rent was to be used for apprenticing one poor boy (£4) and the rest to be distributed between four widows who received no alms from the parish.

In 1837 the Charity Commissioners were unable to establish the name of the founder of the Charity or the founding date. Francis Cholmeley, nephew of the last Englefield at Whiteknights, Sir Henry Englefield who died in 1822, was unable to furnish a copy of the will mentioned or its date (Endowed Charities, 1910). Joseph Goddard had been in possession of the Charity land since 1816 and the Commissioners concluded that maybe the Goddards themselves were in some way beneficiaries of the Englefields as they had been their tenants *upwards of a century*. Since 1816 only two boys had been apprenticed (one in 1821 at £15 and one in 1830 at £20). He paid 40 shillings annually at Michaelmas to the churchwardens who decided to distribute 2 shillings and sixpence to each of 16 widows who had all been in receipt of parochial relief in recent years (Endowed Charity, 1910).

In 1853 Joseph Goddard admitted that he was the tenant of the trustees and promised to pay the balance of money owing (£45); he was also £18 in arrears with his rent to the Charity. This was remedied by paying £26 10s per year in 1854–55 and thereafter £10 per year. Three widows were paid 10 shillings each and £22 9s 0d was paid to John Brown for repairing one of the cottages in 1854. The Trustees advertised for the placement of an apprentice by placing an advert in the Reading Mercury in December 1859 and two months later (7 March 1860) Edward Taylor was

Joseph Goddard's gravestone, Sonning Parish churchyard

apprenticed for seven years to Lawrence Carpenter of Greyfriars, Reading. The first instalment was £10 10s. William Elliot was the next boy to be apprenticed, to Charles Moffat, painter, plumber and decorator.

Joseph Goddard Senior of Elm Farm died in 1867 aged 95 years. His son Joseph Goddard Junior of Coppice Farm took over the Charity land. The rent did not change. By 1898/9 William Goddard (son of Joseph?) was paying ten shillings more in rent and another William Goddard was apprenticed to a Mr Squire of Redlands. The last recorded rent was paid by Mrs William Goddard in 1899/1900. William Goddard died in December 1899 aged 50.

In 1902 the Englefield Charity land was sold for £1080 and the money was invested and administered by the churchwardens of the Parish of Earley.

Church Land

Perkins or Parkins piddle belonged to the Parish from time immemorial. In 1830 the land was rented to Thomas Chapman at £5 5s 0d per year. The rents from these lands were applied to the purpose of a church rate. The land consisting of 1 acre 2 roods 11 perches plus allotments of 30 perches plus 2 cottages and gardens of 34 perches were sold in 1874 for £320 and the money invested.

Earley Poor's Charity

Before the Sonning Inclosure Act of 1816 the commoners of Earley had the right to collect *Turves, Fern [bracken] and other fuel arising from the Lands* on Earley Heath and Earley Lower and Upper Wood Commons. In compensation for losing these rights the Inclosure Act stipulated that one sixteenth of the land was to be enclosed and that the income from this land was intended to compensate the commoners for the loss of these rights. An area of 12 acres, 1 rood and 36 perches was enclosed along the Shinfield and Loddon Bridge Road later Cutbush Lane. Two other allotments of 1 rod 22 perches and 2 rods 11 perches on Earley Heath (along the Drift Road) were included in the Act but Captain Wheble claimed that these lands had been bought by his grandfather prior to 1840.

The Earley Poor's Charity came from an Inclosure award made on 26th April 1820 under the Sonning Inclosure Act, 56 George III, c.36.1816 and covered the ecclesiastical area of the Liberty of Earley. The execution of the award was vested in the churchwardens and overseers of the poor and their successors. The land was *advertised annually for letting in allotments but being a distance from the village [sic], no applications are received* (Endowed Charities, 1910).

Co-opted trustees living in or near the Liberty administered the Charity. In 1852 at a vestry meeting at St Peter's Church the following were in attendance:

George Shackel	*Overseer*
G H Foyle	*Church Warden*
Thomas Harris	*Overseer*
Joseph Goddard	
Joseph Goddard	*(Lower Earley)*
Joseph Gregory	
Thomas Chapman	
Thomas Hathaway	
W. Wheelwright	*(for B. Golding Esquire)*

The Overseers for the Poor produced rate books every year. And based on these records people occupying houses, lands or tenements with a rateable value of less than five pounds per annum were eligible to receive fuel from this Charity.

George Shackel, Overseer for the Poor, brought the accounts up to date in the 1850s. In 1855 Charles Stephens, the banker, sought advice from Robert Palmer MP about the interpretation of the Sonning Inclosure Act for the Poor of Earley. He (Robert Palmer) specified that a person had to be both an inhabitant and legally settled to have a right to the fuel. There was a debate about whether the Poor were entitled to any fuel purchased by the Trustees or they purchase it from the Trustees or the land remain wastes where the Poor may cut it for fuel. Finally he states that *'the industrious Poor Inhabitants of the Liberty mentioned would be held to mean those who are legally settled as persons receiving coals or fuels must be inhabitants'*.

Between 1845 and 1902 a record was made of the people who rented the land and the amount they paid each year. The land was drained and fenced and let to Jonathon Elliott, Thomas Harris, Mr Pither, Mrs Pither, Green, Fawcett and Eighteen. In 1882 onwards the excess money was paid into the Savings Bank (Reading Savings Bank) but by the 1890s the outgoings were greater than the income and in 1898 the vicar returned his tithes and Parish donations and profits from a performance of Dick Whittington by the School Club helped towards the deficit.

In 1903 changes were made to the Charity in accordance with the powers invested in the Charity Commissioners by various Acts of Parliament and the Charity moved into the care of civil parish trustees who met annually at the Porter Institute. The Parish Council of Earley appointed two trustees, Richard Crook Mount of Lakefoot, Earley and Richard Lea of Heathfield, Earley for five years. A Reading representative was appointed to the Trustees and an amending scheme brought in the Reading part of Earley. The names of the poor of Earley seeking relief were put forward to the Trustees by the Parish Relief Officer. In 1903 the Trustees had £100 invested in the Reading Savings Bank and the land was let to John Eighteen for £25 per year. In 1933 the Charity invested £100 in 2½% consolidated stock and £335 in 3½% war stock and the land was let to George Heath for £23 per year.

In 1908 £16 6s 2d was spent on Collector's commission, tithes, rates, land tax, income tax, hedging and ditching and legal costs and £19 10s was expended on the sick and poor fund, clothing club, coal club, coal gift, nursing fund and convalescent fund. So that less than 60% of the income was spent on the people for whom it was intended!

In its last years the Earley Poor's Charity had an income of £200 per year which it distributed in kind to about 40 people each year.

The sale of some of the land in 1985 for housing brought in a huge income. One acre was given as planning gain to Wokingham District Council, the Police Station is now on this land. On the remaining land the Charity built the Liberty of Earley House for residents requiring full time care. The Charity also has its offices there.

Earley Charity

In 1987 the Englefield Charities were combined with the Earley Poor's Charity to form the Earley Charity. The spirit of the apprentice bequest continues in the support of education and the Earley Poor's Land Charity in the relief of hardship for all people living in the area of the Charity. With the increase in income from the sale of the land the boundaries for dispensing the income were widened to the Woodley borders in the east, Shinfield in the south and up to the borders of the Tilehurst Poor's Charity in the west.

Woodley Hill House

Woodley Hill House, originally known as Woodley Hill, is known to thousands of people in the area who have enjoyed adult education classes there. Many had not realised the building was there until they enrolled for classes. In the last century it was certainly a more prominent and visible building and estate in the area, before many of the surrounding roads and houses were developed, and a look at its history makes that clear.

The house was built in 1869 for Messrs F T and J Galsworthy on land they had owned adjoining lands that were part of Erleigh Court, then owned by Lord Sidmouth. The first occupant of the house was the prominent local banker Charles Stephens who first leased the property from the Galsworthy's and then purchased it in February 1876. He also bought the remaining triangle of land between the south boundary and the railway line to make an estate of 26 acres of land. Within these extensive grounds were included tennis courts, extensive kitchen gardens with glass houses, an orchard, together with a stable block and coach house (once Robseal's premises). The Lodge on the corner of Eastcourt Avenue and Church Road was the lodge for Woodley Hill.

Susannah Stephens died at Woodley Hill in August 1914. In her will, she directed that the property should be sold and the proceeds to be

Woodley Hill House
© 1947, Brian Cook

divided between her three surviving sisters. Among a number of bequests made by her was the sum of £3000 to be used for the upkeep of the lifeboat named after her and her husband and *once in three years a good plain dinner should be provided for the men on the station where that boat is kept.*

It would appear that the house remained empty following Susannah's death until it was purchased in early 1917 by the Poor Sisters of Nazareth for use as an orphanage. The house, and in particular the drainage system, needed difficult and expensive remedial work taking some 18 months to carry out. However, the Sisters and boys moved from Leopold House in Tilehurst to Woodley Hill in June 1917 and the first Mass in the new Nazareth House was said by Bishop Cotter on 30 June. Many local

Charles Stephens (1831–1901)

Charles Stephens lived in Earley for much of his life. As a child he lived with his family in Erleigh Court. The census of 1851 records him as being an undergraduate of Oxford University. He later became a banker; and was a partner in the banking firm of Stephens, Blandy & Co. until 1899. As one of the last partners he was appointed as the first manager when his banking firm merged with Lloyds Bank. He was Borough Treasurer for many years and also a Justice of the Peace. He was appointed High Sheriff of Berkshire in 1877.

Charles lived in Woodley Hill with his wife, Susannah. They had no children but there were six servants living in the house and two in the lodge. In total, there were 19 servants and their children.

Charles Stephens played a significant role in the life of Earley and Reading, and was a very active supporter of Earley St Peter's Church; he was a churchwarden there for twenty-five years (1873–1898). He was also closely involved with the Lifeboat Institute. He died at Woodley Hill in 1901 at the age of 70.

The frescos by Ion Pace in the chancel of Earley St Peter's Church were funded by Susannah Stephens as a memorial to her husband. The Lych-gate is also dedicated to his memory.

Mrs Stephens also bought the new Ramsgate lifeboat as a memorial to her husband. This was launched by her on 25th May 1905. The boat was named *Charles and Susannah*.

people, of all persuasions, were generous in their support, including the biscuit manufacturer Huntley & Palmer. The house closed in December 1923 as the expense of the drainage work and the slow increase in admissions affected the economic viability. The boys were transferred to a new house in Southampton, still within the Roman Catholic diocese of Portsmouth.

The house may have been used by another similar organisation during the period between December 1923 and when it was sold again in June 1926, this time to local builder Francis Wilson. It was Francis Wilson and his successors who developed the land surrounding Woodley Hill which now contains Anderson Avenue, Fairview Avenue and Eastcourt Avenue, and utilised the former stables and coach house as his builders yard. The Wilsons never lived at Woodley Hill, but leased the property to the Short family. William Short was from the biscuit firm Serpell & Co. of South Street, Reading and was also active in public affairs, being a member of Reading Town Council for some 18 years and mayor in 1926–7. It was during Short's tenancy that the house was purchased by another director of Serpells Biscuits, Ben Clark. It is not known whether Ben Clark lived in the house for any length of time as he also owned another substantial property nearby, South Lake House, Woodley, now The Thatchers public house in Fairwater Drive. At the outbreak of the Second World War Ben Clark allowed both his houses to be used by the evacuated Archbishop Tennyson School from south east London. Temporary classrooms were built in the grounds of South Lake House and Woodley Hill was used as living accommodation for the Headmaster and a number of the boys.

During its stay in the area the school began to take in local boys of Grammar School age. In 1945, at the end of the war, and with the passing of the 1944 Education Act Berkshire County Council saw the need for a Grammar School in this part of the County. They sought suitable premises for the venture and the nucleus of a new school was temporarily accommodated at the then Woodley Secondary Modern (now Rivermead Primary School). In February 1946, the County took out a lease on Woodley Hill for use as a school. The staff at the time were told that they would have a new purpose built school in the area in 2 to 3 years. The new school, consisting of 25 ex-Tennyson boys and 36 new boys and five masters settled into their new 'temporary' accommodation at Woodley Hill. This became Woodley Hill Grammar School. The School grew rapidly and remained at Woodley Hill until 1957 when it moved to its new premises at Winnersh and became The Forest School.

The County had purchased Woodley Hill from Ben Clark in 1953. When the Grammar School departed, the house was used to accommodate the first and second year departments of Woodley Secondary School (later known as Maiden Erlegh school) until the present site opened in 1962. The outbuildings were used by Earley St Peter's primary school as an annex as there was not enough classroom space on the main site.

Adult education classes started in the early sixties under the direct control of Berkshire County Council with Miss Vivian Davies in charge. Miss Davies took the centre into merger with Bracknell College in 1967 and is still a well-known, popular and redoubtable figure in the local cultural scene, though she retired from her post in the college in 1985.

The University of Reading

The University of Reading began as a University Extension College (of Oxford) in Valpy Street, Reading in 1892. By 1905 the College had outgrown this site and had moved to London Road, the land and buildings being generously funded by Alfred Palmer and family who owned the Huntley and Palmer biscuit factory in Reading. Acacias, a house on London Road and part of the University, was the home of Alfred Palmer.

The University of Reading was incorporated by Royal Charter on 17th March 1926. It continued to grow and became widely known for its courses in agriculture and dairying.

By the end of the second World War more halls of residence were needed for the increasing number of students. Informal enquiries were made about the purchase of land on the edge of the Whiteknights Estate as it was thought to be suitably close to the London Road site for new halls of residence. At one of the meetings held to discuss the purchase of this small piece of land in July 1946, the University's negotiators were informally asked if they would be interested in buying the freehold of the whole estate from its then owners. This was an opportunity too good to be missed. After some negotiation a generous settlement by the Government allowed the University to acquire the whole of Whiteknights Park in 1947 (Holt, 1977). This was an estate of 300 acres (120 ha), the leases on the six properties were nearing their end and there was an agreement that the government buildings at the Earley Gate part of the estate, built and used during the war, would be vacated as soon as was practicable thus the University was to move onto the estate and plan its expansion.

By the late 1960s much of the teaching and research had moved to the Whiteknights campus, leaving only a few departments at the London Road site.

Sadly some of the Victorian houses such as The Wilderness and Erlegh Lodge were demolished as the University developed and new buildings were erected, though some remain. Whiteknights Park House (known as Park House) is used as the Senior Common Room, Blandford Lodge has been used to teach statistics and art history, Whiteknights House to teach law and Foxhill for residence. The various lodges also have a variety of uses, at present Archway Lodge is used as a Muslim Centre and Park House Lodge is the Chaplaincy Centre. The Temporary Office Buildings (TOBs) built during the war are gradually being replaced by new buildings. The War Room first publicised by the Aldermaston marchers was vacated by the Ministry of Defence twenty years ago. It is now used for research. Most of the University is now in Earley!

In 1965 part of Elm Farm (87 acres) in Elm Lane was bought by the University with the intention of building more halls of residence and a Science Park. Sibly Hall, named after the first Vice-Chancellor, Sir Franklin Sibly, was opened in 1967, but government constraints on money prevented the rest of the imaginative scheme from being carried out and the land was sold for housing.

In 1988 Bulmershe College of Higher Education, which was on the site of Bulmershe Court, became part of the University and the Education departments merged on this site.

The University now has over 12,000 registered students. Over the years many well known people have attended the University including, Pippa Greenwood (a presenter on BBC's Gardener's World), Suzanne Charlton (Television weather forecast presenter) and Andy McKay (musician in the band Roxy Music).

Temporary Office Buildings

The Temporary Office Buildings (TOBs) are single storey Government offices that were built at Earley Gate, on the south-eastern corner of

Whiteknights Park at the end of the Second World War. The Kelly's Directory of 1960 lists the Ministries of Education, Health, Housing and Local Government, Labour, Pensions and National Insurance and Power and Works and the National Savings Committee. There was also a unit for fitting artificial limbs. The government closed these departments down in the late 1960s and the University moved into them in 1969, the biggest department being the Department of Agriculture. Some fifty years after these temporary buildings were built, they are now gradually being replaced. The University has plans to replace them all.

Temporary Office Buildings, University of Reading, 2000

The War Room

The former war room is located within the grounds of the University. Close to the Earley Gate entrance. It is located adjacent to the group of Temporary Office Buildings erected at the end of the Second World War. It is a heavily protected surface bunker constructed from reinforced concrete. It was built about 1952 for the commissioner of Home Defence Region 6. It is one of 14 such bunkers built in England at this date.

The bunker is rectangular with one storey at ground level and one below ground level. There are two doors into the War Room at the northern ends of its west and east elevations. These lead into a dog-leg corridor, designed to dissipate blast waves.

The system of War Rooms survived until the late 1950s when it was replaced by a new group of protected headquarters known as Regional Seats of Government. Under this programme the Whiteknights War

Room was replaced by a RSG at Warren Row, Maidenhead. The War Room was retained as a communication centre. In 1964 the administrative structure for emergency government was reorganised as the country was sub-divided into a series of Sub-Regional Controls. Under this system the administration of NW London was allocated to Sub-Region 61 with controls at Warren Row and Whiteknights, which suggest the old War Room had been reactivated. The Warren Row bunker was decommissioned in 1970 and its function transferred to Basingstoke.

At this date the Whiteknights bunker was vacated and during the 1970s it passed to the university. It is now used as a store for the library and for research.

Earley's Museums

There are three museums on the University campus, two of which lie on the Earley side of the boundary. The Cole Museum in the Zoology and Biochemistry Building which has a large collection of zoological specimens, the Ure Museum which is in the Department of Classics which has a collection of Greek and Roman artefacts and the museum of English Rural Life which has many displays covering rural crafts and the rural way of life; including an extensive collection of old carts and carriages.

Part of the **Cole Museum of Zoology** is situated in the foyer of the School of Animal and Microbial Sciences (building No. 7) adjacent to the Palmer building on the map of the Whiteknights campus.

The Cole Museum is a remarkable collection in that it was built up in the period 1907 to 1939 by three people: Professor Cole, Dr Nellie B. Eales and Mr Stoneman. The Museum is matched by an equally impressive collection of books, including many first editions that Cole bought from his own finances. The books were often displayed with many of the museum specimens but when Cole retired in 1939 they were housed in the library that formed a central part of his home. On his death in 1959, the University was able to purchase these books which are now kept in a special private collection in the main Library.

Soon after his arrival he started to build up a museum of zoology and when he retired in 1939 he had the satisfaction of seeing his Department endowed with one of the finest teaching museums in Great Britain. An appreciative Council decreed that it should remain as a permanent memorial to him with the name of The Cole Museum of Zoology.

Small though the Department was, it was from the beginning the special duty of one of the members of the staff to care for the growth and maintenance of the Museum. From 1912 until 1919 this was Miss Nellie B. Eales, and then from 1921 Mr W E Stoneman held the curatorship.

The Cole Museum was described as *being without a rival among its contemporaries* and as a *gem* for the museums of comparative anatomy (*Nature*, 1939).

The Cole collection was based on the model of the Huntarian Museum of the Royal College of Surgeons. It was intended as a place where students could browse and compare their own work in the laboratory with the skilled dissections that were produced in the Zoology Department. A number of excellent technicians assisted in this (initially Mr A H Malpas and when he emigrated to become assistant in the Ceylon Fisheries by Mr W E Stoneman). When the Department of Zoology began to be rehoused on the old site in 1940, a room was provided to house it. The Museum, however, continued to expand and filled to capacity the space that was available on the London Road site.

It was not possible to relocate the Museum until 1971 when the Department moved to the Whiteknights campus. At that time space was made available in the Foyer of the BPZ building. Some parts of the Museum were transported to the new location by hand and a procession of students carried the dismembered elephant up Redlands Road before it was eventually reassembled in its new home.

Several generations of students have *met by the elephant* and because the new location provides much easier access it has subsequently appeared on a number of television programmes.

Professor F J Cole, DSc, FRS

Francis Joseph Cole was born in London on 3rd February 1872. He was not particularly scholarly while at school although he did develop a passion for zoology and converted his bedroom into a laboratory. His early employment found him working for a variety of local newspapers before reaching Fleet Street but he spent his spare time taking private lessons in chemistry, teaching himself Greek and attending lectures at the Royal Institution. He eventually gained entrance to Oxford University, but ran out of money and left to work for Professor Cossar Ewart at Edinburgh University for £1 a week. At the age of 22, he became a lecturer at what is now the University of Liverpool. He was able to combine this post with vacation research and, at the age of 29, obtained a BSc by research at Oxford. In 1906 he was appointed as a lecturer at the University College Reading and the next year was promoted to become the first Professor of Zoology. In 1926 when the University of Reading received its Charter, Francis Joseph Cole was elected a Fellow of the Royal Society (Cole Museum, University of Reading).

The Ure Museum

The Ure Museum is to be found at the eastern end of the northern spur of the Letters Faculty building, in the Department of Classics. It is used by the department from time to time for tutorials so if you would like to visit the museum please contact the secretary first.

It is the fourth most important collection of Greek ceramics in Britain, after those of the British, Ashmolean and Fitzwilliam Museums; and now contains approximately 2000 objects. It is named after Professor P N Ure, the first Professor of Classics at Reading (1911–46), and his wife and former pupil Ánnie D Ure, curator of the Museum until her death in 1976. Between them, the Ures published three books, based on their excavations at Rhitsona in Boeotia, the Homeric Mycalesses, which are still essential reference works for the typology and chronology of Boeotian, Attic and Corinthian pottery, as well as over fifty articles on Greek pottery in general and a volume in the prestigious international series *Corpus Vasorum Antiquorum* (1954) containing about half the present collection in the Museum.

The donations of a collection of Egyptian antiquities by Mrs Flinders Petrie in 1909 and by the British School of Archaeology in Egypt in 1910, a small collection of vases by Percy Ure in 1911 and a sizeable collection of Cypriot antiquities by a Mrs Barry, a relative of Alfred Palmer (of the biscuit firm) were the bases of the departmental museum which was started in 1922. Over the following years the collection has been increased by many donations.

The Ures established good relations with successive curators of Reading Museum. The entire Greek vase collection of the Museum which is based on private collections made in the 19th century by various local personages and bequeathed to the town is now on indefinite loan to the Ure Museum

The Museum of English Rural Life

The museum lies a couple of hundred yards over the Earley/Reading boundary, but we have decided to include it in this history of Earley's Museums for the sake of completeness.

The Museum is now part of the Rural History Centre based on the Whiteknights campus. The Rural History Centre was founded as the Museum of English Rural Life in 1951 and became the Institute of Agricultural History in 1968 to reflect its broadening interests and responsibilities. Its present name was adopted in January 1993 as part of the Centre's development plan.

The Museum has a large collection that spans the last 250 years, illustrating the whole field of rural life and society with particular emphasis on tools and machines, practical farming and rural industries.

Some of the collections such as farm wagons, ploughs and baskets, are of international importance.

The collection includes a permanent display of objects relating to farming, rural industries and country life. The larger part of the Museums collections, however, are held in reserve stores. In addition, there is also a fine collection of oils, watercolours, prints, glass pictures and drawings from the 18th century onwards. Over half of these are animal portraits.

The Rural History Centre is a national centre for the study of the history of farming, food and the countryside and holds documentary, and visual material collections of research resources that are of national and international significance. As well as the Museum the Centre's collections also include a library, business records and archives, bibliographical indexes, photographs and film and video.

Mobile Information Centre

The **M**obile **I**nformation **C**entr**E** now known as MICE first started its life in Earley some 10 years ago as the Earley Mobile Action Group. A small but committed group of Earley people saw the need for access to information in the then fast growing housing development which had few fixed community points. Following a public meeting it was decided that a mobile unit would best suit the needs of the area and the first caravan was acquired to take information to people in their local communities. Within the first 7 years MICE outgrew its first two caravans.

They now operate from a purpose built vehicle bought with a National Charities Lottery Grant in 1997. They offer a one-stop shop providing a very broad range of information including health, education, disability, carers, transport, voluntary groups etc. Although based in Earley, MICE works in Woodley once a week and in other parishes on request.

6 Earley's Community Groups

Scouting in Earley

Scouting was active in this area before the first World War. At a rally in Palmer Park in 1919 the 1st St Peter troop was presented with a troop flag by Canon Fowler. The Anderson Baptist troop was formed in March 1932 and Park Church also had a troop before the Second Word War.

In 1941 two London evacuees Ray Ellis and Norman Lee restarted the St Peter's troop (31st Reading). The Suttons of Erlegh Park gave them full permission to use their grounds for outdoor activities.

Padworth and Eversley were used for camping trips. All the scouts cycled from Earley to their campsites with their camping equipment, a round trip of two hours. Funds were raised with dances, whist drives, annual fete, scout concert and jumble sale. Many people came from the other side of town to these sales as they said that the quality of the rummage was very good in Earley. The two London evacuees left in 1944 for National Service.

In September 1956 the group's Headquarters was opened on University land opposite Beech Lane. This was replaced by another HQ behind St Peter's church hall in the 1980s. The Rover Crew was reformed in the 1950s and was the biggest crew in Berkshire. Beavers, Cubs and Scouts still meet at the St Peter's hut and there are troops at St Nicolas (84th East Reading), Park, and Our Lady of Peace (99th Reading).

Scouts and Guides (Hilltop), 1950s

Guiding in Earley

Guiding in Earley started before the First Word War. Many of the activities took place in St Peter's church hall, occasionally Maiden Erlegh grounds were used. In the 1930s the guides cycled to Arborfield to camp. During Word War II Brownie meetings took place on Saturday afternoons in St Peter's school because the evacuees had use of the church hall.

The 1930s and 40s were the era of large rallies. The Berkshire Girl Guides County Standard was presented by the Chief Guide, Lady Baden-Powell to the County Commissioner, Miss Hanbury Williams, at a large rally in Erlegh Park on Saturday 9th June 1934. Each area of Berkshire, known as a Division, had arranged and organised their own display. There was a presentation of campcraft in the Reading Division arena with East Division, which included Earley, showing tent pitching. Other Divisions sang songs such as *dashing away with a smoothing iron* and *ten green bottles*, physical training, country dancing, team games, outdoor cooking and a complete *Pageant of St George*.

Reading Girl Guides' Rally at Erlegh Park, in Whiteknights Park
© *Reading Standard, July 21, 1939*

In 1939 one thousand Girl Guides and Brownies took part in a rally of the Reading Division at Erlegh Park at the invitation of Mr and Mrs E. P. Sutton. Among the officials there were Mrs St John Atkinson who was to be the new Chief Commissioner of the Girl Guides and Miss Hanbury Williams.

Guide and Brownie Packs meet at various schools and halls including St Peter's, Aldryngton School and Whiteknights School.

Flag of the Earley Women's Institute, *© 1951, Mr T. Ashman*

The Women's Institute in Earley

On 30th March 1938 a meeting was held to consider the formation of a WI in Earley. This was attended by 35 ladies who listened to speakers on the *Aims and Early History of the Movement* and *The Practical side of Running an Institute*. With the enormous growth of housing in the 30's there was a need for activities and interests for wives and mothers outside the home, apart from those organised by the Church, and so on May 11th with an attendance of 80 the new Earley WI had its first meeting to elect the Committee. By November the membership had reached 100.

Led by their President Mrs E.W. Rushbrooke, Secretary Mrs A. Taylor and Treasurer Mrs M. Sturges, they threw themselves into the *War Effort*. (For a full account of the W.I.'s wartime contribution see Chapter 8, Earley at War.) After the war the Institute moved back to St Peter's Hall. During the war the hall had been used for the evacuees and WI meetings were held in the Cricket Club. They carried on with most of their charity projects, helping with the New Branch Library at St Peter's School and organising the distribution of orange juice and cod liver oil. Collecting milk bottle tops and used stamps were popular fundraising activities; later the jumble sale came of age.

Activities such as coach outings to the Wye Valley, Oxford and Stratford-on-Avon were organised as were outings to plays (sometimes coming home with the milk in the morning!). A tennis club, choir, drama group, folk dancing group and handicraft group were all very popular and well supported; many of the groups entered Eisteddfodau and other festivals.

By 1955 Earley WI had to limit its numbers to 150 and for several years had a waiting list. They had enjoyed many garden meetings at the Manor House by kind invitation of Mrs Sidney Cook,in the gardens of Elmhurst and the beautiful garden of Hungerford Lodge where they enjoyed a marvellous day with 50 visitors from other Group Institutes with various stalls and games of skill.

In 1951 the County Federation organised a festival of handicrafts. A local artist Miss Stevens designed a banner depicting the White Knights of Earley, to be made in black and white appliqué. Ten members worked hard on this entry and it gained 95 marks. It was subsequently selected for inclusion in a national exhibition held in March 1952 at the Victoria and Albert Museum.

With the development of the Maiden Erlegh Estate and surrounding areas such was the influx of people that in 1959 Loddon WI was formed meeting at St Nicolas Hall in the afternoons.

By 1962 Gough Cooper had completed the last phase of their development and many new families had moved in, having been relocated to Reading as their firms moved out of London. On the 11th July 1962 the inaugural meeting of Maiden Erlegh WI took place. This was an evening institute which brought the mothers of these young families together. The WI provided an opportunity for enjoyment, education, exchange of ideas and the use of talents together with an opportunity to discuss matters of importance not only to themselves but to the wider world and above all to make friends.

Over the next four years they continued to meet every month at St Nicolas' Hall but in May 1966 they moved to Aldryngton School where they were warned that no stiletto heels must be worn! They remained there until 1978 when they moved back to St Nicolas' Hall.

Over the years they have had stalls in Earley Carnival field and have entered several floats in the procession. Their singers have entertained at many venues in the neighbourhood and for nine years their annual Carol Concert brought the local community together and raised money for various worthy causes. Their members assist at the local WI Market, the Kenton Road Day Centre and do voluntary work at the Royal Berkshire Hospital.

Radstock WI was formed in 1984, 28 members attended its first meeting in the Parish Room of Radstock Community Centre in December of that year.

Current community work includes preparing teas for the Model Railway Exhibition which is part of the local Carnival activities and other events associated with the Carnival Day. A flowering cherry tree was planted in the grounds of Radstock School and another in the wild area at Hillside school during the European Year of the Tree.

Radstock is the only WI within the Berkshire Federation to be *Twinned*. They made contact with Radstock, Avon, ten years ago (1990) and meet annually.

A very important part of the WI movement is the WI Market. Twelve people were present at the special meeting held on the 21st June 1974 to set up the Earley market and it opened on Friday July 5th in the Scout Hut behind St Peter's Church Hall. WI Markets are separate from the National Federation of Women's Institutes and all producers are shareholders. The Market was always looking for alternative premises and in July 1985 it moved to the Silverdale Centre. The Earley Market is one of eight in Berkshire who are all shareholders of Berkshire WI Markets.

The Fundraisers

The Lions Club of Woodley and Earley was formed in 1980 as a spin-off from Reading Lions Club, in anticipation of the significant population growth of both Earley and Woodley. The club is part of Lions Clubs International which comprises some 900 clubs in 185 countries with over 21,000 members. The main activities of the Lions in Earley include running the Earley Carnival, a Grand Car-Boot Sale day, the Model Railway Exhibition and the Grand Fireworks Evening. The proceeds from these events go to local charities.

The Rotary Club of Reading Maiden Erlegh began in September 1988. Its Charter was presented on 16th May 1989. It is one of six Rotary clubs in Reading, the current membership is 47. The club covers the parishes of Earley, Woodley and Sandford, Sonning, Charvil, Twyford, Ruscombe, Hurst and Winnersh. Meetings are held in the University of Reading.

The emblem of the Rotary Club of Reading Maiden Erlegh includes a water wheel commemorating the old flour mill which stood on the site of the present Reading Moat House Hotel at Mill Lane, Sindlesham and a black swan which once was a regular visitor to the River Loddon which flows through the club's territory.

The Earley branch of the Reading Round Table started in 1964 and organises the annual children's float.

The Earley Carnival

In the late 1970s when Eric Jefferies was a member of the Maiden Erlegh Residents Association he was assigned the task of finding a suitable hall in the area for community use. His first task was to assemble funds. He was inspired by the Woodley Carnival to create Earley's own version. He wrote to Earley Town Council and proposed that the first one should be held in 1980. The Council was delighted with the idea but suggested that more time was needed to organise it and that 1981 would be better. Eric, however, was not deterred. Within a few weeks and with the support of many local people and organisations the first Carnival was held near Maiden Erlegh Lake. The monies raised were put towards fitting out the kitchen in the Radstock Community Centre which opened in 1983. The following year it moved to Laurel Park and is now held on the Events Field, Kilnsea Drive.

East Reading Horticultural Society

The Society was founded as the result of *a meeting convened to explore the possibilities of forming an Allotments Association in the East of Reading*. The meeting was held in the East Reading Library at Palmer Park on 8th January 1941. A Committee was formed and a General Meeting arranged for 5th February 1941 formally to adopt rules for the East Reading and District Allotments Association which was changed to East Reading Horticultural Society in 1949.

The principal object of the Society has always been to promote the interests of allotment holders and gardeners and to this end trading and the dissemination of information by means of lectures, garden visits etc. has always played an important part in their activities. During the war years food production – the *Dig for Victory* campaign – was of paramount importance and the Association involved itself in the distribution to members of seedlings of lettuce, cabbage, leeks, grown by Reading University Gardens and in supplying lime (at 1/7d per cwt), fertilisers and sundries.

Midway through the last war the Association had some nine or ten separate allotment sites but many of these such as Dixons Meadow, Shepherds Hill and Wokingham Road were closed in the post-war years. Trading sheds were opened on Bulmershe Allotments and at Mockbeggar in 1942–3 and sales continued to grow until 1945 but then dropped quite sharply and only recovered to 1945 levels as late as 1959. By 1990 sales were almost 100 times the 1945 level.

In 1961 Reading Borough Council built and rented to them the first substantial building on its present site on Embery Way. This is the area of the present large shed where the counter now stands.

Sales of spring flowering bulbs began in 1963, increasing to some 30,000 assorted bulbs by 1990. The range of composts, fertilisers and sundries now compares favourably with many garden centres. This has enabled successive Committees to keep annual subscriptions to almost token levels. Subscriptions have increased from 1 shilling in 1941 to £1 in 2000.

From the beginning the Society included members resident in the Woodley area and a trading shed was erected in the Reading Road allotments for their benefit. Woodley members were represented on the Committee and took over the trading facilities at Reading Road. A series of lectures were organised at the Coronation Hall and by 1965 there were no fewer than 415 Woodley members out of a total membership of 1175. Accordingly in March 1965 it was decided that Woodley should form an independent Society and the Reading Road trading shed together with stock was formally handed over.

The Society circulates a monthly newsletter and organises a programme of lectures and visits.

Maiden Erlegh Bowling Club

On 18th July 1939 a public meeting was held in St Peter's hall to discuss the formation of a bowling club. Mr S. Cook offered land at £700 in the Wilderness Road/Aldbourne Avenue area. At a second public meeting on 3rd August 1939 the purchase of another piece of land in Beech Lane from Mr Duguid was considered but turned down. At a third meeting later on that year on 22nd August held at Mr Bunce's garage (Wilderness Road) the Maiden Erlegh Bowling Club (MEBC) was formed. Alderman George Ford was elected Chairman, Mr G. Barnett Secretary and Mr H. J. J. Hobbs Treasurer plus 10 committee members. A registration fee of one shilling was levied and the first year's subscription was 35 shillings. In September 1939 further proceedings were deferred due to the outbreak of war and the committee requested Mr S. Cook to hold the land in abeyance.

The club considered Mr Cook's site again in 1942 but the walled garden off Beech Lane, formerly part of the Maiden Erlegh estate, owned by Mr Bunce was offered to the club for £700. Agreement was reached after Mr Bunce insisted that the sale of intoxicant drinks on the premises would be available to Club members only. The sale was agreed at £700 with the inclusion of the extra frontage at £3.10 shillings per foot.

In March 1943 a £70 deposit was paid and Barclays Bank acted as Trustees and provided loan facilities of £1000 at 4.5% interest. The purchase was financed by a mixture of a bank loan and money raised by members.

The green was set up at 42 yards square. One existing greenhouse was let and the other one reserved for a temporary clubhouse. Messrs Sutton's and Sons won the tender to lay the green. Ladies were able to play only in the afternoons, if the rinks were available. The club was officially opened on 9th September 1944. The President of the English Bowling Association brought a team of 24 players to play at the Club and presented them with a flag.

The first Annual General Meeting was held on 9th April 1945. Loans from members totalled £845 and the bank overdraft was £314. The green was opened on 5th May 1945. A score board and scoring boxes were purchased for £17 from the late Park Institute Bowling Club which donated cups, photographs and equipment. In July 1946 a suitable building for use as a pavilion was purchased for £420. It was erected by members and voluntary labour during the winter and was officially opened on 19th May 1947.

Whiteknights Indoor Bowling Club

In 1964, a member of the Maiden Erlegh Bowling Club (Mr Wilfred Chaffey) approached J. D. Warren, who had been involved with the Wokingham project, with the idea of using land adjacent to the MEBC outdoor green to build an indoor club. In 1966 outline plans for the bowling club were referred back but following pressure through the press outline planning permission was approved. Full planning permission was granted in May 1970 and a form of lease was agreed with MEBC.

With the promise of funding from individuals and prospective loans from the Sports Council and Wokingham Rural District Council it was decided to proceed and on 18th May 1971 Reading and District Bowls Club Limited was formed. The first Bowls Committee adopted the name Whiteknights Indoor Bowling Club. By 1982 the club had paid all the loans back. In 1989/90 the facilities were upgraded. It is a very active club with between 600 and 700 members and a long waiting list. It is one of the biggest bowling centres in the country with seven rinks.

Sutton's Bowling Club

Sutton's Bowling Club was formed in 1906. Its first home was Cintra Park. The club moved to Earley in 1956 when Sutton's Trial Grounds, London Road became their new home. They stayed at the site until 1989 when Sutton's Seeds moved to Torquay and the grounds became an industrial estate. Wokingham District Council offered the club a new site at Chalfont Way, Lower Earley.

Sutton's Bowling Club

The Club has had many successes since its formation. The members have won 53 Berkshire County competitions. Additionally, the Club has had one England international player, J. R. Haines from 1982–1986, an England Trialist K. Nash in 1987 and most recently, in 2000, an Under-25 England trialist S. M. Jones.

Reading Cricket and Hockey Club

Reading Cricket Club. '*The Club has a beautiful ground at Church Road, Earley which has become very popular*'. *Early 1950s.*

The Reading Cricket and Hockey club was based in Church Road on land adjacent to Highwood. The club applied for permission to extend its grounds into Highwood in the 1970s which would have meant the loss of about one sixth of that area (6.25 acres). The local authority refused planning permission and the club moved to more commodious grounds. The ground on Church Road was sold for housing, now HighTree Drive. Barrington Close, one of the roads, makes reference to both the cricketing connection and to the Surrey County Cricket Club in particular. The club ground is now in Sonning Lane.

Earley Home Guard Social Club

After the D Day landings of 6th June 1944 the threat of invasion retreated and the need for the Home Guard disappeared. Over the years a strong sense of fellowship had been forged between members who decided to keep in touch and meet regularly socially. So an Old Comrades Association run by Earley Platoon which had been affiliated to Sonning company was formed. The first General Meeting was held on Tuesday 17th October 1944 in the Palmer Park Institute. The next General meeting was held two weeks later on the day that the Home Guard was disbanded (Tuesday 31st October). All past and present members of Earley Platoon were invited to be members as were ex members of the forces, Civil Defence, Police and Fire Services.

Meetings were held initially in members' houses and later in the Old Café, also known as Jack's Café on the Bath Road (now the site of the Brunel Diner). Many social events were organised but the Fete held on Solly Joel field on August Bank Holiday 1945 was one of the most successful events ever held in this area. It was a very hot day and people came in their thousands from all over Reading, by car, tram and on foot. Earley School playground was a bicycle park at 3d a bike. It was soon full! Special trams were put on from Reading to the turntable/terminus (now a petrol station) at the junction of Wokingham Road and St Peter's

Road. Extra police were drafted in on over-time. The crowds had a wonderful afternoon. The Treasurer, Mr Pound, had to have a police escort to take the cash, over £1100, to the night safe in Reading. It was the biggest and best thing to happen in the area since before the war. It cheered people up and Reading Corporation and Wokingham Rural District Council wrote to congratulate the club and to offer their assistance in any future events of a similar nature that the club planned. The club made a profit of over £500. A similar event was held the following year and the Fete closed with the biggest firework display that the town had ever seen. The final profit was £432.

By the end of January 1945, a possible site in Pitts Lane, owned by Mr George Barker, a retired Police Sergeant, had been found. The land had formerly been used for allotments. It measured 180 feet in depth with an option to purchase a further 50 feet at a later date. More importantly the land was on the right side of the road. Special clauses written into the deeds of all the land on the opposite side of the road forbid the sale of intoxicating liquor. Hence there is not one public house in this large part of Earley.

Mr Ben Clark, a wealthy local landowner, offered a large building formerly used by Tennyson School at Southlake, Woodley provided it was dismantled and taken away at the club's expense. The hut was duly dismantled and re-erected on the Pitts Lane site. It was officially opened on Wednesday 23rd July 1947, less than two years after the founder members started the club with absolutely nothing.

Over the years the building was extended and on Friday 23rd September 1964 a brand new building was opened. The building was refurbished in 1988. The clubhouse has been, and still is, a social centre for many residents.

EARLEY HOME GUARD SOCIAL CLUB.

The Management Committee requests the pleasure of the company of

Mrs. E. A. Watts

at the Official Opening of the Club Premises in Pitts Lane, Earley, by

MR. BEN CLARK

on Wednesday 23rd July 1947 at 8 p.m.

Invitation, Earley Homeguard Social Club

7 History on the Edge

Whilst writing most of this book we have confined ourselves to the modern day political boundaries of Earley. During the time that we were doing research for the book we were often asked if we were going to include many places that border against, or lie just over these boundaries. Our initial response was to be puritanical and somewhat parochial and stick rigidly within these boundaries.

However, upon further reflection, we decided that whilst we were happy to stay within these invisible boundaries, most of the Earley residents who live near the edges of Earley do not see these boundaries in their everyday lives. Their world rotates around their own individual houses paying scant regard to the artificial boundaries created by politicians.

For this reason we are including in this chapter brief descriptions of the history of those open spaces, buildings and institutions that are closely associated with Earley.

European Centre for Medium Range Weather Forecasts

The European Centre for Medium-Range Weather Forecasts (ECMWF) is an independent international organisation, supported by 18 European Member States and four European Co-operating States. Its basic document is its Convention which defines its objectives as providing accurate medium-range weather forecasts for industry, agriculture and commerce.

In the 1960s weather forecasting was identified as an area suitable for co-operation between members of the European Economic community. Weather does not respect national boundaries. Furthermore it was already clear that to make sensible use of supercomputers the nations of Europe should combine their scientific and technical resources to extend the range of useful weather forecasts.

It was decided to locate the Centre in Shinfield because there were centres of excellence in the field of meteorology and related disciplines in the vicinity i.e. the Meteorological Office in Bracknell, Oxford University, the University of Reading and Imperial College, London. The site at Shinfield Park on Earley's western boundary also has good access to Heathrow airport *via* the M4 motorway.

The Centre's staff are recruited from the various member states. They normally work at the ECMWF for several years before returning to their home countries. Of the Centre's 142 staff, 55 are from the UK.

Meteorological Office College

The Meteorological College at Shinfield Park celebrated its 60th anniversary in 1996. But it was in 1971 that it moved to Shinfield Park which had just been vacated by the RAF Training Command.

The Meteorological Office Training School was set up in1936 to provide weather forecasts for an experimental flying-boat service as British and US Governments were planning the first scheduled commercial flights between Britain and North America. Very few people had flown across the Atlantic and little was known about its weather, let alone how it might be predicted. The School was initially set up at Croydon Airport by C. J. Boyden but it then moved to rooms over a Lyons teashop in South Kensington.

When war was declared in September 1939 the forecasting courses were suspended but this created an immediate need to train officers of the newly formed RAF Volunteer Reserve (Met) branch. The Meteorological Office Training School was quickly re-established, this time in Berkeley Square.

After the war the Training School moved sites several times. In 1971 new premises were found for the school at Shinfield Park. The residential Meteorological Office College was established there. The traditional syllabus was reviewed to familiarise new-entrant meteorologists with computers and electronic instrumentation. Over the years students from more than 80 countries have visited the College. As well as training its own staff the college has hosted teachers, pilots, sailors, engineers, TV presenters and managers in industry.

Shinfield Players Theatre

On 12th January 1956, a small group of potential thespians met at the St Mary's Church Hall in Shinfield and formed **The Shinfield Players**. Such was the enthusiasm of this small group that three months later they put on their first production, a three act farce *Tons of Money* at the St Mary's Church Hall with a cast of 10. The ticket price at that time was the enormous sum of half a crown and the programme cost 3 pence!

By 1969 the Players felt they needed a permanent home. During the Second World War years Shinfield Park had been the home of the RAF Bomber Command (Training) Headquarters until its closure in 1968 when the site was earmarked for the new Berkshire County Council Headquarters, Shire Hall, and the proposed Meteorological College. These proposals obviously required the removal of temporary buildings on site and in 1970 the Ministry held an auction of all unwanted buildings.

One of the members Derek Wood, the local newsagent, was at the auction to purchase a garden shed for himself and found that the NAAFI, affectionately known as the Eagle Club to the many serving members of the RAF, was also under the auctioneer's hammer. Having performed in this building in the past, he realised the potential of this building as a theatre. Unfortunately this building had already been sold to a group of travellers whose only interest was to remove all the metal from the building for scrap and burn the remainder. Derek Wood felt that the purchasers would sell the building less the scrap metal and a hurried meeting of the Players was held and it was agreed to offer up to £100 for the building, a large sum of money to this small group in those days. Derek returned to the auction and after a certain amount of negotiation purchased the building for the sum of £72.

Unfortunately one of the conditions of purchase was that the building must be dismantled and removed from the site at the earliest opportunity. Negotiations with the local Parish Council for a piece of land on which to erect this building dragged on for three months with no decision being made and pressure was being brought to bear for the removal of the building.

At this point the members were desperate as they feared the loss of this building altogether, being unable to comply with the conditions of sale. In desperation they approached the Ministry and explained their problem to them and received a sympathetic hearing. The Ministry agreed to make available approximately a third of an acre of land facing Whitley Wood Lane and which had originally been the main entrance of the RAF base on a five year lease. The Ministry insisted that it must be surrounded by a wire and concrete security fence to their own high standards. The Shinfield Players have been on the same site ever since with the lease being renewed every five years.

The site was cleared, the security fence erected, foundations laid and the building erected, at the same time converting it into a Theatre boasting a 30 foot square stage, a naked auditorium seating 160, a large foyer with bar facilities, dressing rooms, workshop and all the other offices of a building such as this.

Although the group was only small at the time, they recruited many volunteers from the locality to assist them over a two-year period. All this work cost a great deal of money and the members spent many hours in fund raising, achieving the sum of £1,800 by their own efforts. The Theatre was officially opened on Friday, 9th March 1973 by Ald. R.H.C. Seymour, Chairman of the Berkshire County Council. On the 12th April 1973 the Theatre opened its doors to the public with their first presentation in their new home of the James Bridie play *Tobius and the Angel* and they presented their first musical, *Merrie England* in 1974. They further extended their repertoire by presenting an annual traditional pantomime, the first being *Aladdin.*

Since opening its doors the Shinfield Players have done much work not only in maintaining the building but incorporating many things for the benefit of its audiences and has spent well in excess of £50,000 on improvements and equipment. Currently the Theatre boasts a sophisticated computerised, digital lighting system which is the envy of a lot of other groups; full theatre sound; and has recently been refitted with theatre seats obtained from the Theatre Royal at Winchester, giving a seating capacity of 156. The Shinfield Players and its Theatre is a true Community Theatre, catering for all tastes with its extensive annual programme and presenting annually four plays, two full stage musicals, a pantomime, the Shinfield Festival and fund raising concerts in aid of Charity. It also hosts other groups who wish to perform in a theatrical environment, a regular group being the nurses and doctors from our two local hospitals who present their own brand of humour for a week in January, raising much needed monies for the hospital charities. The Theatre also believes in initiating young people into the arts and currently has four youth groups, aged between 8 and 18 years who meet weekly, culminating in two or three productions every season (Hawes, 1999).

Dinton Pastures Country Park

Dinton Pastures Country Park is situated on a narrow strip of alluvial meadowland that lies between the eastern bank of the River Loddon and a slightly raised gravel terrace. It was on this higher and drier land that the farms and hamlets, which made a living from the grazing land and the river, were located.

The area of land that today comprises the Country Park lay mainly within the liberty of Whistley. Whistley was one of the four liberties of Hurst. The area was obviously well wooded when the *Domesday Book* was compiled in 1086 and this situation must have remained much the same until the 19th century (VCH, 1923). This ancient landscape of woodland and meadows has been preserved for posterity in the names of the villages in the area. Whistley is derived from two Anglo-Saxon words *wisc* and *lei* meaning marshy meadow and a clearing of woodland for settlement, respectively. Hurst is derived from the old English for a wooded hill and is therefore the settlement built on the wooded hill.

Whistley's ancient Manor House, which was situated on a site on the River Loddon just north of what is today Lavell's Lake, was demolished in the middle of the nineteenth century. Today almost nothing remains of the hamlet of Whistley, which at one time must have had a successful economy based on agriculture, timber, basket-making and fishing.

The Domesday Book states that:

In CHARLTON hundred

The Abbey holds WHISTLEY itself, and always held it. Before 1066 it answered for 10 hides; now for 7 hides. Land for 12 ploughs.

16 villagers and 1 smallholder with 9 ploughs.

a mill at 5s and 250 eels; meadow 10 acres;

woodland at 50 pigs; a fishery at 300 eels.

The value was £10; now £6.

(Morgan, 1979)

As the centuries went by the balance of these local industries continually shifted. The predominant land use changed from arable to pasture and then to gravel extraction. Another major change was the considerable reduction in the area of woodland. Despite the general decline of the timber industry the growing of osier willow for basket making continued up to recent times. The 1842 trade directory recorded a hurdle-maker and two basket-makers in the Whistley and Twyford area; a basket maker worked in Winnersh until recent times. Old tithe and sale maps of the area show where the osier beds that produced the necessary raw materials were located.

Fishing on the River Loddon has been important as a dietary supplement to the local people since ancient times. At the time of the *Domesday Book* it was eel fishing that was recorded, but when the Manor of Whistley was auctioned in the late eighteenth century, it was ponds containing carp, tench and perch that were highlighted. The old trade directories mention several local rod makers and the remains of old fish traps can still be found near Sandford Mill.

All of this industrious activity in the area should have kept the local population in a comfortable lifestyle. However, as was common in those days, a considerable portion of wealth was paid to the church and, in particular, the Abbot of Abingdon, who had been granted the land in 978 and who continued to benefit from it until the dissolution of the monasteries in 1538.

The land in this area lay within Windsor Forest until 1700 and so the King retained rights of ownership over it. The relationship between the monarch and the local people did not always run smooth. For instance in 1392 the bondmen and bondage tenants went on strike. They *met in assembly and swore to refuse to render their accustomed services*. Despite the fact that powers were given to imprison them, they were not to be bullied and the following year found them continuing to rebel. Further unrest was also stirred up at this time when the traditional rights of the foresters were taken away from them. In 1396 the King chose to release the Lord of the Manor from his then obligation of supplying them with sustenance known as metecorn which until then had consisted of two weekly meals for themselves and their servants.

Whistley Manor was given to Richard Ward of Waltham St Lawrence by Henry VIII. This was followed over the centuries by many ownership changes as fortunes for the successive owners fluctuated, but as faces changed, the manorial rights continued to provide each new owner with free fishing, free warren (control over local rabbits, an important food source in years gone by) and view of frankpledge (a system by which each member of tithing was responsible for the good behaviour of every other).

After the Manor House was pulled down the two main building

complexes in the area were Sandford Mill and High Chimneys. John Nordorn's map of 1609 shows Sandford Mill to have been in existence at that time. As a punishment for supplying corn to the Royalists the mill is supposed to have been sacked and burned by the Parliamentarian troops. The current mill not only gained its income from grinding corn, but also collected tolls from those crossing the River Loddon at this point in the late eighteenth century. The mill, which continued to operate until 1919, has in the past been recorded as belonging to the Manor of Sindlesham and as being part of Winnersh. From 1785 the mill became linked with the Manor of Whistley and the estate of Bill Hill.

The other major building in the area, High Chimneys, was built in the early seventeenth century by the Barker family. High Chimneys dairy farm, now the Country Park Centre, was built in 1904 to serve the growing local population's demand for dairy produce. The farm was sold by auction in 1919 and again in 1926. By 1926 the farm had diversified to some degree with the addition of piggeries, poultry houses and additional stabling, but the main farm income was still derived from dairy farming. The whole property was described in the sales catalogue, in typical estate agency terms, as *a first class dairy farm and gentleman's residence.*

A history of Dinton Pastures Country Park would not be complete without mention of the gravel workings that not only led to the formation of the lake dominated landscape we see today but also limited the land's potential future uses and thereby indirectly leading to the eventual decision to create the Country Park.

By the early 1960's the demand for sand and gravel for building houses, offices, hospitals and roads had led to the need to extract gravel from new quarries. For instance 10 km of motorway requires one million tonnes of aggregate.

The Thames Valley gravels are a legacy of huge ice sheets that reached down into this area between two million and ten thousand years ago. The eroding action of these ice sheets produced a mixture of sands, gravels, boulders and clays. During warm inter-glacial periods, huge amounts of this material was dumped in layers, two to four metres thick, at the edge of the ice sheets forming today's plateau gravels which are often found well above present day river levels. Further sorting of this material by later rivers led to the formation of the valley gravels that are a feature of the present flood plains of the Thames, Kennet and Loddon.

Early in the plans it was decided to create one large lake that would be suitable for sailing (Black Swan lake), White Swan Lake and the River Loddon were designated for angling and the smaller lakes were given over to wildlife conservation. The remainder was made into a golf course and used for walking, nature observation and picnicking. Horse riding was prohibited due to destruction of the pathways. Wokingham District

Council completed the purchase of the 230-acre site at a cost of £150,000 and began to develop it in 1978.

Today's use of the land as a Country Park continues the recreational theme that was a feature of the area when it was a King's hunting ground. However the emphasis has changed today from shooting the deer, wild duck and snipe to conserving the area's precious wildlife.

Highwood Local Nature Reserve and Bulmershe Heath

Highwood is the last remaining remnant of the once extensive Bullmarsh/Earley Heath which extended over much of what is present day central and north Earley and Woodley.

Bulmershe Heath was created by Neolithic man over 4,000 years ago, when he started to clear the area of its trees to create more open space for his livestock. The gradual change from a nomadic hunter-gatherer way of life to a more settled farming existence continued for several thousand years and by the Bronze Age, the heath would have been almost entirely cleared.

For nearly 2000 years the heath would have provided the local peasants with both firewood and grazing land. As was the case in much of the rest of Britain, this way of life came to an end in the 18th and 19th centuries when wealthy landowners began to enclose large areas of heath land. The then owners of Woodley Lodge, Henry Addington and James Wheble, applied to enclose parts of Bulmershe Heath in 1794 and 1816, respectively, thus depriving the local population of its ancient fuel gathering and livestock grazing rights.

James Wheble, when he was owner of Woodley Lodge, commissioned J. C. Loudon, the famous horticulturist, to re-landscape the grounds to *look at how the heath of Bulmershe may be united with the Park*. Part of Loudon's work was to create an arboretum, planted with many of the

Bulmershe Heath

It is probable that much of Bulmershe Heath, including the area now known as Highwood, would once have lain in the ancient manor of Bullmarsh. Highwood and nearby South Lake were purchased in 1789 by Henry Addington and by 1796 had become part of the 285 acre Woodley Park. James Wheble purchased the property in 1801.

It achieved local fame when on 25th July 1799 King George III and the then Prime Minister, William Pitt, inspected 1,000 members of the Berkshire Volunteer Corps. This included Addington's Woodley Cavalry who performed sword exercises in full speed at attack and advance (Reading Mercury, 1799). In the early 1800s the heath was the site of the famous Reading Races which were known locally as the Bulmershe Heath Races. The races were run over a three mile course and were well attended. The races ceased after the Heath was enclosed (Lloyd, 1977).

new exotic introductions of the time such as monkey-puzzle trees, giant redwoods and rhododendrons. Some of these trees can still be seen in Highwood.

Today Highwood consists mostly of woodland. Despite the attempts of its 19th century owners to garden it, it forms a very valuable natural habitat that supports a thriving community of wild flowers and animals. Parts of the woodland have been coppiced (cut periodically to the ground) to provide a steady supply of raw material for building, fencing, tool handles, etc. The area is now mostly managed as high forest with some coppiced areas. Highwood also contains a small fragment of the dry and wet heath land. This is particularly precious, as it is the last remnant of heath land that still exists in this part of Berkshire, with most of the rest lying along the Hampshire and Surrey borders.

The wood came under threat in 1982 when the Reading Cricket and Hockey Club applied for permission to extend its ground to take in part of Highwood. This would have meant the loss of about one sixth of the wood (6.25 acres). Planning permission was refused, but this threat to the wood galvanised a group of local residents into action and in 1982 Friends of Highwood was formed. The area was given some additional protection in 1992 when it was designated a local Nature Reserve (see also chapter 6).

Holme Park

The earliest references to Holme Park ('holmr' meaning meadow) can be traced back to Saxon times when the Bishops of Sunning had their country estate near the River Thames. More accurately, these bishops had their see originally in Ramsbury and later in Salisbury. Many parishes in Berkshire came under the jurisdiction of the diocese of Salisbury and it wasn't until 1836 that these came under the See of Oxford. Such anomalies were called peculiars. The lands which composed the Bishop's demesne had been granted to them by the Crown from a tract of the huge Windsor Great Park. Over the centuries, and given its many Church connections, Sonning came to be an important meeting place for various political and religious figures of the day. King John was reputed to have lodged at the Bishop's Palace before he set off to Runnymede for the signing of the Magna Carta in 1215.

In 1399, national events once again intruded into this rural backwater. After Richard II's deposition, and subsequent banishment to Pontefract Castle, where he was ultimately murdered, his child-queen, Isabella of Valois was placed under house arrest. She was detained at Holme Park and placed under the custody of the Bishop of Salisbury whose watchful eye even foiled an unsuccessful attempt to rescue her in 1400. This incident, coupled with Henry IV's personal insecurity, persuaded the authorities to send Isabella back to her native France as quickly as possible. Her sojourn at Sonning, brief though it may have been, was lonely and anxious, and gave rise to a local legend that the exiled queen's ghost still languishes along the quieter reaches of the Thames.

Despite the turbulence of the Reformation in the 16th century the Bishops retained their estates at Sonning until 1574 when Queen Elizabeth exchanged some of her properties in Wiltshire for the Bishop of Salisbury's at Sonning. From 1574 to 1628, when the Crown's revenues were falling sharply, the Holme Park estates provided income for successive monarchs including Charles I's elder brother Henry, Prince of Wales.

In 1654, at the height of Oliver Cromwell's protectorate, the two London merchants who had acquired Holme Park from the Crown decided to sell to Sir Thomas Rich, a member of the Vintners' Company of the City of London, and later a City of Gloucester alderman. He had amassed a considerable fortune from trading with Turkey. Rich, whose ornate memorial can still be seen in the vestry of Sonning's St Andrew's Church, was created a baronet by Charles II, a year after the Restoration (1660) in recognition of his loyalty to the Royalist cause. As a well known benefactor, both Reading Blue Coat School and the Sir Thomas Rich's School in Gloucester received bequests after his death in 1667.

Successive members of the Rich family remained in occupation of Holme Park until the fifth baronet, Admiral Sir Thomas Rich, sold the estate to Richard Palmer of Hurst. Palmer's father had accumulated a growing income, having served as land agent to the Duke of Bedford in Great Russell Street.

One of the first things Palmer did after moving to Holme Park was to demolish the old Rich family mansion which had been situated near the ruins of the Bishops' Palace just to the north side of the estate close to the river. In its place, work began on a Regency-style house in 1796. This Palmer family had no connection with the Palmers of Huntley and Palmer's the Reading biscuit producers! Richard married and had several children, one of whom was Robert. Due to Robert Palmer's involvement in Tory politics at both local and national levels, Sonning again became something of a social centre for public figures of the day.

From 1825 to 1859 Robert Palmer was Member of Parliament for Berkshire. A man of great integrity and generosity, a true patrician from all accounts, he was described by contemporaries as The Great Squire. Amongst his and his sister, Susannah Caroline's many endowments were St Peter's Church, Earley (1844), and the Robert Palmer Almshouses in Sonning village (1850). Caroline Palmer was especially interested in education and was instrumental in founding both Earley St Peter's School and the Woodley Church School. Significantly, when other places up and down the county were troubled by rural violence in the *Hungry Thirties and Forties*, few if any serious incidents of disorder occurred in Sonning. Palmer presided as Chairman of the Quarter Sessions, and dealt out justice to poachers and other miscreants from roundabout.

The Palmer estate extended into present-day Woodley and Earley. Sonning Golf Club still has a cottage within its grounds which was the game-keeper's home. Much of the area's rural isolation continued into the present century despite the digging of Sonning Cutting in 1838 for

Holme Park, Sonning, May 1911
Sales catalogue, © Martin & Pole, Nicholas

Brunel's Great Western Railway. Palmer and his country friends objected to the railway because they said it would *scare away his game birds*. In 1872, at the age of eighty, Robert Palmer died leaving the property to a brother, Richard and sister, Susannah Caroline.

After 1880–1882 the main buildings of Holme Park assumed their present recognisable form. Back in 1880 the Rev. Henry Golding-Palmer, Rector of Stratford St. Mary in Essex for thirty-six years, was bequeathed Holme Park in the will of his aunt, Susannah Caroline. Reluctantly, he left parishioners and friends to take up residence in what must have been a draughty and rambling old country house. He resolved to redesign it in consultation with the architect, Henry Woodyer, who according to the fashion of the time remodelled the house in a mock Tudor style. Woodyer was also the architect of St James Church Woodley and Christchurch, Reading. Within two years the original Regency fabric was transformed into its present, familiar red-brick and flint-faced appearance at an estimated cost of £40,000, a small fortune in those days during which time Golding-Palmer and his wife went on an extensive tour of Italy, Egypt and Palestine.

The essential fabric of the big house has remained unchanged since 1882. Particularly striking are the Elizabethan-style wainscoting in the stone floor with its Italian marble flooring, the plaster mouldings in the ceiling and the heavy panelling which was so much a feature of the original Elizabethan country houses.

On the north side of the main building, a conservatory was constructed containing a wide range of tropical plants and a fountain. This was demolished in 1914 and was situated at the organ-side of the present Buttery. Most vestiges of the original Richard Palmer Regency house were destroyed during Golding-Palmer's adaptation of the house.

By 1911, it was clear that the costs of running such a huge estate were prohibitive. Indeed, at about this time death duties and inflation were taking their toll on similar properties up and down the country. In April 1911, these considerations amongst others persuaded Ruth Wade-Palmer and her sons, Robert and Aubrey, to auction off their properties in Woodley, Twyford and Hurst. Holme Park was purchased by a local syndicate.

Owners followed in quick succession, but the one who probably left most of a mark was Captain Walter Fryer who bought the estate in 1924 and kept a string of racehorses. When Fryer died deeply in debt in 1933 the property was bought by the Farnborough House Preparatory School.

During the 1939–1945 war the estate was let to the Royal Veterinary College which was evacuated from London. Teaching and lecturing were conducted in the main building, whilst staff and students some of whom returned for a brief reunion in December 1982 were accommodated in various rooms upstairs and downstairs. In August 1940, many of the original glass windows were shattered when a low flying German bomber released a stick of bombs into the woods near Sonning Lock. Fortunately the fabric of the building was undamaged.

Reading Blue Coat School

The Reading Blue Coat School Association began in 1946 when the Trustees of Reading Municipal Church Charities sold the old school buildings in Bath Road, Reading in order to meet the requirements of the 1944 Education Act. After an appeal and after much speculation over just whom or what was going to buy Holme Park (one rumour was that Holme Park was going to be an asylum!) the school raised enough money to purchase the house and grounds. By a nice historical accident it could be said that the Rich connection was revived when the school which Sir Thomas had endowed all those years ago took up residence on January 21st 1947.

Palmer Park

Palmer Park was part of Mace Field and contained the mace or maes holes (see Chapter 4). It was part of a greater piece of land bought from Francis Cholmely in the 19th century by George Palmer. The 49 acres of land were donated in perpetuity to the people of Reading as Palmer Park and George Palmer paid for the land to be enclosed with railings and planted with trees. The citizens were so grateful that they erected a monument to him in Broad Street which was unveiled on 4 November 1891. Later it was placed near the stadium in Palmer Park itself.

George Palmer's motives were not wholly philanthropic!

> *Huntley and Palmer ruthlessly maintained their monopoly over labour. When the London, Brighton and South Coast Railway planned to construct a railway works on land adjacent to what is now the Reading to Guildford line, the Palmer's feared competition for labour and pressure on wages. They bought up this proposed site and, with a stroke of genius, donated it in perpetuity to the people of Reading (Hobson,1995).*

Palmer Park entrance from Wokingham Road
Postcard, 1904

Mockbeggar Farm

Mockbeggar estate, and its associated farm, at one time lay south of Wokingham Road, close to Whiteknights Park. Before Whiteknights Lake was made and Whiteknights Road built across the dam the stream would have run naturally down the hillside across the fields to the Kennet: *It was an ancient enclosure lying to the south-east of Hawthorne Field, one of the six open fields of Earley and identifiable with Arleghfield (Earley Field)* (Dormer, 1931). The 1887 boundary changes moved this land from Earley into the Borough of Reading.

Mockbeggar had originally been known as Aleyn's farm after Thomas Aleyn (or Allen) who farmed the land in the early 1500s when it formed part of the possession of the Abbey of Reading.

At the time of the dissolution, Henry VIII granted Aleyn's Farm along with other possessions of the Abbey including land at Bulmershe to William Gray, ballad writer and MP for Reading. Gray died childless and Aleyn's Farm passed to the Blagrave family, to his wife's children from a previous marriage.

By the 1742 Inclosure, part of Hawthorn Field was added to the farm. The Blagraves continued to hold the estate until 1792 when George Blagrave's wife, Martha and daughter Jane sold it, to Henry Addington (later Viscount Sidmouth).

By the time that James Wheble purchased the property in November 1801, the property had become known as Mockbeggar. During the Whebles' ownership between 1820 and 1860 a brick kiln was built on part of the estate (now the field bounded by Green Road and Wokingham Road). The concave hill, formerly convex, below Whiteknights lake was dug out for clay and made into bricks which were used in the expansion of house building in Newtown and Earley Rise. In 1861 part of the western side of the estate was sold by auction, soon after this Hamilton Road and Bulmershe Road were built on this land. The Wheble family held on to the property for nearly a century until 1896 when they sold it to Oliver Dixon who ran a riding school from the farm until the 1950s.

Documents from the end of the 17th century onwards often refer to the property as Aleyn's or Allen's alias Mockbeggars. Dormer (1931) postulates that Mockbeggar refers to a house that has an appearance of wealth, but is either deserted or else inhabited by miserly or poor persons and this could cause disappointment to passing travellers or beggars. He suggested that after William Gray died there was lengthy litigation before the Blagrave family finally secured their inheritance, and that *it is possible that between the death of Gray and the death of his widow that Alleyn's farm was left untenanted and derelict and came to be known as Mockbeggar from this circumstance.*

Mockbeggar seems to have had a strong connection with Whiteknights. Before Gray purchased Aleyns, the farm had been let to Thomas Beke or Bek who may have been related to the same Beke family that at this time was in possession of the Manor of Whiteknights. In 1833 James Wheble, the then owner of Mockbeggar, wrote:

> *The farm called Allen's Farm, or Mockbeggars, adjoined Whiteknights, and on it a farmhouse and buildings stood. The greater part of this land has been planted and forms part of the Whiteknights woods and is fenced off from Mockbeggars. The buildings were moved to another part of the farm, where they are now.*

The Wokingham Road School, later called Alfred Sutton Primary School was built on the Wokingham Road side of the farm at the turn of the century after the area moved into Reading. The boys' and girls' secondary schools were built in the 1960s and had a very short life of less than 20 years. It was decided to close these two schools because of the falling numbers of secondary-aged children in this part of the county and its former catchment area was distributed between the two nearest secondary schools. Reading Technical College moved into the buildings.

In the 1960s Berkshire County Council bought the Edwardian house called Mockbeggar and the LEA used the property as the Administrative Headquarters of its County Music Service and also, from the mid-1980s, as offices and teaching rooms for its local music centre, the Central Berkshire Music Centre. In 1990 the Berkshire Young Musicians Trust took over the music provision for the County's schools. The Trust continued to rent Mockbeggar from the County/LEA until December 1998 when the Trust moved to Stoneham Court, Tilehurst. The building remained unoccupied and was substantially burnt by two fires on successive weekends in December 1999 and pulled down in October 2000.

At the time of writing the future of most of this site is under discussion. Offices, housing, a mosque and open space have been suggested.

Pepper Farm/Leighton Park

Leighton Park was previously known as Pepper Farm. Whiteknights Park was to the north and the borough boundary with Earley to the east. For centuries the eastern boundary was also the parish boundary between the parishes of St Giles, Reading and Sonning.

There are other interesting features of the lanes around Leighton Park. Pepper Lane to the west of the borough boundary and along the entire north side of Leighton Park was a late addition. This western end of Pepper Lane in Reading is first hinted at in a map of 1756 and is clearly shown in a map of 1843. Prior to this approximate date Pepper Farm extended slightly beyond the present line of Pepper Lane to follow the borough boundary northwards as it began to make angles through Whiteknights Park. More surprising is the track which used to run from the original Whiteknights House due south down the eastern boundary of Leighton Park to Elm Road via what is now South Drive. What was formerly the track is now no more than an unusually deep ditch and is largely hidden in undergrowth. Half way along it and within the grounds of Leighton Park is a shallow gravel pit, sufficient to have provided good clean builder's sand and gravel and surface for tracks and lanes for the immediate area.

This track also provided access to what seems on Rocque's map of 1761 to indicate Pepper Farm. The earliest evidence of buildings is within what is now the (Leighton Park) School's maintenance department. So far it seems that the main structure of one of the single storey buildings round a farm yard may be late 18th century and parts of what became the Stable Block in 1856 (inscribed on the keystone) may be from the period when a large walled garden was added. While there is still some doubt about the origins of the Stable Block, there was certainly a farmhouse immediately opposite it to the west and built in about 1830.

The new mansion was built by 1860, possibly by 1856. In 1863 Captain Alexander W. Cobham from the family which owned Shinfield Manor moved into Leighton Park with his young wife. The estate was a marriage gift to him from his father-in-law. Sadly Alexander's wife died the following year, but he continued to live at Leighton Park and married again. The old farmhouse became the laundry. The Cobham family household was a large one. The census of 1881 lists seven children (by his second marriage) and eleven servants; and above the stables were a coachman and his wife, a groom and two laundry maids.

All these gentlemen's estates came with the development of the Great Western Railway and the demand for houses by the new commuters at the richer end of the middle classes. Sometimes this involved the splitting up of much larger estates, such as Whiteknights Park established a century or more earlier. An ambitious advertisement in the Reading Directory of 1845 had announced a project to turn Whiteknights into a miniature town of 150 villas built in Elizabethan style. In 1886 Leighton Park itself was offered up for sale by the Cobhams in five lots.

The advertisement in *The Times* of 24th June 1886 gives the flavour of the period:

> *Berkshire, close to Reading. – Important Notice of Sale of the finely timbered Freehold Residential Estate known as Leighton-Park, with the modern, substantial, and very commodious mansion, stabling, lodges, and gardens, lying on the south side of the county town of*

Reading, and at a convenient distance therefrom. The property lies in the midst of a high-class residential district, immediately adjoining the properties of M. Lonergan, Esq., and Sir R. Kelly, and contiguous to the Whiteknights estate. It is within easy reach of the meets of Mr Hargeaves' and Mr Garth's foxhounds, and possesses a very long and highly valuable frontage to the high road and also to Pepper-lane…

Leighton Park School

The Leighton Park estate put up for sale by the Cobham family in 1886 was bought in 1890 with the aid of the proceeds from the sale of Grove House School in Tottenham, north London, a Quaker School which had previously closed. Leighton Park School is a Quaker Foundation; it opened on 22nd January 1890 with four pupils, one of these, Edward Hodgkin, was a nephew of Elizabeth (née Hodgkin) wife of Alfred Waterhouse (see chapter 3).

Alfred Waterhouse, who lived in nearby Foxhill and who had been a former pupil of Grove House School was responsible for the early alterations and extensions of the original house for the school. In a style quite different from his usual neo-Gothic he designed the extensions to the Leighton Park mansion. In 1894 he drew up the plans for Grove House, the second boarding house named after and constructed with the remainder capital which survived the closure of Grove House School, Tottenham. He gave this building such clean and simple lines that it almost belies the early date of its construction.

In 1940 H. R. Smith (at the School 1894–98) recalled the neighbourhood as he remembered it:

When the Governors purchased Leighton Park it was a gentleman's country seat [J. Edward Hodgkin had called it a very ordinary gentleman's house!] really in the country. On the Shinfield Road between the Green at the end of Christchurch Road and the hamlet of Cressingham by The Merry Maidens there were no houses at all except the two lodges of Whiteknights and the two lodges of Leighton Park [the two latter long since demolished and replaced]. At the Green itself there were only four ancient cottages, three villas and some antique pitch-covered cowsheds which stood out odoriferously far into the road. There was no Northcourt Avenue or Cressingham Road. All that now populous area was grass and plough, owned by the Palmer family [and Shinfield Road and Pepper Lane were unmetalled]. The South Berks Hunt used to finish their Point-to-Point Races close to where Dr F. Gilford's Clinic now stands [near The Merry Maidens]. On the western edge of Shinfield Road was thick undergrowth in which stood young larches; some of these larches, grown big, survive in the House gardens. Pepper

Lane has changed little save as the School has changed it. Wilderness Road and Elm Road were real country lanes with harebells and primroses.

A favourite walk that can still be taken was to the Sonning Cutting and it was a country walk the whole way except in the immediate neighbourhood of Earley Church. Here was the village general shop of Mr Toop. From him we used to purchase biscuits. He never had the sort we really wanted: 'We don't keep the Nice, we have the 'ousehold and the Garibaldi, or as some of you young gents calls them Squashed Fly Biscuits'. He then endeavoured to get us to purchase Penny Dreadfuls, 'the papers condemns them, but some think they're rather good'. New boys used to be lured into a walk to Sonning 'to see the treacle mines'. Another favourite walk that can still be taken, now, alas, between posts and wires but then over open fields, was the path to Arborfield Old Church. There were no buses, only a few boys had bicycles. In the frosts of 1891 and 1895 a lot of skating was done on the lakes of Whiteknights and Bulmershe as well as over flooded land in the latter year. Whiteknights was not the half-derelict place it now is but a well tended Park. Nightingales and hawfinches nested where Wantage Hall now stands and wild hops grew in the hedge above the broad ditch on the western side of Redlands Road.

Briggins and Shrublands

Immediately to the east of Leighton Park and just over the boundary into Earley was another large house, originally called Briggins, it later became known as Shrublands. In 1888 General Sir Richard Kelly is recorded as living there (Steven's Directory 1888). Later it was occupied by Mr George Bird (Kelly's Directory 1907).

In the 1950s Shrublands belonged to Sir James Miller who was a builder and property developer. Sir James had been Lord Mayor of London and Lord Provost of Scotland in successive years. Sadly Sir James's son died in a car accident on his way up to the family's estate in Scotland to celebrate his 21st birthday. Sir James retired to his Scottish estate, Shrublands was demolished and the whole estate was developed for housing. Copperdale Close and the flats, the houses in Harcourt Drive, Falstaff Avenue, Felstead Close, Flaxman Close and Rowland Way occupy the land where the house and grounds once stood.

Crosfields School

The roots of Crosfields can be traced back to a school in Castle Street, Reading, called Marlborough House which had started in the early 19th century, and which, by the early 1920s had moved to a large house in Parkside Road.

At the outbreak of the second World War the Headmaster of Marlborough House approached Leighton Park School to ask if they would take over Marlborough House, thus ensuring a continuity of education for the pupils at the school. The take over was agreed and the school became Leighton Park Junior School, moving into Townson House at Leighton Park and taking their meals in the cricket pavilion.

After the war the Leighton Park governors acquired an RAF Officer's convalescent home on the Shinfield Road. The property, a site of 66 acres costing £25,000, was originally known as Goodrest and was the home of the Englefield family in the early 1600s before they acquired the Whiteknights estate.

Leighton Park Junior School was moved to the newly acquired site and was re-named Crosfields School in memory of Hugh Crosfield an old Leightonian and governor who had been killed in an air raid in 1944.

In 1957 the Governors of Leighton Park set up Crosfields as a non-profit-making Trust with a separate Board of Governors so that it became entirely separate and independent of Leighton Park, except for the use of some of its facilities. In the following decades the school grew under successive headmasters, with the demolition of old and out-of-date buildings and the addition of new ones, some of the expansion being funded by the sale of trees and land. At this time the school still thrives and is looking forward to the addition of a Music School and Theatre.

Reading Cemetery

The Reading Cemetery Company was established by Private Act of Parliament in 1842 and the first interment took place the following year. In 1959 it was taken over by Reading Corporation in whose control it remains; there are still occasional burials in family plots.

The cemetery was built on a field called Hattons Platt, part of the open field called Mace Field. The land was purchased from Francis Cholmeley. The triangular site lies between the London Road (A4) and Wokingham Road (A329) with the Entrance Lodge at the intersection, now known as *Cemetery Junction* on the western edge of Earley.

An advertisement in 1843 said that the ground *is ornamentally laid out with walks, trees and shrubs*. A very low boundary wall divided the consecrated ground with its Episcopal Chapel from the unconsecrated ground near the Entrance Lodge, with a Chapel for Dissenters. Both chapels have now gone, but the wall still acts as a divider between sections 23–30 and 32–60. The graveyard was laid out with 65 sections, each with its own plan of grave plots.

The graveyard as originally planned was soon found to be too small and the garden area to the east of the Episcopal Chapel was brought into use, section 66 onwards.

Reading Cemetery
Postcard, early 20th century

Separating Sections 71 and 72 is a hedge enclosing a Sword of Honour and War Memorial, erected and maintained by the Commonwealth Graves Commission, on which are recorded the names of 99 British and Commonwealth service men, including a Serbian Sergeant, who died in the Reading area during the first World War. Some of the men are also in named War Graves or family monuments elsewhere in the cemetery (Berkshire Family History Society, 1997).

8 Earley at War

Boer War

A number of Earley residents went off to fight for Queen and country in the Boer War; some never returned. To commemorate their fallen neighbours, the parishioners of Earley St Peter's Church erected a gilt bronze plaque in their memory behind the lectern on the right of the chancel. Bertram Reynolds of Victoria Street, Westminster was commissioned to both design and make this plaque. Captain Denis Menezes Miller who had been in the 14th Hussars carried out the official unveiling of the plaque on Sunday, 1st May 1904. The unveiling of this memorial must have been particularly poignant for the Vicar, Charles Firmstone, as two of his brothers were amongst those who were besieged at Ladysmith waiting relief troops to arrive.

In addition to the cost of the plaque, the memorial fund raised a further £2 3s 7d. This money lay untouched for a number of years but eventually in April 1913 it was decided to put the remaining money into the fund for repairing and resetting the church clock.

War memorial, St Peter's churchyard, 2000

World War I

There are now very few residents living in Earley who have memories of Earley during World War I, however, Mrs West recalls:

> *In WWI I remember the sirens going off and the gas lights being put out. I was so frightened that I clung to my mother. My younger sister was not the least bit frightened. Food was short and we would walk across Palmer Park to buy potatoes. When our corner shop had a supply of jam, our empty jars were filled at the back of the shop; we entered by the front door and left by the back door.*

Many Earley residents went off to fight for their country never to return. There was much discussion once the War was over as to how best to remember and commemorate the fallen heroes. Finally, on 27th December 1920, after ideas such as a cottage hospital had been discounted, the diocese decided to erect a stone cross in the churchyard of St Peter's Church and a tablet in the porch. Both the cross and the tablet were designed by Mr H.R.R. Blacking of Quarry Hill Lodge in Guildford. The cross itself was carved out of Cornish granite and stands 15 feet tall. The finished cross was unveiled on 14 February 1921 by Colonel Leslie Wilson and then dedicated by the Vicar, Canon Fowler.

There was another war memorial in the adjacent church school which was lost when, in 1962, the beautiful old school building was demolished.

World War II

It is now over 50 years since the residents of Earley have had to live their daily lives with the threat of invasion by a feared enemy at the back of their minds. We are very grateful to the following five Earley residents for giving us a glimpse of an era where air raids, food rationing, evacuees and blackouts were a part of everyday life.

In November 1940 a stick of bombs fell on Earley. One fell on Bulmershe Park, a second exploded in Milton Road, damaging several houses. Another scored a direct hit on a fish pond in Erleigh Court Gardens scattering fish everywhere! And a fourth hit Sutton's trial grounds.

A stick of bombs fell on central Reading on Wednesday 10th February 1943. One bomb scored a direct hit on the People's Pantry café in Cross Street causing serious loss of life as it was full at the time. The offices of Blandy and Blandy and Wellsteads shop were destroyed. The Town Hall and St Laurence's Church were also badly damaged (Hilton, 1996).

Margaret Fairburn I was ten years old at the beginning of the Second World War and my first memory is of walking to church along Wilderness Road with my oldest sister and seeing searchlights sweeping the sky. She told me that they were practising in case there should be a war.

At the end of August in 1939, my grandparents were with us on a summer holiday from their home on the North East coast. On 3rd September my father set off to drive them to London to catch their train, but returned later with them saying that war had broken out and he thought the coastal areas would not be safe. I have heard the famous broadcast by Neville Chamberlain many times since then but I did not hear it on that Sunday. However, the next day relatives arrived from London, and our three bedroomed house was full to overflowing.

The other residents of Earley were soon accepting evacuees, school children and mothers with babies, into their homes, as Reading and the surrounding villages were officially a reception area for evacuees in spite of our proximity to London.

Earley indeed turned out to be an area almost untouched by enemy activity. There was one serious incident in the centre of Reading when bombs were dropped in daylight on the main street causing deaths and injuries, and thought to be a returning bomber jettisoning its load. Later, near the end of the war, when V1 and V2 rockets were causing death and destruction in London and the South East, one stray V1 landed in a field at the top of Beech Lane, just behind the farmhouse which now houses the Town Council Offices. There were some broken windows and a few cuts, and a big crater almost immediately cordoned off by the American Army, but that was all.

For families like ours with no young men called up, life for the first months of the war went on much as usual, except for blackout, and the beginning of rationing which was to become much more stringent as the war progressed and for several years afterwards.

In Earley we began to see soldiers appearing as Wilderness House was taken over by the army and a series of troops were billeted there with, towards the end of the year, the Americans.

At the height of the war we sometimes lay in our beds listening to flights of German bombers droning overhead to the Midlands and returning in the small hours having caused untold suffering.

At the bottom of Beech Lane near the fork in the road, some tank traps appeared – large concrete drainage pipes about three feet across, filled with cement and with metal loops protruding from the tops so that they could be dragged across the road to block it if need be. I had a touching faith in these objects and always imagined German tanks coming up the lane and being stopped by the tank traps. Luckily, they were never tested and became a meeting place for the local children to gossip and jump from one to the other.

As the war went on and food and fuel became scarcer, we children spent a lot of our time picking blackberries for jam, acorns for pig food and rose-hips to be made into a vitamin rich syrup for babies and all collected at school.

We went around with prams collecting wood for the fires as coal was rationed and, as the most junior member of the family, it was my Saturday morning job to queue outside a fish shop in Wokingham Road with a carrier bag and newspaper to buy any fish and as much as I was offered. Fish was unrationed but often scarce. Our diet was stodgy and monotonous, based mainly around potatoes and corned beef with some meat, cheese and bacon, and visitors, mainly young relatives in the Forces or friends and family from London as air raids got more severe, brought their rations with them.

However, I never felt hungry or deprived and, since by the end of the war more than a third of my life had been spent that way, it felt quite normal. As the war drew to an end, clothes rationing was stringent and I had my school uniform and one other dress made for me by my mother from an odd collection of remnants. A bolt of grey cloth bought for a tailor to make an overcoat for my father before the war was dug out and the tailor made a coat for me. I must have looked like a Russian General in it but it was warm and all my friends were in a similar state, so we never worried about competing on the fashion front!

One unforgettable memory was at the start of the invasion in 1944, when we stood out on our back lawn in Beech Lane and watched a huge fleet of planes towing gliders filled with soldiers literally filling the sky, the ground beneath our feet throbbing. The war ended it seemed to me quite suddenly and we were sent home from school for a celebratory day's holiday. As I rode home on my bike I was astonished to see every house, including ours, draped with allied flags. The next day there was a huge bonfire lit at the junction of Beech Lane and Wilderness Road, and peace returned to Earley.

Thinking of the suffering of people in other parts of the country, we were very fortunate in Earley.

Ada Little née *Mears* I was 17 years old when the Second World War began. On the day that war was declared, September 3rd 1939, I went to Sutton School (Alfred Sutton School), where dozens of London children had arrived, they all looked very sad. We found homes for them with the local people.

Later, I went to work at the Munitions Factory at Burghfield. Later on I also became an Air Raid Warden. Several of us also helped to prepare vegetables in the kitchens at the Royal Berks Hospital which we did until the end of the war. As Air Raid Wardens we had to go to training at Reading School, we were trained to fire Lee-Enfield rifles and Ross rifles, and also to throw hand grenades. We often took part in parades through Reading. I remember the day that Reading was bombed, it was in February 1943, a month before I got married. When I got married the wardens formed a guard of honour for us.

We were rationed of course, but we seemed to have enough to eat, we grew our own vegetables. I walked into a brick wall once during the blackouts, – I had two black eyes for a week!

Right: Ada Little with her father and brother, 1942

Below: ARP, WWII, 1941–42
Ada Little, 4th from the right, in the middle row

Mrs West

In WWII I had two boys billeted on me. The government paid for everything for the first 10 weeks. When their parents were asked to contribute towards their keep they came and collected them, even though they were from a well-to-do family. The boys attended school at Woodley Hill House. They had good appetites! Afterwards I had two little girls aged 5 and 6. Their parents came most weekends. When there was a lull in the bombing the girls returned home. That was shortly before the V1s and V2s were dropped on London. In 1944, the week before my daughter was born, we heard a plane drone overhead, then silence, followed by the bombs exploding. We learnt later that they had been dropped on the fields between Beech Lane and Radstock Lane. Many years later the last occupant of Radstock Farmhouse pointed out the damage to the chimneystacks caused by the bombs. People living in Beech Lane said that the noise was terrific.

Mrs Marsh

It was the start of the war and I had four young boys, evacuees from London, to live with us. We ploughed up the garden and grew our own vegetables and fruit. We had a cow in milk. She came from a farm in Little London that we owned. The parents would not let the boys milk the cow as they said it was too dangerous! The boys went to school in the morning or in the afternoon in Woodley. I remember it as very hard work, made harder by the frequent visits of their mothers. One of the boys had medical problems but his mother would not let him have the operation he needed.

Marjorie Culham (from her wartime diary)

September 1st 1939

I took my car to St Peter's Hall to help with the evacuation, and could have wept to see small primary children arriving clutching their luggage and iron rations – a tin of corned beef and a bar of chocolate and sundry other groceries. We took the children to various billets round the village.

September 2nd 1939 (Saturday)

This was the day that mothers with under-fives arrived and billeting these was far more difficult!

August 16th 1940

The sirens went off at teatime. I was at a party in a friend's house in Wokingham Road, we heard a plane and rushed into the back garden and watched it circle round and then head off in the Woodley direction. It dropped four bombs and then disappeared from sight (it was like a chicken laying eggs!).

February 10th 1943

I was attending a meeting at the General Post Office in Friar Street. Just after 4.30pm when the meeting finished, the sirens sounded. The noise of bombs dropping and anti-aircraft fire was incredible and we stayed in the basement until the ALL CLEAR, we emerged to a scene of absolute devastation, Friar Street was covered in broken glass and the council brought out snow ploughs to clear it so that the buses could run. My office at 38 Friar Street (the Collector of Taxes) was unscathed. The next morning one member of staff, Mr Moncur, travelled to work with a friend who asked him if his office had been hit, when Mr Moncur replied that it hadn't the friend said *what a pity*.

Some twenty years after the war finished, the residents who lived in the dip in Beech Lane were given a small reminder of how scary the war years would have been for Earley residents. Mrs Brooks recalls the time when an old war time bomb was discovered on the corner of Radstock and Redhatch. 'This would have been some time around the mid-1960's, my parents moved to Beech Lane in 1964 and although a little vague, it is believed that this event was during the early part of the year, possibly 1966–7. I recall that the houses in Beech Lane, up to and including 55 were evacuated and despatched to the Bowling Club to partake of tea and biscuits. My parents were not quite so fortunate and were instructed to leave all doors and windows up to prevent damage when the blast occurred – not a welcoming event in the depth of winter'.

Bomb disposal from Radstock Lane, 1970
© *Reading Chronicle* *13 February, 1970*

The first meeting of the Women's Institute in Earley was held on 30 March 1938, and so many of their earlier activities were directed towards the war effort. They were soon not only having keep fit classes but also first aid and gas classes under the leadership of Mrs Rushbrooke and Mrs Rutter, in order to assist the local authorities with their ARP work. A detachment of the Red Cross was formed and the members assisted with canteens and sewing parties for evacuees and their parents.

1939–40 was a difficult year with a lower membership of 84. Due to war conditions, most members were busy with work of national importance or with the Red Cross or WVS. They had to meet earlier as many members were looking after evacuees and others found the distance to walk in the black out a handicap. Many members assisted Mrs Colebrook with the evacuees.

Through the War years, their voluntary work and fundraising was beyond belief. In 1940, 33 members attended the Canning School at Reading Cricket Club and the result of 2 days work was 334 cans of fruit. This became a regular event and in 1941 they bought their own canning machine.

They had a comforts box to raise money for the Army Comforts Department. From the sum of £4. 1s. 6d *The Daily Sketch* appeal received 21 pairs of socks, 2 scarves, 7 helmets, 6 pairs of mittens, 2 pairs of gloves, 1 pullover. The Royal Berkshire Regiment appeal for Prisoners of War – 6 helmets, 6 pairs of mittens, 6 pairs of gloves, 6 pairs of socks and the Secretary still had 12 shillings and 2½ pence in hand! Later knitting sessions produced garments for Prisoners of War, and the Navy. For Liberated Europe 12 members knitted 12 shawls, 24 coats, 24 pairs of knickers and 24 pilches (vests).

Gardening became very important and the Garden competitions began. Packets of seeds were ordered. Every year Mrs Waight presented the Institute with seed potatoes. The results from the competition to grow the heaviest crop were sent to the Royal Berkshire Hospital, usually 1½ to 2 sackfulls; this was before the National Health Service. Money from the egg collection and the Annual New Year Party was also sent to them. Mrs Hopcroft laboriously collected and sorted stamps for their appeal. 35lbs of onions were sent to the Red Cross. There was also a very active trading stall at each meeting.

A regular house to house collection was organised for St Dunstans for the Blind. Their first collection raised £35. The amounts increased every year to £85 10s in 1944. A phenomenal sum for those days and even today we would be pleased with that.

There were whist drives, bring and buy stalls, raffles, trading with a shilling, which all brought in money for the Institute, The Red Cross, Queen Charlotte's Hospital, Aid to China Fund and others. A War Savings Group was started and the sum accumulated rose to four figures. Rural Pennies raised £240. The Treasurer and assistant treasurer Mrs Petty took on this enormous burden with a very good will and ability, but it must have been one big headache.

There were many meetings in homes for making slippers, dressmaking classes and *make do and mend*. At these sessions they would undo old garments and make new ones from the good pieces.

The subjects for the talks at the meetings reflected many of the important issues of the day, like Home Nursing, The Home Front, Evacuees Problems, Wartime Economies, and Poultry keeping. However these were interspersed with subjects on crafts, making gloves, slippers, dressmaking and cookery, plus lighter subjects like Lantern Slides and talks on holidays, *The Adventures of a Suffragette* and a debate on whether they should have double summer time after the war.

There were varied monthly competitions and outings, one to Messrs Sutton's Trial Grounds also to Littlehampton to Messrs Shippams Factory and Kew. In the summer they picnicked at Southlake in Woodley and had their June meeting in the garden of the Manor House, members carrying their chairs across the road to the garden. The most enjoyable and financially successful event was the Annual New Year Social, especially when the troops, or as on one occasion, a group of American Soldiers, were invited as their guests. In 1940 the Choir was formed under Mrs Case. In 1941 Mrs Case and Mrs Gilbert had attended Variety Entertainment Classes. In 1944 the Drama Group was at last formed with Mrs Brown as their Producer. Entertainment was recognised as a vital morale booster in the War years. The Secretary had in her mind the Social Half Hour when she wrote in her annual report about the emergence of the Drama Group, *We look forward to this and the Choir for a tower of strength and help.* They had struggled to get these two groups going, and they were rewarded well with entries in the drama and music festivals and entertainment at meetings and group meetings.

From reading the Annual Reports, a wonderful sense of very charming, caring, gifted people comes through and was a strong foundation for the future of the WI. After the war Mrs Prouten and Mrs Shave went to Buckingham Palace to receive War Service Certificates.

The Earley Home Guard

Britain had no need for resistance or underground movements because unlike other countries such as France it had not been invaded – it was free. But its citizens were organised to form local defence groups – the Home Guard.

The Earley Platoon of the Sonning Company of the Home Guard was based at a garage at Shepherds House Hill (now the BP Petrol Station) which had closed down due to the shortage of fuel. From there nightly patrols were made covering the railway line and bridges, Sonning Lock and the Gas Works. Each member of the Platoon would be on duty two nights a week, a little sleep might be possible, whilst colleagues kept an eye on things, but frequently little or no sleep was had.

Every Sunday the Platoon met at the garage then marched smartly to

Company HQ, at the Blue Coat School in Sonning Lane, for parade and training. Training was rigorous, the men were required to keep fit and regularly attended a camp at Warfield on Saturday night. The following morning they had to run a tough army assault course. Shooting practice was held on the Berkshire Downs near Didcot, or at the Bisley range. An Efficiency Course consisted of firing 15 rounds from 500 yards in three minutes then to run 100 yards, lie down and fire another 15 rounds, again within three minutes and so on. All this using a heavy bolt action rifle and in full kit. After four and a half years many men had become expert marksmen!

On one night a German bomber dropped two bombs, one fell into the River Thames and the other exploded on Sutton's Seeds trial grounds. Someone (Ed Watts) was half way up the gasholder at the time and was nearly blown off. If that bomb had hit the gas works, everyone at the works would have been blown to bits!

Compared to many other Home Guard Platoons, particularly those based on the south coast or in industrial areas of the country, the Sonning Company of the Home Guard and Earley Platoon had a quiet war (Clayton).

9 Earley from the Air

Aerial photographs of Earley taken between 1947 and 1996, which show the development of Earley

1947: The whole of Earley from the Thames in the north to the Loddon in the south. Palmer Park is towards the top of the picture, with the wooded Whiteknights Park below it.
© *RAF*

1947: North Earley with smoke rising from Earley Power Station and a train passing in front of it on the Paddington line. The Earley Court estate is beginning to be developed for housing. Woodley Lodge is in the centre towards the bottom.
© *RAF*

1947: Maiden Erlegh House showing the extensive stables and the lake. Beech Lane and Radstock Lane can be clearly seen.
© RAF

1947: The Wokingham Road. Hungerford Lodge is still standing; Solly Joel field can be seen. Building is going on around the Maiden Erlegh estate. Maiden Erlegh House is in the bottom left hand corner.
© *RAF*

1961: The development of Maiden Erlegh housing estate. The fields of Lower Earley and the Stud Farm can be seen.
© Crown Copyright MOD

1963: North Earley. Ideal Windows is north of the railway line, the large greenhouse at Sutton's is between the railway line and the A4 and the housing is complete across the Earley Court estate.
© Ordnance Survey

1963: Showing the Three Tuns crossroads (*centre top*); the Temporary Office Buildings and Erleigh Park House in Whiteknights Park; and Maiden Erlegh school at the centre of the completed Maiden Erlegh Estate.
© *Ordnance Survey*

1963: The fields and farms of Lower Earley.
© Ordnance Survey

1996: South-west Earley, bordered by the M4 and Shinfield Road.
Aerial photographs reproduced with permission from Wokingham District Council rectified with permission of Her Majesty's Stationery Office, © Crown Copyright, N/C/00/1037

1996: South-east Earley. Wokingham Road is running parallel with the A329M at the top with the M4 at the bottom.

Aerial photographs reproduced with permission from Wokingham District Council rectified with permission of Her Majesty's Stationery Office, © Crown Copyright, N/C/00/1037

1996: The Three Tuns is to the top centre of the picture, the University park is to the top left hand side and ASDA at the bottom, centre.
Aerial photographs reproduced with permission from Wokingham District Council rectified with permission of Her Majesty's Stationery Office, © Crown Copyright, N/C/00/1037

1996: North Earley. Sutton's Business Park is in place, bisected by the A329M; work on the Thames Valley Park has started.

Aerial photographs reproduced with permission from Wokingham District Council rectified with permission of Her Majesty's Stationery Office, © Crown Copyright, N/C/00/1037

10 Earley on the Ground

A series of maps covering Earley from 1776 to 1998

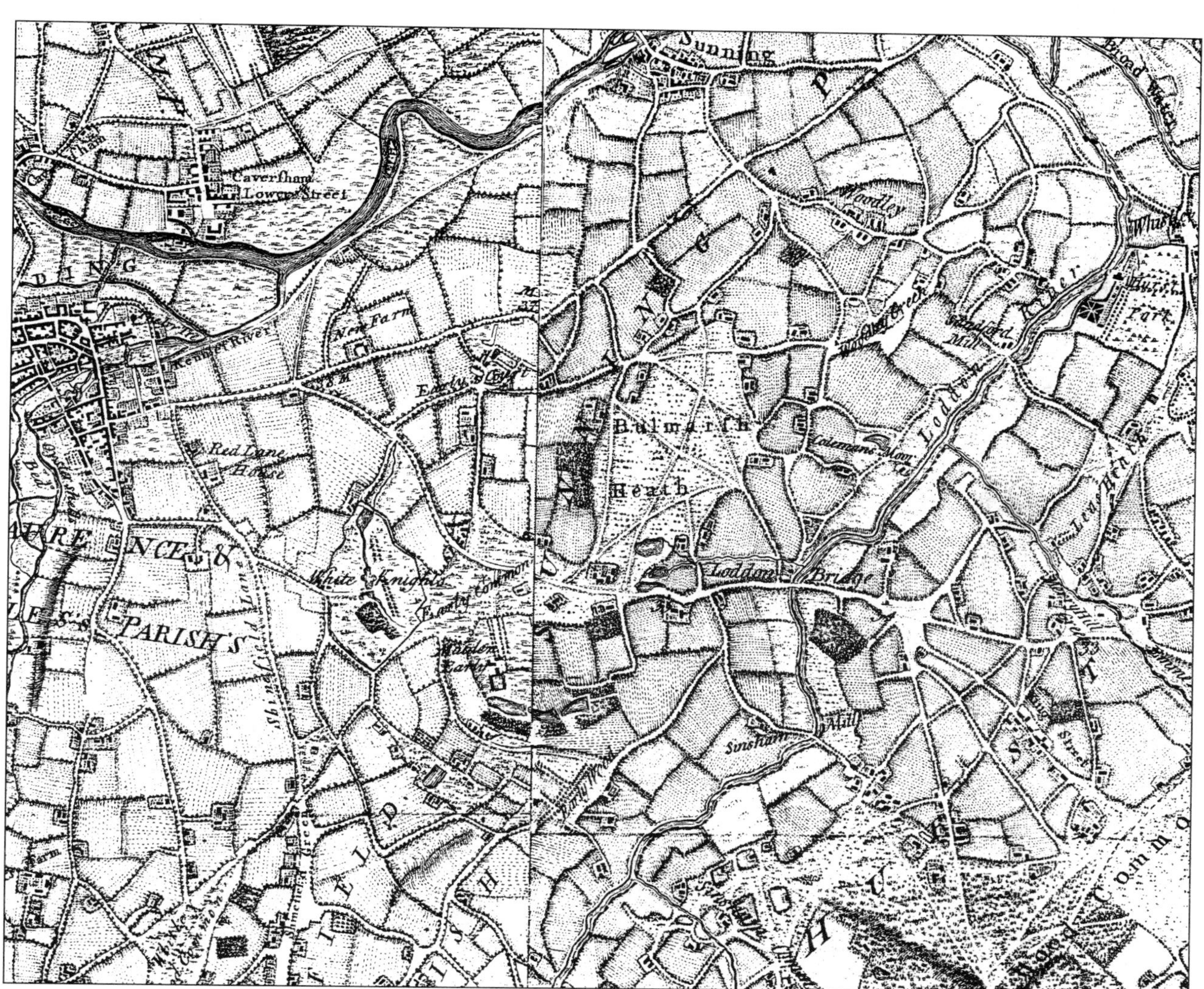

Earley 1761, *Survey of Berkshire* (2nd and 3rd sheets).
© *J. Rocque, RLSL*

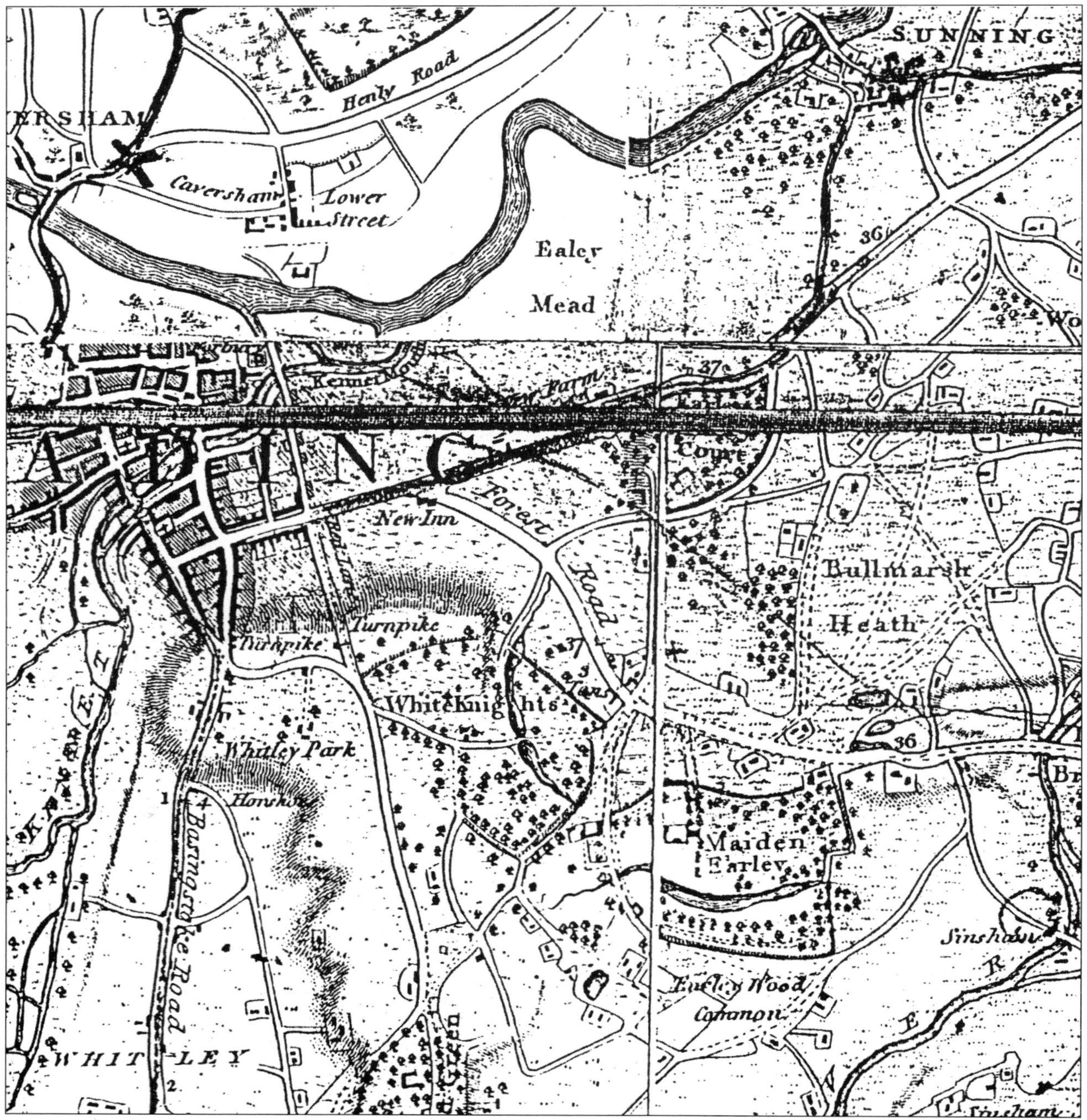

Earley, 1790: A Topographical map of the town of Reading and the County adjacent to an extent of ten miles.
© T. Pride, RLSL

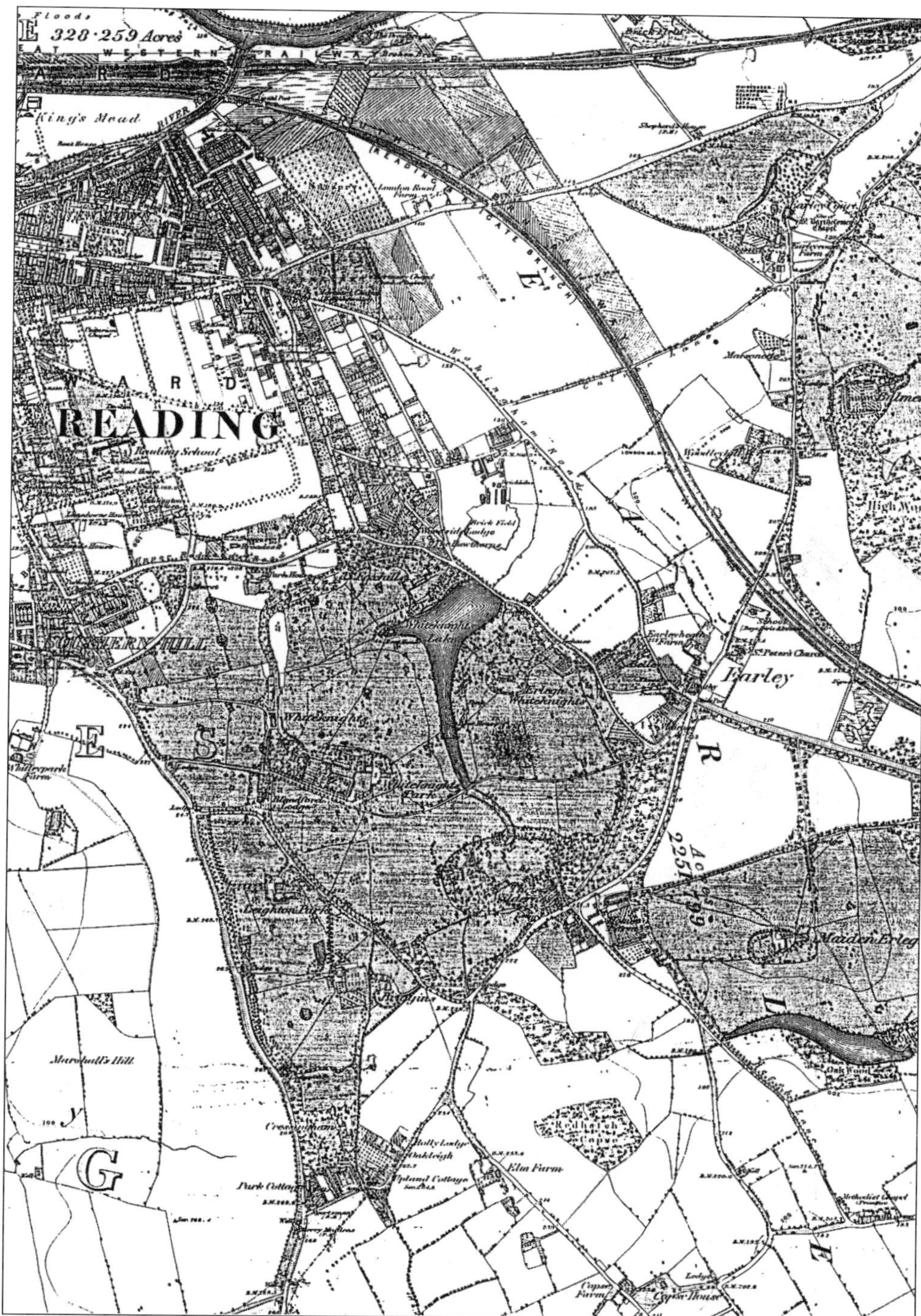

Earley, 1883; surveyed 1872.
Reproduced from first edition, 6″ to one statutory mile, with permission of Her Majesty's Stationery Office, © Crown Copyright NC/00/1037

Earley, 1913; surveyed 1877–78. *Reproduced from first edition, revised 1909–10; 6″ to one statutory mile, with permission of Her Majesty's Stationery Office, © Crown Copyright NC/00/1037*

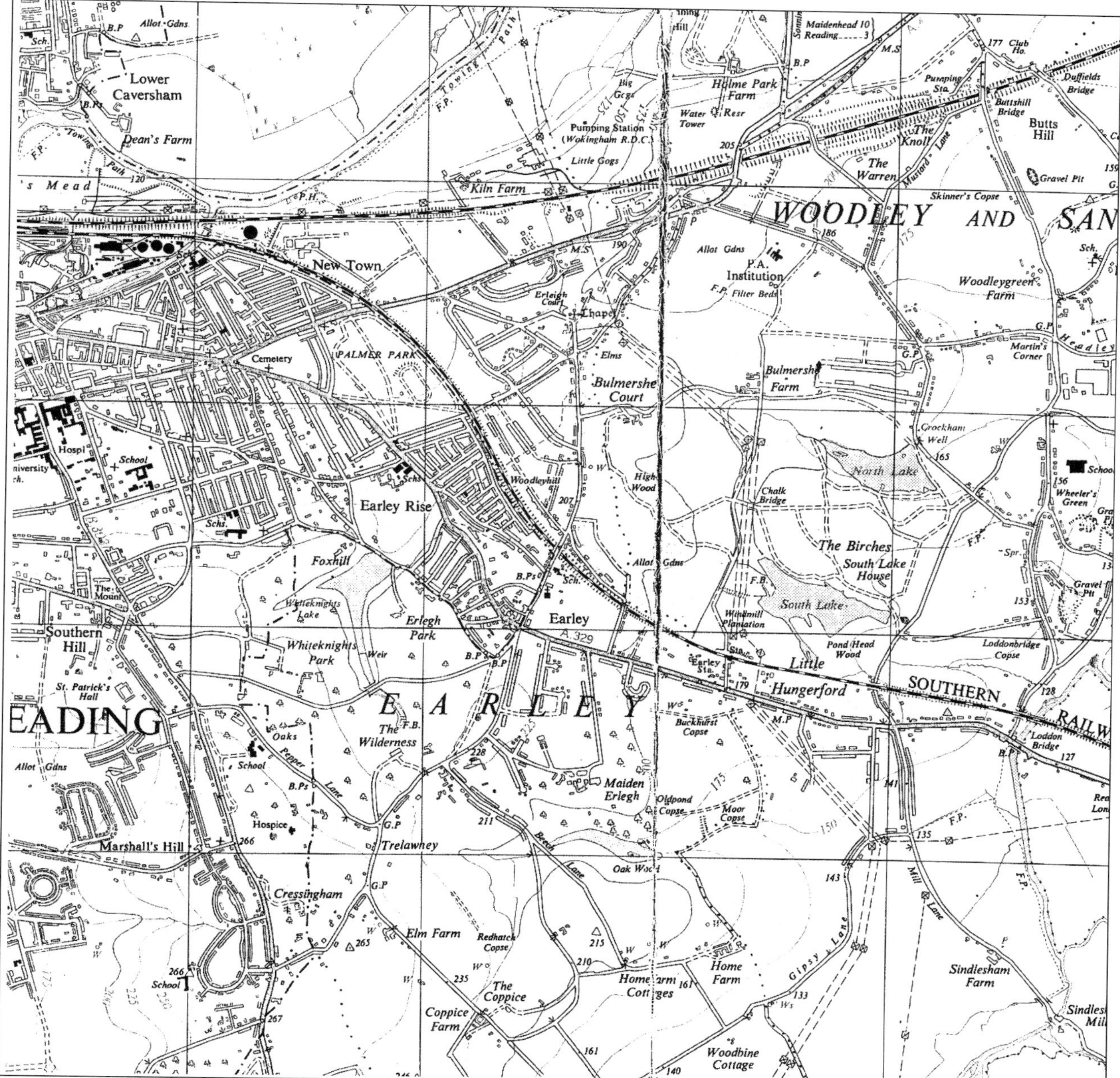

Earley, 1947

Sheet 41/77, printed and published 1947, 6″ to one statutory mile, with permission of Her Majesty's Stationery Office

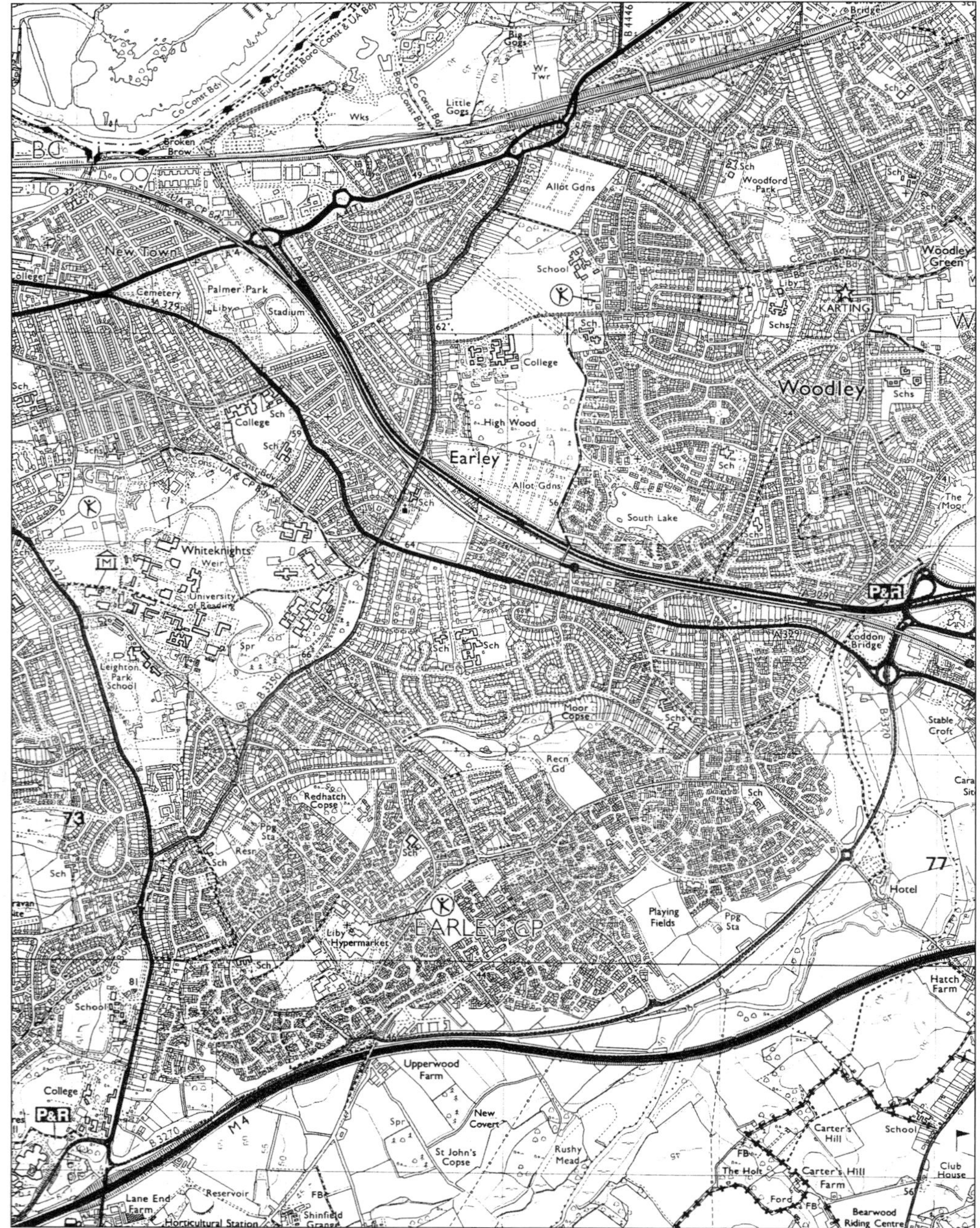

Earley, 1998.

Reproduced from Explorer Series 159, Edition A, revised 1998, 1:25000 scale with permission of Her Majesty's Stationery Office, © Crown Copyright NC/00/1037

11 Living Memories

In this part of the book a number of local residents who have lived in Earley for some time have recorded their memories of the area which give a greater understanding of everyday life in 20th century Earley. In living memories the smaller, more mundane events of society are recorded giving a more detailed chronicle of everyday events. These memories were recorded between July 1998 and May 2000.

Mrs Ethel West

I was born in 1910, the third of four daughters. We lived in Pitcroft Avenue. My father was a baker and worked at Harry Mabey's on Queen's Road opposite Huntley and Palmer. The baker is still there under different ownership. My father joined up in November 1914 and was killed in August 1918 in France. My two older sisters had left home by this time but my widowed mother was left with two young daughters to bring up.

My grandmother had been in service. She told us about how she used to sit at the back of St Peter's Church. A young man started to sit next to her. One day he put his hand on hers, she was very embarrassed. They married in 1875. They lived in a cottage on Cutbush Lane. My grandmother was widowed when my mother was seven years old.

She talked about walking behind the horse-drawn hearse from Cutbush Lane to St Peter's Church. My grandmother worked in a laundry in a large house nearby until she married again. My grandfather and my step-grandfather were both farm workers.

My mother went to school at St Peter's or the Earley School as it was called then. They walked from Cutbush Lane in all weathers. In the winter it was a relief to them when they saw the lights of Culham's shop at the Three Tuns crossroads. Wokingham Road was mainly fields at this time and my mother and her sister were frightened to go along it, as they didn't see anyone.

I started my schooling at Alfred Sutton's Nursery School or the Wokingham Road School as it was then called. But the First World War interrupted my schooling and I attended Redlands School mornings or afternoons until the school was taken over as a hospital for wounded soldiers. I passed my 11+ and attended the Wokingham Road School until I was 16.

On a Thursday my younger sister and I walked down to our grandmother's house. We did it in all seasons and weathers. We walked out of the back of her house across the fields down to the Loddon. We picked armfuls of Loddon lilies when they were in flower. My grandmother grew fruit and vegetables and she organised us to pick gooseberries in season. On her brick-floored kitchen she had a stone jar in which ginger beer was brewed.

When I left school I worked at Pulsometer Engineering Company on Oxford Road for four years and at Freeman Hardy and Willis until I was married. My husband worked at Huntley & Palmer's all his working life and we lived at St Edwards Road all our married life. I moved to Earley in 1972. We were married at St Peter's Church, as were my grandmother, my mother and my daughter.

My sister and I went to Sunday School at 10 am. The boys were in the old school and the girls in the hall. At 11 am we attended the Church service. I used to dread the long litany as we had to kneel for such a long time; if we moved we were chastised by Mr and Mrs Waight, the Sunday School superintendents. One Sunday we decided not to go to the Church service and went for a walk. We were surprised to meet people coming out of Church early. Canon Fowler had died and there was no service that day.

We used to go for walks in Palmer Park and the Woodley Woods (where Woodlands Avenue is now). In the summer holidays my mother and our neighbour who had young children would take us for picnics in Woodley Woods and we would spend all day there. One of our favourite walks was the path to Sonning along the Thames. For a treat on a Sunday summer's evening we would have a 6d ride on the steamers on the Thames from Caversham to Sonning or Mapledurham. A favourite circular walk was to walk down the Wokingham Road, under the railway line, through the woods and along the public footpath from Bulmershe to Pitts Lane. In the season we would stop and pick wild strawberries on the railway embankment.

My husband's family came from Wokingham. He was a chorister at St Peter's. He attended the Bluecoat School when it was based on the Bath Road on the other side of Reading. They had to walk to St Laurence's Church across Reading each day. This experience put him off church forever. In later life he would only go to the Harvest Festival.

I remember the stables on Wilderness Road. My mother's sister and her family lived in a house behind the stables, on Beech Lane. They had 10 children, five boys and five girls. All the boys worked with horses. We used to talk about *going up by the four-face clock*.

There were no houses on Wilderness Road when we walked along. There was a ditch which we used to jump in and peer over the fence to look into Solly Joel's. My mother remembered doing the same thing when she was a girl.

Joe and Phyl Pettitt

Phyl and Joe Pettitt came to Earley (Woodley until 1986) in 1948. Joe was teaching at Woodley Hill Grammar School. They could not find a house to buy in the area so they parked their caravan on a site on Gypsy Lane near where Silverdale Road now joins it. They lived there, with their two dogs, until they moved into their new house on Silverdale Road in 1954. At this time Silverdale Road had eight houses on one side and bungalows opposite and the only access was from Hillside Road. Hillside Road and Meadow Road were unmade roads, in perpetually poor condition and never dry. Springs appeared everywhere and Phyl said that she always had to wear Wellington boots and take her shoes with her, all the year round. The houses were not connected up to the main sewers until the mid-fifties. The smell from the cesspits was very strong in the summer months.

The ruins of Solly Joel's grandstand were still evident between Hillside Road and Finch Road as well as buildings, which might have been barns, and they remember two big oak trees in this area being felled. A second 'Maiden Erlegh Drive' ran from the station, along Finch Road towards the stream where it forked. One fork went to Maiden Erlegh house and the other went across the stream, along the hornbeam track, presumably to the stud.

In 1952 they bought land from a local builder, Mr S. R. Brown, who had bought a lot of land in the area before the war. The builder managed to gain access from Gypsy Lane and so the southern section of Silverdale Road was built. A Mr Crook built a lot of houses in this area.

The 18-acre field opposite their house was formerly part of Maiden Erlegh Stud. It had been bought by the Hon. Mrs Beatty in 1932 and sold in 1970 for eight million pounds. It is now covered with Egremont Drive plus other Cumbrian names. This field had been ploughed up during the war and the first year that they were there it produced a natural crop of heartsease, *Viola arvensis*, a sea of yellow, blue and green. The freshly ploughed field gave a wonderful patchwork effect of different browns. They enjoyed watching the thoroughbred mares grazing or galloping in the field. One man hay making made Joe very sad as he remembered hay making from his youth in Sussex as being a community effort.

Mrs Mollie Marsh

I was born 90 years ago. My father and grandfather were jobbing builders. I was twelve years old when we moved into a house that my father had built on the corner of Kendrick and Morgan Roads. I went to Kendrick School which was then in Kendrick House, now Watlington House, in Watlington Street. I remember playing at 'wounded soldiers'. My kindergarten teacher, Miss Corbett, made me write right-handed although I was left-handed. I stayed at school for dinner on Mondays, as it was wash day at home. I loved the beef stews and ginger puddings.

I met my first husband, Sidney Cook, in 1930. I was invited to a birthday party at St Peter's Church Hall, but my current boyfriend was not. I danced with one of Sidney's brothers during the evening and I first met Sidney at the end of the evening. He offered me a lift home – with four of his friends. It was 28th January, a cold miserable, winter's evening. We had a puncture at the tram terminus on Wokingham Road. Sidney set off to Holmes Road, where the family had their yard and offices. He didn't want to leave me with his friends so I had to walk with him in my strappy, silver shoes and my lovely coiffured hair getting wet and the curls straightening out! Meanwhile his girlfriend gave up waiting for him to return to take her home and had to make her own way back. A few months later we started going out together and we were married in 1937.

Our first home was The Homestead on Wilderness Road. The Homestead started off as a dairy. The owner, Mr Bunce, asked my husband to alter it into a house for a son who was getting married. The son had the work done whilst the father was away and had no money to pay for it, so Mr Bunce decided to sell the house and Sidney bought it in exchange for two building plots.

Our next home was Hungerford Lodge on the Wokingham Road which we bought from Mrs Heelas in 1940. It had 6½ acres of land and it was in a poor state. It was a Georgian building with a long drive from the Wokingham Road to the house. There was also a path from the house to the station. We paid five shillings a year for the right to walk straight on to Earley Station. We became used to the trains and missed them if a train did not run!

In early 1945 my husband came home and asked if I would like to live in the Manor House. Mr Percy Colebrook wanted to exchange the Manor with 3½ acres of land, including an orchard along Heath Road, with Hungerford Lodge as Mrs Colebrook wanted a bigger garden. I reluctantly agreed. I was sorry to leave Hungerford Lodge as the house was very comfortable and I loved the garden.

The Manor House was in very poor condition when we moved in. It had not been painted for 27 years and it was alive with cockroaches and mice. And I was ill. It was another month or so before I realised that I was pregnant. The next year I gave birth to twin boys. My husband was in shock for three months after their birth! When my health recovered we held at least two social events every week for various charities. I prepared the food myself. I'd weigh out all the ingredients the night before then bake batches of 200 scones, 8 cakes etc.... fresh for the event that day. I employed two gardeners to maintain the gardens. My husband was always working and our social life only started when we moved to the Manor House.

We were unable to trace the history of the Manor House. The foundations are very old, of flint and rammed chalk, and the small bricks used indicate it was built before the 1600s. There are the remnants of wattle and daub walls. There had been a fire many years ago, and whole branches and tree trunks were used to repair the damage. When carrying out some alterations we discovered an underground larder full of broken china and 17th century coins. The roof contains huge timbers. We re-tiled the roof with tiles that we brought from another house. We spent 27 years getting the house as we wanted it. The Manor House had previously been known as Earley Heath Farm. At one time its land stretched down as far as the Gallows Inn, named from the gallows which stood nearby – near to the present day Cemetery Junction. The farm was part of the Manor of Erleigh Whiteknights and was in the possession of the Englefield family from the 17th century until it was acquired by the Marquis of Blandford in 1798.

I decided that I wanted a window in the larder. Sidney asked a friend to teach him how to make a metal-framed window. He had just bought the builders – *Toogood* at 99 Whiteknights Road, and they had a blacksmith's forge. The window was a great success so he decided to make metal-framed windows for his houses. Initially the factory was set up in the grounds of Toogood's yard, but later he bought Colebrook's Farm next to Sutton's land near the Thames and so *Ideal Casements* was started.

We had always wanted to see the tower of St Peter's Church restored. When, in the early 1960s a new roof was required, the vicar came and discussed the work with my husband. At the same time I asked him to complete the tower while he was alive rather than as a memorial to him. My husband agreed. An old parishioner produced original drawings to show how the architect had intended to finish it. The work was held up by strikes and bad weather but at 4.15 on Friday 11th September 1964 the scaffolding came down and my husband came home early to see this happen. I remember that it was a beautiful September evening and we were both thrilled to see the finished tower. My husband died the next day.

I was a widow for ten years before marrying Julian Marsh, an old family friend. We moved into a new house that I had built next to the Manor House. Three more houses were built in the Manor House grounds.

The entrance to the Manor House was originally by the lodge on Church Road. We knew Mr Dormer very well. He lived at 29 Church Road, next to the Lodge. The house had been made into two after the Beauchamp sisters left. Mr Dormer was very interested in furniture and initiated in us a life-long interest in it. Mr Dormer never wrote on Mondays so we went together to sales looking at and buying furniture. He was an eminent academic and a Fellow of the Royal Historical Society.

When we first moved in, Church Road was a country lane with lots of big houses around. It was a small community and everyone knew each other. We were unusual as we had a car but most people walked a lot or bicycled. The baker came every day. Culhams and Browns ran the shops either side of Church Road at the Three Tuns crossroads, and there was a greengrocer, a butcher, a do-it-yourself shop, which we built for the Wards who ran it, and a Post Office. The cottages next to Culhams were called the Dripping Cottages – the owner sold dripping for a living. I'd 'phone up Colebrook's in Broad Street to send up chops and David Grieg's in West Street for pheasants. Baylis, the grocer, called twice a week for orders.

We were coming home one day when we saw someone skulking in the bushes at the bottom of the garden – it was the Headmaster, Mr Willoughby, from St Peter's School. He was checking up to see if the grounds were big enough for country dancing! They were, and his pupils then came every May for dancing around the Maypole and the crowning of the May Queen.

I was always thrilled to see the advertisement *Cook's Craftsmen Built Houses* on the sides of buses. My husband's firm built large numbers of houses in Reading, Woodley and Wokingham. He built on the orchards along Heath Road. Reading was threatening to build council houses there so he got in first. He bought back Hungerford Lodge from the Colebrooks when they retired to Bexhill, Sussex. The lodge was pulled down and houses were built there – on what is now Stanton Close. Wilderness Road was largely fields up to the end of the Second World War. Sidney built houses, which cost £1020 each; anyone who helped to make a sale received £5. People were frightened to pay those prices after the war. He was very careful about waste. He found that the men were taking home bundles of wood left over from cutting the timbers for the eaves. After that he had the wood cut to size before being delivered to the site!

Behind Wilderness Road are Aldbourne Avenue and Ramsbury Drive. In those days the builder named the new roads and he named those. The Cook family came from Aldbourne, a village near Marlborough, and the family of my in-laws, the Goodmans, came from Ramsbury in Wiltshire.

Liz Vincent

I came to Earley in 1969. Up until that time I had lived in or around the big northern cities. Earley in those days was like living on another planet! I cycled to work every day along the lanes and after a short time recognised and waved to the few cars and tractor drivers who shared the lanes with me. I look back over 30 years and I am very grateful that I had a year to appreciate Lower Earley before the M4 came through and the housing started. I enjoyed cycling along Elm Lane and Cutbush Lane; I first started bird watching along these lanes. I nearly ended up in the ditches on a number of occasions as I was watching the birds rather than the road! I watched a stoat dragging a dead or dying stoat across Elm Lane and into the steep banks. I was very surprised by the depth of the ditches along the lanes, until it rained and the ditches filled up immediately. I found out that the area was full of running springs. Even during long hot dry summers some residents on Redhatch Drive had to pump water from the backs of their houses and residents in other parts of Earley were accused of watering their lawns during hosepipe bans and others have had their drives dug up looking for leaks!

Part of Coppice Farm, Elm Lane was used by a group of vets. They had a surgery and operating theatre for horses. A farrier worked in another building. Many horses were brought there to be shod.

When my bicycle had punctures I could walk to work along the public right of way from Elm Road across the fields to Cutbush Lane. This lane was the boundary between Earley and Shinfield and on some maps is called Pigwash Lane (after pightle or piddle meaning a piece of land). The farmer (Mr Colebrook, I think) moved part of the footpath a few feet to the east onto a higher, drier area. I was told that he had a huge battle with the local authority but it was much easier for walkers as the lane was wet most of the year. When Lower Earley was built most of the footpath disappeared and was never reinstated!

One of the sights of Earley was the mares and foals in the fields of Maiden Erlegh Stud. The stallions had gone before I had arrived but my colleagues told me that they used to see them being exercised along Cutbush Lane. The large oaks along Cutbush Lane were cut down just before I arrived. We were able to walk to Rushy Mead and down to the Loddon. The woods were very wet, and full of primroses in the spring.

None of my colleagues believed that the M4 would be built. The line of the road had been proposed in the 1930s but the present A4 was upgraded through the middle of Reading instead. During the building of the M4 I remember the noise, Cutbush Lane was permanently wet, daily punctures and a feeling of loss of an area that I'd known for such a short time but had come to enjoy.

A motorway service station was proposed for Upperwood Farm/Cutbush Close area. The local Residents Association battled for many years to have that moved. The then Minister of Transport promised to get the issue sorted out very quickly. It was another 16 years or so before the motorway service station was built at Burghfield.

When I first came there was pavement only along one side of Elm Road from its junction with Elm Lane. The number 20 bus ran every 40 minutes, along Shinfield Road and down Elm Road/Wilderness Road to the top of Beech Lane. It broke down frequently.

Erleigh House on Cutbush Lane was burnt down in 1975. We were told that the house had been empty since its elderly occupant had died and that squatters had occupied it. I can't remember much about the house. It was a large redbrick Victorian/Edwardian house but the barn next door was interesting and though dilapidated, it looked like a late mediaeval hall house that I had seen at the Weald and Downland Museum, Singleton.

After the M4 was built, Earley was cut off from the land next to the Loddon and the remaining fields were designated white land, i.e. this land was to be developed. We were all sent copies of the Barton and Willmore plans, which showed how the area was to be developed. At local meetings the developers, planners and politicians sold the plan to the local people. We were sceptical but agreed, after all the Lower Earley Planning Development Brief was clear and coherent: 6 primary schools, 2 secondary schools, lots of open space…

The first planning permission was given for ASDA to build a superstore. The local residents association had asked for mixed shopping as in Woodley but Wokingham DC refused to buy the land. I remember coming back from the planning meeting and listening to the first episode of *Hitchhiker's Guide to the Galaxy*. It seemed to be a replay of what I had been listening to earlier on in the evening! So the field where I had watched the ponies and where my dog had chased rabbits disappeared. The little settlement on Elm Lane was boarded up and the houses pulled down. The Cottage is the only property to remain on the lane itself.

The stud farm fell into disrepair. The lovely house associated with it with its magnificent views across the valley deteriorated very quickly after the roof tiles were vandalised. The wooden loose boxes were burnt down. The planners tried to put the line of Rushey Way through the pond twice but a fine rearguard action by local residents, particularly the late Eddie Dawson of Trelawney saved it.

William Breadmore

I was born in one of a pair of cottages on Beech Lane on 4 November 1920. I was one of 5 brothers and 3 sisters. The cottage was part of the Wilderness Estate which was then owned by Mr Ingram. It was

Bill Breadmore, on his mother's knee, with his parents and brothers, Beech Lane 1921

the normal practice that all tenants were thrown out of their properties when estates changed hands. When Colonel Butler bought the estate my family was given notice to quit. But one of my brothers had diphtheria and my family refused to move. We were threatened with the bailiffs so my father contacted the local policeman, Mr Dean, who stood guard outside the house all day and eventually the bailiffs went away and we became the tenants of Colonel Butler. The rent remained at 4/– per week.

There were obviously no hard feelings between Colonel Butler and my family. I remember how one day he called all the children into the walled garden and lifted up the strawberry nets and ordered us all to eat as many strawberries as we wanted. The gardener had a face like thunder! I liked Colonel Butler a great deal. We had the freedom of the estate.

The two white lodge houses on Wilderness Road were the lodge houses for the Wilderness. The lodge nearest the walled garden was the home of the gardener and the groom lived in the other one. The stables (on the south side of Wilderness Road) were huge and there were stalls for 15–20 horses on each side. There was a clock tower on top of the stables. On three faces the time was correct, on the fourth it was five minutes fast. Owls, bats, swifts and swallows lived in the tower. At the back of my cottage was the generator for the big house. The electricity cable ran across to the big house. The electricity was for the big house only; our house was lit by oil lamps, later on by gas. The Wilderness was pulled down in the 1940s and the fittings were sold and exported to America. It was a lovely house and I was very sorry that it was removed.

I went to St Peter's school. My first memories are of my brothers and mother telling me to put my hand up if I wanted to go the lavatory. I never learned much but loved it. My teacher, Mr Willoughby, used to chastise me for being too interested in the girls!

My father was a gardener for Solly Joel, then a groom for the Colebrooks. Later on he worked at Woodley aerodrome. He told them that he was 60 when he was actually 70. He finally retired at 80. He grew all our vegetables and fruit. All his life he went to bed at 10 p.m. and rose at 5 a.m. He died aged 94 and my mother aged 93.

As children we used to watch the big cars going in and out of Maiden Erlegh estate and we marvelled at the peacocks and Afghan hounds. We used to 'borrow' rowing boats and row across to the islands on Maiden Erlegh Lake. We were in full view of the house but we were never stopped.

In the season we'd collect elderberries to make elderberry wine and blackberries which our mother turned into blackberry and apple jam. If we had any blackberries left over we took them down to the jam factory in Reading where we received 6d/bag.

Wilderness Road was called Pepper Lane when I was a lad but we used to call it by its present name. Is that why the authorities renamed it?

I remember the milkman coming around in his pony and trap and ladling milk out from a churn into a jug. We had five cottage loaves every day which we bought from a baker on the Wokingham Road. Hens scratched around the estate and we knew where to look for their eggs. I remember being permanently hungry.

Farmer Mowlan, who rented the farm from Colonel Butler, made me a cricket bat which kindled a life long love of cricket in me, and he made fireworks for us on bonfire night. I used to help him milk the cows. We played football and cricket in the field in front of the stables (corner of Beech Lane and Wilderness Road).

Farmer Mowlan used Shire horses for ploughing, haymaking and harvesting. I led the cart one day when the men were haymaking. But the horse refused to move when I wasn't with him so I was told to clear off. Mr Mowlan used to pick me up and put me on the backs of these huge horses. I had a wonderful view of our garden and I could see my father working on his vegetables. In the summer the fields were full of colour and flowers. We played in the meadows and everywhere there were hundreds of grasshoppers, butterflies and swifts and swallows flying low catching insects.

The first policeman in the area, Mr Dean, lived in the cottage on Elm Road on the edge of Earley. One day we were playing about by leaving a parcel attached to a piece of string in the middle of Wilderness Road. We hid in the bushes and teased passing folks by tugging the parcel out of reach as soon as they bent down to pick it up. Mr Dean and his wife came by. He stopped and looked at the parcel which we duly whipped from under his nose. He walked away with his wife laughing.

I loved attending the Sunday tea parties at the Manor House (then the home of the Colebrooks). We had teacakes and tea in delicate cups. Everyone was dressed up, except for me. I was a scruffy little urchin, but I enjoyed the high life!

On Sundays lots of people used to go for walks through Whiteknights Park. Anyone caught cycling was asked very politely to get off and push their bikes. The Suttons family lived in one of the big houses on the (Whiteknights) estate, Erlegh House. My friend's father was their chauffeur and his family lived on the estate.

Lower Earley was very quiet and we all enjoyed going for walks along the lanes and paths. I remember scrumping apples in the Wilderness with a friend and going to Lower Earley to eat them.

There used to be a huge oak on a piece of land which jutted out at the corner of Elm Lane and Elm Road. I remember having my photograph taken with a friend standing on the stump of the tree – 60 years ago. We were told that prisoners were brought out from Reading gaol and hung from that tree early in the morning. Older people talked about the hangings that used to take place outside the Marquis of Granby on a Saturday. The farmers and their families used to turn up for a drink and to watch the prisoners, who were brought from the gaol, being hung.

I was called up when I was 20 years old. I spent seven months in Brock Barracks in the Infantry before being sent to Cornwall, Ireland and then Burma. I ended up in the Signals Regiment. The Berkshire Regiment that I was formerly in was nearly wiped out in Burma but I was in the Borders Regiment by then. I didn't like the war and I was very lucky to survive.

When I was first married we bought a piece of land at the bottom of Andersen Avenue and had a bungalow built. Shortly after we moved to the present house near to where I was born and brought up the route of the A329M was published and our bungalow later disappeared under it.

I love Earley and I love Reading.

Wilderness Stables on the corner of Beech Lane and Wilderness Road
© Dann/Lewis 616 Rural History Centre, The University of Reading

Matilda Roberts

I was born in Earley 79 years ago and lived with my parents, three brothers and four sisters at No.6 Maiden Erlegh Terrace. The cottage was part of Mr Joel's Maiden Erlegh Estate and leased along with Loddon Bridge Farm to a man called Mr Hissey, who lived on the farm. My father worked for Mr Hissey and rented the cottage from him.

The cottage had five rooms and we collected water from an outside pump. There was a ditch that ran along the side of the Wokingham Road and a little wooden bridge went across to each pair of cottages. After the war Wokingham Road was widened and the ditches and bridges disappeared, although the cottages can still be seen along the Wokingham Road today. My mother bought the cottage for £400 but I cannot remember when she had a bathroom and toilet built on. My sister remained in the cottage until she died 10 years ago. Our mother was a courageous woman who only had one leg (one had been amputated when she was six years of age) and a wooden crutch, she would go on the bus into Reading to do her shopping and I remember how kind bus drivers were, because they would stop right outside our house and help my mother with her shopping.

As a child, I remember climbing over the fence and into the woods at the back of the terrace. This was Mr Joel's land and we were not allowed onto it. We would play until we heard the gamekeeper's dog barking and then we would quickly scramble back over the fence. A friend of mine's father worked as a gardener on the estate and I accompanied her when she took him his tea, the gardens were beautiful, full of lovely flowers. Also when I was a child, there was a copse at the end of Mill Lane which was full of pink, white and blue violets. My friends and I would pick them and sell them to our neighbours for one penny a bunch.

I saw Mr Joel on many occasions usually during Ascot week as he rarely stayed at the house any other time during the year. During Ascot week he would entertain guests at Maiden Erlegh House. The first time I saw him he had a little dark beard which got whiter the older he got. I used to stand outside and watch the charabancs pass taking Joel and his guests to Ascot each day. One year there was torrential rain and when the party returned in their charabancs there were ladies' stockings hanging out of the windows to dry. I never saw Joel's wife or any of his children only Joel and his guests, usually ladies in all their finery.

When Joel died the contents of the house were sold at auction, once the auctions had finished the people who lived on the estate were allowed into Maiden Erlegh house to choose one thing to keep from what was left. I went up to the house and remember it was mainly small pieces of furniture and it was mainly the children living on the estate that went up to choose something. I chose a small wooden stool which I later gave to my nephew, unfortunately he threw it out because it had woodworm.

The tenants in the cottages also gained bigger gardens when Joel died, as part of the woods that ran behind the cottages was added onto them.

As a pupil at Earley St Peter's school I was sent once a week to Newtown school for lessons in laundry and domestic science. We were given a penny for the tram and I used to run all the way and spend the penny on sweets. When I left school aged 14 I went to work as a housemaid at a house in Whitegates Lane, for a lady called Mrs Ross, who had three daughters.

During the war I joined the Land Army and worked at the Ministry of Supply at Binfield. My brother worked for the Bunces on their farm and he was working in the cow shed when the Germans dropped bombs around it, fortunately for my brother, none went off. I also remember a doodlebug being dropped somewhere along Beech Lane.

Probably my most frightening memory was trying to return to my parents' home one evening after visiting my sister who was living in a cottage in Beech Lane. As I cycled along Beech Lane I was confronted by a bull belonging to the Bunces which had escaped from its field and was grazing on grass along the side of the road. Unable to pass, I decided to go along Gypsy Lane and when I got there I found that Mrs Beatie's bull had also got out and was waiting for me there, I didn't know what to do, so I decided I'd have to pass it. Somehow I managed to get past and lived to tell the tale.

Keith Pope

I was born in Earley in 1943 and as a boy I worked for the Co-op Dairy as a milkman. My milk float was a four-wheeled cart drawn by a horse. In 1950 the Co-op stables were to the side of Maiden Erlegh Mansion House and on the return to the stables we turned into Betchworth Avenue and just past the old oak tree was a farm gate, and a gravel drive which curved to the left of the house. As I remember, you could not see much of the house as it was surrounded by very high laurels or rhododendrons. The stables were quite large with approximately 100 horses that delivered milk and bread throughout the Reading area. The milk carts were open-sided and the bread carts were enclosed. The best horses were used on the milk rounds and the frisky horses were used for delivering bread.

In the 1950s I belonged to the RSPCA which was in Whiteknights Road, near Earley Gate and used to visit the riding stables on the corner of Beech Lane / Wilderness Road. We also went fishing in Maiden Erlegh Lake. It was very overgrown and the Lake was full of small roach and goldfish. At the Beech Lane end of the Lake was a hill covered with trees and underneath was a beautiful flint cavern with two small arches and one central larger arch. It had a sandy floor and water bubbled out from the sand, and along a reed bed nearly to the small island where there was a wrought iron silt trap. To the reed side there were wooden boards just under the water and, as boys, we used to follow each other across the lake and the whole thing used to sway. The frightening things kids get up to!

To the rear of the houses in Beech Lane were lead-lined tanks which were apparently used for rearing trout.

We moved house in deep snow just before Christmas in 1963 to Lakeside when it was still a building site – no street lights, no footpaths, it was a mess. The Gough Cooper houses, with the exception of the most expensive cottage style with integral garage, were not built with two pathways for a car or with a garage. They had just one single path to the front door and a single path through the double gates round to the back door. They had solid fuel (coal) boilers too. Through that bad winter of 1963–4, the house where I now live in Lakeside was left half built, open to the elements.

I remember the two earth moving machines that started to fill in the lake. They made a start to fill it in where the weir is now. The lake was about 100ft longer than it is today with a small third island with bamboo growing on it and a willow tree.

To the rear of my garden there was a wooden boathouse which fell into the Lake around 1970 and was dismantled. I have heard that it is still in Earley somewhere as a garden shed. By this time the thatched cottage on the large island was no more, only the concrete base still remained. To the far end of Old Pond Copse was a brick arch sluice gate to control flood water between the lake and the stream that runs to the river Loddon. To the right of Old Pond Copse was the Maiden Erlegh Stud. The horses would come right down to the corner of the field by the Lake. When the stud closed in the early to mid 70s, I would collect the horse manure from the old half round corrugated building in my Triumph Herald and trailer – good stuff!

When I started as groundsman for Earley Town Council, we had a 6ft × 8ft garden shed in the corner where the Environmental Interpretation Centre stands today and an old Briggs & Stratton walk behind grass cutting machine and nothing else.

With the introduction of the Bylaws in 1973, Bailiffs were appointed for the first time. There were three original bailiffs.

In 1964–5 fishermen would arrive in Lakeside on a Saturday night in London Transport buses. As a result of the noise from their transistor radios, many of the houses had a rate reduction, including myself, which stood until the introduction of the poll tax.

The large willow tree at the inlet of the Lake I planted myself some 25 years ago. Children persistently tried to break it down but fortunately it did not stop it from growing. It has since been cut back as it was getting too top heavy.

As a young motorcyclist I used to go to the Terminus Cafe which was the Old Tram Terminus in Wokingham Road where the BP petrol station now stands near the Old Alfred Sutton School. Previously it was an allotment site and a horse racing circuit before that.

In the old stables and barn we played on the old Reading open top trams which were stored there in Crescent Road. The barn was also used for Reading Model and Experimental Engineers of which I was a member for many years.

There are so many things to write about, it is difficult to know where to stop. All the changes in Earley from the Mansion House being blown up with dynamite, together with so called preserved trees to the development of Lower Earley. The stone lions from the house are now at Child Beale Trust near Pangbourne.

Brian Stone

I was just three years old when I moved to Earley in 1953. The parish at that time had remained unchanged for many years and it wasn't until about 1956 that the Maiden Erlegh development started. When we moved to The Crescent the adjoining Kenton Road was a dead end onto the Sol Joel estate. The fields behind our house (now the playing fields to the School) were used as a paddock for horses from the estate. Looking back on those years, life seemed rather tranquil, stress hadn't been invented, the number of car owners were relatively small and very few people worked further away than a trolley bus ride into Reading. Supermarkets were still a few years away but the Baylis Mobile Shop and the Browns bread van travelled around the streets bringing the shop to the housewife. In the summer the Corona fizzy pop lorry would come round. This was quite a luxury item in the fifties and a far cry from today's cans of Coke which appear to be part of the staple diet. It doesn't seem possible that the Co-op dairy still delivered milk by horse and cart. I can remember being fascinated how the horse would plod along the road on his own knowing where to stop, while the milkman ran in and out of each house in his brown overall with his leather satchel jangling with small change. He always appeared exhausted trying to keep up with the huge animal. When he arrived outside our bungalow the horse, being a creature of regular habits, would more often than not leave a deposit and without doubt my Dad had the best roses in the road! The only commercial competition appeared to be whether the consumer bought Esso Blue or Pink paraffin both of which did brisk business before widespread central heating became available.

At the age of five it was time to start school at St Peter's in Church Road. Pre-school nursery education was virtually non-existent in those days and visits as a rising five in the previous term unheard of, so it was in at the deep end on day one. I can remember queuing on that first day to register. The lad in front of me was called Richard and we were destined to be in the same class all through junior and for a majority of secondary education too. Although I can't remember it affecting us greatly, for many of the new entrants it was a harrowing experience being the first time the maternal bonds had been broken. Very few women worked in those days and had dedicated their time to raising the family so on this first parting emotions obviously ran high. The Headmaster at the time was a Mr Willoughby who used to frighten us to death with his loud booming voice. Of his teaching staff I remember Mrs Gould she was, in our eyes, very old and quite deaf. Obviously as lively youngsters we took full advantage of the situation. She had the knack, however, of restoring order by retrieving a cane from behind the blackboard and waving it at us menacingly. All these years later my memory of her reminds me of the Grandma character from the Giles cartoons. Although corporal punishment was still used in those days I don't recall her implement ever being used in anger!

Another lady who put a huge input into school life was Miss Barnes. I'm sure she is remembered by many as she taught there long after I left. I recall shortly before Christmas one year Richard and I were summoned to go to see her to audition for the role of one of the three kings in the annual nativity play that was held in the church. We each had to sing a verse of the carol *We three kings* which had to be sung very slowly, the object being to walk from the vestry to the nativity scene before finishing the verse. My inability to master this feat cost me the chance to take part in that year's production.

Although not a Bank Holiday as it is now, May Day was celebrated each year with country dancing in the grounds of the Manor House opposite the school. One year I was picked for the maypole team. Everything went fine until the final dress rehearsal when a stray arm from a fellow team-mate knocked one of my front teeth out, this caused the white smock outfit we all wore to turn a speckled scarlet. Needless to say I was relegated to the role of human ballast at the bottom of the pole.

Most youngsters today are ferried to and from school by car. Back in the fifties the best on offer was a carrier on the back of your Mum's bike. It wouldn't be uncommon to see thirty or forty mothers with similar contraptions waiting for their children at the school gate. How things have changed today, nobody turned a hair when at the age of eight I would frequently walk the mile home on my own across the then docile Wokingham Road. This journey would often be broken to visit the local paper shop near the traffic lights for fruit salad or black jack chews (four for one old penny – what value). A few years later I was to get my first job there as a paper-boy for the princely sum of 12/6 a week.

During this time, Gough Cooper Homes made relentless progress developing the Maiden Erlegh estate. What a great place to play, with the old derelict mansion and its neglected terraced gardens down to the lake. Perilous trips were made to the island in an old discarded water tank, a journey not recommended as leaks were common along with wet clothing. As today, a building site attracts children like a huge magnet and we spent many hours in the evening and holidays playing there. The highlight to these sorties was the day in the early sixties when the grand old mansion house was razed to the ground with explosives. With hindsight this was a travesty. I am sure in these more enlightened times it would have been converted into a community centre along with its beautifully ornate marble swimming pool.

By way of a change, we also spent a lot of time at Earley station waiting for the steam locomotives to pass through. Occasionally an engine would arrive to do a spot of shunting in the coal yard adjacent to the station and we used to pester the life out of the drivers to give us rides on the foot-plate. I can still smell that lovely aroma of steam and hot oil now. On a really good day we would be invited to share the driver's breakfast cooked in the engine's firebox on a shovel. Believe me you haven't lived until you've tasted bacon cooked that way, what a delicacy.

St Peter's was, of course, a very old Victorian school with outside toilets and ancient heating. In winter the free school milk would often freeze. These occasions were instantly recognisable because the contents would ooze out the top in white stalagmite formations, the foil caps forming a silver peak. The smell of those crates gently thawing against the huge radiators still turns my stomach. With no kitchen facilities, school dinners were delivered each day by lorry and I am sure this is where they gained their dubious reputation. The gastronomic delights of lukewarm cabbage and tapioca pudding will be ingrained in the minds of my generation forever. All this took place in St Peter's Hall and if you had PE straight after lunch it could be quite hazardous.

You had to become quite adept at dodging the deposits of mashed potatoes etc. that had found their way onto the floor if slipping up while hopping around the hall was to be avoided. It wasn't until soon after we left that a programme of redevelopment was instigated. It didn't worry us however, as we were about to be the trailblazers of the brand new secondary modern school being built at the bottom of my garden. Somehow the ignominy of failing the Eleven Plus didn't seem to matter.

By the summer of 1961 it was apparent that the new Maiden Erlegh Secondary Modern School would not be ready on time, so arrangements were made to spend the first two terms of our secondary education at Woodley Hill House in Fairview Avenue. The three teachers allocated to us, Miss Clarke (later to become Mrs Munday), Mr Watts and Mr Lowson were later to join us at the new school. I don't think the old lady caretaker was sorry to see ninety eleven year olds leave her premises just before Easter. I can still hear her now standing at the front door of the old house barking at us to 'scrape and wipe' our shoes before crossing her pristine threshold.

Before our transition to the new school, it was apparent from meetings our parents attended that a strict school uniform code was to be adopted. I remember my Mum and Dad returning one night to announce that boys might have to wear straw boaters, thankfully this was later to be relaxed to caps. Looking back on old photographs it is apparent that short trousers were still worn by the boys. I think I was well into my second year before I started to wear long ones. Street credibility was a long time coming in those days.

Eventually the big day arrived, and after all the build up it was a slight anti-climax. Apart from being photographed as we entered the premises for the first time I do not recall any official ceremonials. Those early days were obviously well planned because the transfer appeared seamless, the same three teachers carried on and were joined by James Dunkley who was to become the first headmaster of Maiden Erlegh Secondary Modern School. He was a strict but fair disciplinarian and if you were called out of assembly it was with some trepidation that you awaited your fate outside his office.

By the end of that first term we began to appreciate how lucky we were to have the first use of the school equipment and facilities, everything was there from cricket nets to pottery kilns. All the equipment was new and in plentiful supply. In addition, the school now had its own kitchen for school dinners and for several years it became tradition for the pupils to form an orderly queue to stir the Christmas pudding each year. The reputation of the school rapidly grew and has never looked back nearly forty years later. During that first term, the school was ours, it was never quite the same in the following September when the new intake of first year students came and to add insult to injury a year group was slotted in above us. It might appear selfish, but I think this was a shame as it would have been nice for our year to have led the school through to its first full complement.

If the school lacked one facility it was a swimming pool and to get over this problem we were bussed to Martins Swimming Pool in Wokingham in the old Smiths double-deckers. These vehicles were very top heavy and we soon discovered that with a little effort they could be rocked quite precariously. Along with several others, this prank resulted in us being called from assembly the following morning for an appointment with the head. I wonder how many poor souls have followed since?

Cross-country running was a popular activity with the games staff as we were just dispatched to run around the country lanes while they sat in a nice warm gym awaiting our return. The route was fairly pleasant however, once you had run through the footpath between the lake and Beech Lane you were into undeveloped farmland. It was then up Radstock Lane, left into the dip and left again into Beech Lane before returning to the school. There was never any escape from this arduous activity; even with a sick note you were dispatched to act as a Marshall half way round the course. Sadly, the rural route we used to plod round has been swallowed up in the Lower Earley development.

Looking back now, Maiden Erlegh was quite progressive, it offered pupils the chance to travel abroad at reasonable cost and many took the opportunity to travel to Switzerland. Although it may appear a bit tame now, in the early sixties it was quite an expedition. The Tirabad centre in Wales offering outward-bound activities was to follow in a joint enterprise with the neighbouring schools of Emmbrook and Charters at Sunningdale. Sadly this was not up and running before I left. My own children were later to enjoy the experience however during their own school days at Emmbrook.

On May 9th 1997 over sixty of the original pupils and staff of Maiden Erlegh Secondary Modern met for a reunion in the Maiden Over Public House: a venue purposely chosen as it had been strictly out of bounds years ago and it gave us all a feeling of rebellious nostalgia. It appears that most of us have turned into reasonably well-balanced adults and I guess we have to thank our Earley childhood for that! In fact the evening was such a success that another was held in 2000.

May Staley

The following memories are an amalgamation of a 1983 Reading Chronicle article and May's current recollections.

I came to Earley in 1904 at the age of thirteen months and have lived here ever since. My parents lived in Sussex, my father was a policeman there, and I was sent to live with my grandparents because my parents had had another baby. My parents had more children, three or four girls I think, but these stayed with my parents. I went to stay with my parents and sisters for holidays but as I grew up in Earley I regarded here as my home.

My first memory is of going to St Peter's School, Church Road in 1908, the old school is now demolished and a new one has been built on the site. I used to walk home and back again for lunch. The headmaster was Mr H. J. Wooldridge and during the winter months we were let out of school early in the afternoons because Wokingham Road was wooded on both sides and was a lonely road to go home. You met the occasional tramp, but they were quite harmless.

Wokingham Road was then a gravel road and was mostly used by horse traffic. An old chap, Mr Wingfield, with his four-wheeled barrow used to scrape up the horse manure, and if anyone wanted it for their gardens he would sell it for a few coppers. The road was tarred some time between 1912 and 1914.

Travelling up the north side of Wokingham Road from Ward's shops by the traffic lights, there used to be allotments which reached back to the churchyard. Adjoining the allotments was the common which later became Sol Joel Playing Fields.

Rumour goes that the vicar of the parish refused some money from Mr Joel, a racehorse owner, because he did not believe in gambling, so the playing fields were given to the Borough of Reading and were opened by the then Duke of York, later George VI.

At the corner of the common was a pond, beside Mays Lane, which was a great attraction to us children in icy winters. Mays Lane was named after two families named May who lived in two cottages over the railway line and at that time there were no other houses on Mays Lane. Further along Wokingham Road from the junction with Mays Lane, there were more allotments until you reached Hungerford Lodge which was occupied by Major Wheble who looked after the Bulmershe Estate.

Hungerford Lodge was knocked down before the war and Stanton Close was built in its grounds. Further up Wokingham Road was a small paddock until you reached five cottages by Station Road where the South Berks Hounds often met. The village policeman, PC Harris, occupied one of these cottages.

My grandfather was a gamekeeper on the Sol Joel Estate and we lived in Keeper's Cottage in Maiden Erlegh Woods. My grandfather let the hounds from the East Berkshire Hunt on the estate and he was given £1 for every fox that was caught.

Earley Station itself was in the parish of Woodley. After Station Road there were two more cottages and then about half a mile of copse and bogs until you reached a stile which led to a path to Woodley, now called Henley Wood Road. After the stile there were eight bungalows which were semi-detached and each had four rooms and a small scullery. They had one well between two houses and the water was pulled up by a bucket on a rope. The bungalows were built to accommodate the men who built the railway, the first occupant being 'Ginger' Stevens and the bungalows were called Ginger Terrace until about the 1930s when they were given numbers. These bungalows have been modernised and are still occupied. We also lived in Ginger Terrace at one time. Near the bungalows was a wall which ran around a field and parts of this wall are still standing and are used as front garden walls. At the end of the wall there was a Lodge on the corner of a cart track over the railway line to Woodley which is now called Pond Head Lane. The Lodge became Nelson Balls' Coal Depot.

Travelling down the south side of Wokingham Road from the traffic lights at Church Road, there was about a quarter mile belt of trees with deep ditches at the roadside until you reached Maiden Erlegh Lodge. The entrance to the drive led to the mansion which was occupied by Mr S. B. Joel.

I remember Solly Joel quite well, and I especially remember him riding around the estate on a white donkey.

Every year, on the Sunday before Ascot races, Sol Joel gave a big party at his house for the racehorse trainers and jockeys. It became known locally as Ascot Sunday, and local children waited at the Lodge gates, very excited to see the motor cars, a rare sight in those days.

Each year Sol Joel gave all the school children of Earley a treat – a picnic in the grounds of Maiden Erlegh and 6d (six old pence). When Sol Joel's daughter married the annual treats stopped because he did not approve of her choice of husband!

After Mr Joel's death, the mansion was used as a private school and later by the Church Army until it was demolished in the 1950s.

After the Lodge there were more woods until you reached a small gate in a wooden fence which led to the keeper's cottage, where I lived. At that time it was an old thatched cottage, which was later condemned, and a new one (still in use) was built. Many pheasants were bred there every year for the annual shoot in October. On one such shoot 599 pheasants were shot in a day and my grandfather who was the Gamekeeper, went out the next morning and shot one more to make the total 600. Local men were employed as Beaters to drive the birds towards the guns. The men were paid 2s 6d a day and boys 1s.

From the keeper's cottage you travelled about half a mile passing woods all the way, until you reached two bungalows and eight houses built to accommodate the workmen on the estate. These houses had wells to supply their water, but were fitted with pumps to pump it up. Today I live in one of these houses and one of the original pumps is still in my garden. After more woods you reached a gate where Groves paper shop now stands, which led to the racecourse (now Meadow Road and Sutcliffe Avenue) where races were held annually. After the estate was broken up, the grandstand on the racecourse was dismantled and taken to Newbury racecourse. The racecourse was bounded by Mill Lane and Gipsy Lane and then on to Beech Lane where you reached the stud farm where the racehorses were bred. At that time the stud groom was a Mr Hallaway. In Beech Lane there was a forge and a laundry for estate use, as well as large kitchen gardens now all built over.

I remember that there was a pond at the corner of Mill Lane and the Wokingham Road. Wokingham Road was tarred for the first time after the First World War, liquid tar was sprayed onto the road and gravel was spread on that. In those days the small number of people living in Wokingham Road did not have the living standards expected today.

There were two milkmen in Earley who fetched their milk from Sindlesham Farm House daily. One of them was J. Lewington with whom I worked for seven years. We drove a pony and two-wheeled cart with a step at the back and had no protection from the weather. The milk was collected in 10 gallon churns and then put into buckets which we took up to customers' doors. The smallest quantity sold was just over half a pint for ½d. In later years I worked at Huntley and Palmer's as a dough checker.

A baker with a horse and covered cart called on customers three times a week. Most of the traffic on Wokingham Road was horse drawn heavy carts from Sindlesham Mill (which is now a restaurant in Mill Lane) carrying corn and flour to Reading. A coalman with a horse and cart called on customers once a week with coal at 1s per cwt.

I also remember that a May Queen was crowned in the school playground every year on May 1st. I had that honour in 1917. Patriotic songs were always sung round the flag on Empire Day, 24th May. A popular vicar of the parish, the Rev. Canon Fowler, died in Church during the morning service.

Earley had no public house, no shops or public transport. To go shopping meant a long walk into Reading and took most of a day. There was no television or radio and telephones were few and far between. Boys and girls could not go out together as they can today, even when I was 18 I could only go out with other girls and I had to be in by 8 pm. Yet I remember we were very happy (apart from the terrible loss of many of the men we knew in the war). I believe that at 17 I was much younger than a 17-year-old is today. I worked hard but I was not subject to the stress and emotional problems of today's teenager. A girl in the early 1900s had no career problems, she was expected to marry and have children.

Harry Harris

I came to live at Maiden Erlegh mansion house at the age of 12, along with my mother and brother. My mother worked as a Housekeeper/Matron for Captain Waterlow Fox at his boys' school in Sutton Courtenay and when he moved the school to Earley we moved with him. My Father was in the Royal Flying Core (which later became the Royal Air Force) at the time and when he came out of the forces Captain Waterlow Fox gave him the job of head gardener.

When we first moved to Earley we lived in the main house along with Captain Fox and the boys and staff at the school. This meant that during school holidays when everyone had gone home and Captain Fox was away on his travels abroad (usually lasting around 10 weeks) my family had the house to ourselves. I had been told that Sol Joel had hidden diamonds in the house and I searched every nook and cranny of that house looking for them, but I never found one.

I had only had limited schooling in Sutton Courtenay as it was a small village school so when I started at Earley St Peters at the age of twelve, I had to start at the bottom and work my way up. Fortunately, I was a quick learner and quickly moved up through the school. I was good at football and St Peter's had a good football team run by the Headmaster, Mr Rutter, which I joined. I have happy memories of my time at school and often stayed until 5 o'clock in the evening playing football. By the time I left at age fourteen, I was top of the school. The Headmaster Mr Rutter left to go to Australia or New Zealand some time after I left (1939) he was replaced by Mr Willoughby.

I had great fun growing up at the Mansion House, I felt as if I owned it and spent many hours roaming the estate. There was a punt on a rope which I used to go across to the Summerhouse. It had a lounge and kitchen downstairs and a bedroom and balcony upstairs. There were 32 deer on the estate and 32 maids working at the school and there were lots of pranks played on them. One evening two maids were returning up Maiden Erlegh Drive after a night off, when a ghost appeared out of the bushes. One froze and the other ran to the house for help, on their return the ghost had vanished, resulting in the butler getting the sack and Earley getting a new postman and the ghost was never seen again!

Although Maiden Erlegh was now a school, it remained a stately home and was maintained in the highest decorative order as it had been during the Sol Joel years. On the lawn to the right hand side of the main entrance stood a statue of one of Sol Joel's horses which had won the Derby. Waterlow-Fox kept the fine library and the rooms as they had been, I remember palm court well. There was a white marble statue of a nude girl with swans around her feet and a jet of water came out of their mouths. In the middle of the room was a domed ceiling and secluded lighting came from behind white marble shells. I swam in the swimming pool on many occasions, it was the most elaborate pool I've ever seen. The ceiling was covered with oil paintings of topless mermaids with their tails painted as waves. On the floor of the pool was Sol Joel's Crest and the room was full of marble. There was a trapeze, diving board and a chrome bar which ran across the pool pouring a fine mist of water into it through five holes. From the poolroom, stairs led up and out onto the roof where you could sunbathe. The pool's temperature was controlled by coal boilers underneath.

A man called Jimmy Black, who was the landlord of the Three Tuns public house rented stables from Captain Fox and he and his daughter Cynthia Black trained ponies which drove two wheeled buggies, like Prince Philip does today. The stables were tiled in dark green and red tiles thought to be Sol Joel's racing colours and I remember the floor looked like chocolate bars, it was kept spotless. At weekends Jimmy Black would ride around the estate on one of his horses, he was always smartly dressed with a red rose in his buttonhole.

The gardeners and staff were not allowed to be seen by the upper classes so when they saw Mr Black coming they would have to hide. One weekend a group of staff decided to ask Mr Black for a tip for the 3.30 race at Ascot, one brave member approached Jimmy as he rode up Maiden Erlegh drive, he looked up and down and told him which horse to back and said 'don't ever ask me again.' The group each put sixpence on the horse and it won.

The Co-op had bought the other stables (called the Homestead) and they used the back drive. At Earley cross roads there was Jarvis Garage on one corner and Culham's grocery stores and post office on the other. There was a RAC blue and white traffic control box which a man stood inside. He took great care of his box and the garden around it, he had white stones leading up to it and he won a prize for best garden around a box.

When I left school I went to work at Woodley Aircraft before joining the Airforce which I served in for 5½ years during the war. I used to cycle there every day on my bike. My parents moved into the Lodge in about 1940 because although we enjoyed living in the big house it did mean that my parents were at Captain Fox's beck and call 24 hours a day, so when the lodge became vacant they asked if they could move into it. I met my wife, who worked in Woolworths, while we were still living in the big house and we married in 1942, to begin with we moved in with my parents in the lodge. In 1947 we moved into a house in Salcombe Drive where we stayed until my father's death in 1979 when we returned to the Lodge.

My parents worked for Captain Fox until he retired and the school was closed in 1945. My father remained head gardener on the estate until ICI sold it and moved their offices to Elvetham Hall in Hartley Witney. My father continued to work for ICI at their new premises until he retired and for his loyal service they agreed to sell him the Lodge house.

When my father died in 1979 he left me the lodge so we sold our house in Salcombe Drive and moved back here. We extended the original house to its present size and my wife and I have lived here ever since. We have seen many changes and I was very sorry when they pulled the big house down. My son remembers that they had to blow up the big towers of the house because they were too solid to knock down with the bulldozers. In its years after Captain Fox the house was let go by its owners and the Canadians that stayed there during the war ate the deer from the Deer Park. The gates were removed during the war, sawn off with a blow torch and taken to Jackson's Scrap metal merchants where they remained until after the war, ICI were asked if they wanted them returned but they didn't so they went for scrap.

Renee Smalley

My memories of Earley date from the early 1930s. My father used to take me for walks along Cutbush Lane from Shinfield Road, to Beech Lane and then along Wilderness Road. In those days Cutbush Lane ran from Shinfield Road to Gypsy Lane, long before the M4 was constructed. It was a lovely country lane. The University raised plants in huge greenhouses near Shinfield Road and I remember going just inside the grounds to admire the beautiful rose beds, sadly it's all now derelict.

My father used to pick wild roses and honeysuckle from the hedgerows for me. There were some cottages along the lane, one was Maydene the home of Mrs Nellie Webb and her sister. These two ladies started the Sunday School in Maydene in the 1940s and their house became the nucleus of the church in Lower Earley, later St Nicolas' Church. The clergy and members of St Peter's used to process round the fields in Cutbush Lane at Rogation time with the local farming community.

Beech Lane was a lane bordered by deep ditches and open fields beyond; part way down, the lane made a sharp turn to the left then it turned right before carrying on to join Cutbush Lane, there was no Rushey Way in those days, now Rushey Way runs parallel to the part of Beech Lane where it turned sharply to the left and crosses it as it turns right, the lower part of the lane is now called Carshalton Way. Beech Lane was tree lined – huge trees – until it passed the lake. I can remember the houses in Wilderness Road, between Beech Lane and the (Earley) crossroads being built.

In 1962 I moved to Beech Lane to live in number 31, a house I had seen being built in my childhood. It was a very pleasant quiet road. There were riding stables at the top of the road (Wilderness Road end) and it was lovely to see the riders pass the house. Turning left into Wilderness Road from Beech Lane just past the white house, there were fields until where Douglas Court now stands, where there was a very grand house standing back from the road – with a large garden bordered with conifers.

In the 1960s Radstock Lane was rural and there was a farm on the left, and our milk and our eggs came from there. Later when the land was sold for building they discovered several unexploded bombs. We were among many households evacuated while they were made safe!

Elm Lane was surrounded by farmland, the lane originally went behind what is now Larkesmead and took the route which is now the pedestrian route past the Salvation Army Centre, it was used by traffic in those days. Males, the veterinary surgeons had their practice where the Salvation Army is now. There was extensive farmland at the back of it, plus the large house – the Males family home – they were devoted members of St Peter's Church.

Mrs Heather Witt

I lived in Earley from the age of two until I was eight in the years 1924–30 when my father was head gardener to Mr E. P. F. Sutton at Sidmouth Grange.

We lived in one of four estate cottages in Church Road occupied by employees at Sidmouth Grange but were called Erleigh Court Cottages. I never knew why, but I presume there must have either been some previous arrangement where they were built on Erleigh Court land or they were so named because they were nearer to Erleigh Court than to Sidmouth Grange. At that time Church Road and Mays Lane were the only tarred roads between St Peter's Road and what is now the A4. Everywhere else was unmade roads or gravel tracks. I expect I could pick out one or two landmarks but it was a long time ago and according to street maps I have seen, a lot has changed. The owner of Sidmouth Grange was Mr Philip Sutton (EPFS according to all the etchings on Dad's tools). His brother, Mr Noel Sutton, owned Whiteknights. They of course were part of the family of Sutton and Sons the seedsmen. I think there were other brothers but not living locally to my knowledge. I would expect that their father or perhaps grandfather was Alfred Sutton, the school in Wokingham Road being named after one or other gentlemen. My two older sisters attended there after they won their scholarships. When we moved to Earley those sisters started at St Peter's School on the same day as the new Headmaster, Mr Rutter. He had taken over from Mr Browne who had moved on. Ten years later when I went to senior school in Wokingham, the Headmaster was Mr Browne! My *only claim to fame* was during the May Day celebrations at Earley School (Earley St Peter's school) when I was chosen to be crown bearer, but as the procession accompanied the May Queen across the playground for the crowning ceremony, I was so busy looking around for my mum in the spectators that the crown slid off the velvet cushion onto the ground. My memory goes a bit hazy there but I think everything ended up all right! We were all asked to bring what flowers we could for decorating the May Queen's rostrum, etc, and of course at that time lilac was well in abundance. My mind still goes back to the classroom set aside for these flowers every time I smell lilac even after seventy years!

Peter and Margaret Martin

Peter and Margaret have lived in the Wokingham Road since 1976.

MM – I lived at 2, Farm Cottages, Radstock Lane, my father was a cowman. We lived there until we were bombed out in 1942. Four bombs were dropped, two detonated. We went to live with my grandparents in Whitley Wood and I had to ride my bike from there all the way to St Peter's school.

PM – We lived in Yattendon for nine months, then Broadmoor Farm for about five years, then we moved back to Reading in the late 1950s.

MM – I worked on a farm, then at the National Institute for Research in Dairying (NIRD) in the goat shed. I also worked for a large dairy, Emmerson and Jones which sold milk direct to the public. I had to keep the records for the cows, and take samples for butterfat, there was a Milk Marketing board in Christchurch [Road]. I had a job sampling raw milk for testing, it was the milk quotas that drove a lot of farmers out of dairying.

PM – The Palmer family owned Shinfield Grange, Mr Palmer was Master of the South Berkshire Hunt. The family owned three farms, Old House Farm, Upperwood Farm and Lowerwood Farm, Lowerwood was subject to flooding.

MM – Old House Farm was supposed to have the biggest tile barn in Berkshire. The farmhouse was said to be very old, there was a frame to hold the house up. Milk from Upperwood was sold to Jobs Dairies, now part of United Dairies.

PM – The Palmer's gamekeeper was very strict, when we went beating for a shoot the reward was five shillings and a rabbit. The Crocker family rented Upperwood Farm from the Palmers. Horses worked the fields as they were too small for tractors. The Colebrook family owned all the land from Radstock Lane to Shinfield Road to Cutbush Lane, they owned the vet's house in Elm Lane and the Spinney which is now surrounded by houses. The vet's house was near where the Salvation Army building is today, the veterinary surgeon was Mr Male. Bunces bungalow at the lower end of Beech Lane used to be the Primitive Methodist Chapel. Mr Halestrapp who lived in Arborfield Hall was a cattle dealer. Mr Lucas was at Brookers Hill, he took threshing machines to work on farms everywhere, he had three machines. I worked at the Farm Institute at Hurley and at Darvalls on Saturday and Sunday to earn extra money, and eventually in 1962, I was able to buy the cottage, it was very basic and had no sanitation. The cottage was sold to Cooks who sold it to the council.

Doris Taylor

I recall that Mr Waight and family moved into a largish house on the corner of Salcombe Drive, built on land sold off from the Maiden Erlegh Estate. He became Head Air Raid Warden for the area centred on his own home. The only other warden I can recall was 'La' Bennett. The wardens fitted us all with gas-masks and later on, the filter bits to tape on to the end of the mask.

Street fire watching parties were formed and we patrolled in pairs during the hours of darkness. My sister and I were a *pair*. Our boiler suits hung on the bedroom door ready for us to hop into them in an emergency. It did not dawn on any of us that if there was enemy action our parents would, no doubt, lose two daughters in one go!

There was no main drainage then – only cesspools in the back gardens. I can tell you – there were no *sweet night airs* in those days! One didn't notice it in the daytime hours, but in the still night – ugh! It was a great comfort to all to hear the wardens laughing and joking together during *alerts* when they were out of doors. I joined the ATS so memories of daily wartime events were really non-existent after that.

I live in Wokingham Road near the shops at the Three Tuns. The deeds of my home are interesting. The land used to be Earley Heath, and then the Act of Enclosure changed all that. By some means or other (the deeds are at the solicitor's office), the land on this (south) side of the railway line had to be sold off to settle a gaming debt to Monte Carlo!! A Mr Foster bought the land. He had a greengrocer's shop at the bottom of St Peter's Road and grew all his own produce. He sold off the front land (fronting onto the Wokingham Road) in 1928 and my father

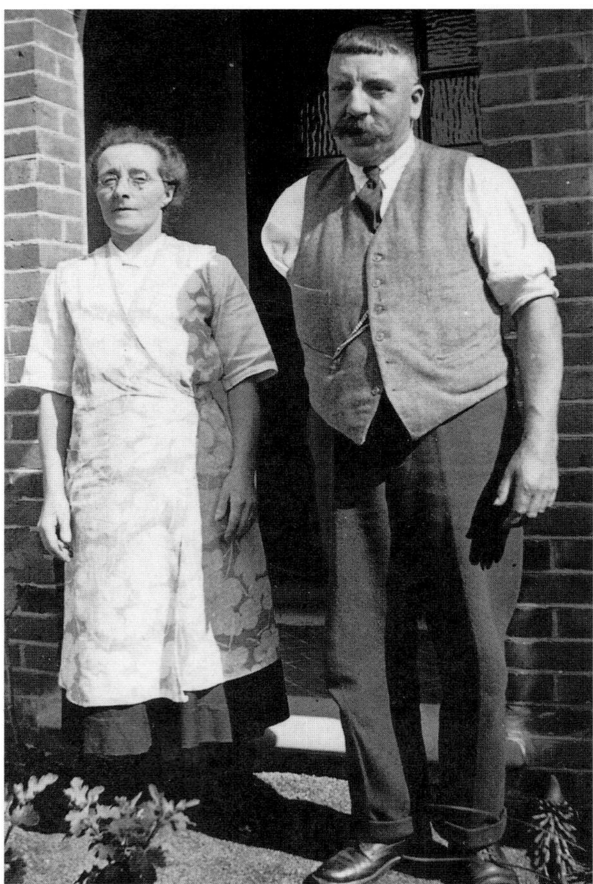

Doris Taylor's Mum and Dad, 1934

bought a plot 30ft by 180ft for £100–£120: a fortune! My mother and father had saved very hard to realise their dream of owning their own home so when the opportunity to buy a plot of land came up they took it. My father had served with the army in India for nine years and my mother was a cook and they had saved every penny possible. When my father built our house he kept an account of everything in an old exercise book this included the wages for the men, all the stamp duty and bus fares to the council offices etc. and all the materials and their cost are listed. He had to learn to write with his left hand as he lost his right arm. The total cost of the house was £622 2s 7½d. This included £126 5s 0d for the cost of the plot of land and took account of a subsidy grant of £50 from the council (a grant to encourage people to build their own homes) and £1 1s 3d in returns (materials not used). The number of bricks bought was 23,700 and the number of roof tiles was 6,600! Work on the house began in about October 1928 and we moved in on July 11th 1929. We had very little furniture to start off but we did have our own home.

The market garden owned by Mr Foster was worked by **hand** (sic); Mr Foster, Evelyn, his niece, and Ned Pawsey (who lived at Whitley and rode a ramshackle bike) did the work, although most of the digging was done by Evelyn. Ned looked after the pigs, goats and chickens so there was plenty of manure for the plants! When Mr Foster retired the land was developed for housing and became Courts Road. It was called Courts Road because Mr C. Allen George, a local builder, had some of the land and laid out some tennis courts; it cost six (old) pence per person per hour to play there.

Jean Fostekew (née Nelmes)

From 1934–52 I lived at 95 Wokingham Road, from 1960–2 in Mays Lane, during 1974–5 in Heath Road, from 1975–6 at 687 London Road. Two of my children went to Earley St Peter's School. The ashes of both my parents are interred at St Peter's Church, Earley.

The famous test pilot, Harold Penrose lived at 100 Hamilton Road and he was lifted up by the man flying kite of S. F. Cody in Palmer Park in the early part of the century, he remembers seeing an aircraft make a crash landing in the grounds of Whiteknights.

Trams ran up the Wokingham Road to the Terminus Café which was situated at the junction of St Peter's Road. They were extremely noisy and the cups and saucers used to rattle as they went past.

The field bordering Green Road was called Oliver Dixon's field and was a riding stable.

The shops now in the parade in the Wokingham Road opposite what was Alfred Sutton School were originally houses and some retained their small front gardens until after the Second World War.

There were two funeral directors, four general grocery stores, a chemist, a hardware shop, a gentleman's outfitter also selling ladies shoes, two butchers, a dairy, a bakery, a drapers, two newsagents, a wireless shop, a greengrocers and seed merchant, a post office and a library where you paid about 3d for each book you borrowed.

The muffin man came round each Sunday with his tray of muffins or crumpets on his head, ringing his bell in the traditional way. He seemed to come from St Peter's Road so he was probably based at the bakery which was halfway up that road. The Walls Ice Cream *Stop me and buy one* also came round with a little truck propelled by a bicycle. The water ices were delicious. The chimney sweep lived in Pitcroft Avenue. The cobbler's shop was also in Pitcroft. The window cleaner was silent and I could never make out if it was a man or a woman. Further up the road between the bottom of St Peter's and the junction with Green Road there was a sweet shop and a bicycle repair shop called Kittowes.

The headmistress at Alfred Sutton Junior School was Miss Wooldridge and the reception class teacher was Miss Huddy, in 1936 other teachers included Miss Medhurst, Mrs David, Miss Pope, Miss Lasky and Mr Chandler.

There was the Eleanor Austin School of Dancing at the top of St Peter's Road. This was very popular with mothers and daughters and the occasional son. She put on shows and displays in church halls.

Ada Little (née Mears)

I was born in Clarendon Road. I remember the very thick fogs when I was young, the worst ones were in November. In the summer a man selling ice cream came round each day on his 3-wheel bike *stop me and buy one* – it was a penny for an ice-lolly. The muffin man came on a Sunday carrying muffins on a tray on his head. People used to come round the streets singing, walking slowly down the road,

'Stop me and buy one', ice cream seller, late 1920s. Marjorie Culham is on the right hand side.

children ran out and gave them a halfpenny or a penny. Lamplighters came each evening with a long pole to light the streetlights which were gas lit.

We only bought hot cross buns on Good Friday morning, we would go and get them at 8.00am from Brown's bakery in St Peter's Road.

I was nine years old when I had my first car ride, only one man in our street had a car. The coal man delivered the coal and the children stood outside and counted the sacks as he took them through the house to the coal cellar. I remember the milkman, he came each day and measured out one pint of milk into our jug, the baker also came each day, and both of these had a horse and cart. Two penny worth of vegetables, carrots, onions, parsnips etc, with the meat, would make a lovely stew for our whole family of seven.

We all loved May Day at Earley School (Earley St Peter's School was originally called Earley School), each child took a chair with their mother's name on the bottom of it. Every class took part; there was country dancing, including the Maypole. The choir would sing, they were conducted by the headmaster. This all happened after the May Queen had been crowned; then she would sit with all her attendants and watch the afternoons entertainments. I was fortunate to meet my old teacher, Mr Rutter (who had been the headmaster), in the early 1960s when the old school was pulled down ready to build the new one. I had four cousins and two sisters at the Earley School. I used to take my Mum's flat iron to school to press our needlework.

A great day out for all the family, cousins and friends was to take dinner and tea down to the river, we even took the wind-up gramophone, that was in one pram with all the food and the babies were in another pram. We had a sing-song and played all sorts of games, those were the days – and it didn't cost much!

Ada was 17 years old when the Second World War began, and her wartime memories are included in the chapter *Earley at War*.

Marjorie Culham

I was born over the village shop on 2nd August 1914 and I started school at St Peter's in September 1919. I was in Miss Hinkley's class and I had to wear a white pinafore over my dress. When I was about six I caught diphtheria and had to go to the isolation hospital at Tilehurst. I was taken in a brown horse-drawn ambulance! I can remember having green liquorice powder – it was horrid! There was no public transport between Earley and Tilehurst but my mother had a friend with a pony and trap who twice a week would take her to the hospital to look through the window at me! I suppose I was lucky to survive as seven of my little friends died.

I remember following the lamplighter with his long pole. I also remember jumping in and out of the spray from the water cart that was used to water the roads.

One of the highlights of our year was watching the horse brakes bringing racegoers home from the Ascot races, we called out 'penny for the Ascot races' and scrambled for pennies! It supplemented our 'income' which was our Saturday penny spent at Miss Fulbrooks shop on 20 aniseed balls or sherbet dabs or fairy whispers which had little love-messages printed on them. Snowfruits from the *Walls stop-me-and-buy-one* cycle were also good value for one penny.

When the old Three Tuns Pub was shut we used to play in the arbour there – here I sampled beer from dregs left in one of the glasses by a pub customer – I did not like it!!

Once a week a musician would visit the Tuns and play old songs on some sort of brass instrument – so nobody got to sleep before ten o' clock! We did not have wireless and television so we made up our own games – of course we had hoops and tops in their season, *tag-over-the-rails* and *here-we-come-to-learn-a-trade* were two of my favourite games. How lucky we were to be able to play in the country safely, no one interfered with us and our parents did not worry about us, knowing that we would come home when we were hungry!

David Brown

Mr Brown was born in the Royal Berks Hospital and lived in Pond Head Lane, Earley, which, in the Domesday Book, is known as Dead Man's Walk. The footpath is still in Pond Head Lane and it goes to Woodley underneath the railway and underneath the A329M. In earlier times, it was used for carrying the coffins from Arborfield Church to Sonning.

Mr Brown was a pupil at Earley St Peter's School and he particularly remembers being taught by Blanch Annitts who was 6 foot tall and 6 foot round. The children did Maypole Dancing in the Manor (owned by Mr Cook who owned Ideal Casements) opposite Sol Joel Park. One boy who made a mistake was put across Blanch Annitt's knee and spanked in front of everyone. She was an evil woman.

Mr Brown and his father worked on Maiden Erlegh Stud Farm which belonged to Mrs Beatty who bought the Chapel Cottage in Beech Lane for one of her employees. Mr Brown's father had the builder's yard at the bottom of Mill Lane for thirty years.

Some of Mr Brown's memories of local characters: Nelson Bull the coal merchant whose coal yard was in Pond Head Lane for about thirty years and Mr Jack Moles who was the Station Master at Earley. Mr Moles kept an allotment between the railway and the coalyard as well as bees and rabbits.

Dunaways (after which Dunaway's Close was named) Scrap yard was on the corner of Hillside Road and Sutcliffe Avenue. Georgie Dunaway had land on the corner, owned a parrot and lived in a house in the middle of the scrap yard. After the war the land was filled with tanks.

E. Butler

Having spent all my life in east Reading and Earley, I have seen many changes. I well remember being one of the many children from Alfred Sutton Primary School who lined the route when the Duke of York (later to be King George VI) came to open the Sol Joel Playing Field. Subsequently, I spent many happy hours playing on the swings and roundabouts and later on playing tennis. In turn, my children greatly enjoyed these same facilities and then, in their turn, my grandchildren. One of my memories is of being brought up to the gates of the mansion during Ascot week to see the house party returning after a day at the Races. How I admired the ladies' lovely dresses! Oddly enough I never remember any envy, they had their place and we had ours – times change.

Of course, in the 1920s and 1930s Earley was still fairly rural and Church Road was not even made up. As far as I can remember, there was one large house called Maisonette which I believe was occupied by the Dunlop family. Culver Lane was known as Gipsy Lane and there were hedgerows full of dog roses on either side. Again, we children of Alfred Sutton School walked along here and through what is now Whitegates Lane, to form a guard of honour when the Prince of Wales visited Suttons Trial Grounds. I felt very let down over this, as I told my parents on being asked, *Well, did you see him?* I replied *No, he didn't come, they were all just gentlemen.* Obviously I had expected a Prince to be in robes and a coronet as seen in the picture books.

Wokingham Road from the Three Tuns to Loddon Bridge was still rural. There was a large house known as Hungerford Lodge, occupied by Mr and Mrs Percy Colebrook, well known for many years for their lovely shop in Broad Street, where at Christmas time a wonderful array of turkeys and game birds were for sale. No-one of my generation had heard of oven-ready birds. We brought them home, plucked them and drew them ourselves.

When we moved to Allendale Road in 1973, what a pleasure it was to walk along Radstock Lane, past fields of barley, into Gipsy Lane and back. It was an idyll soon to be lost forever under a sea of bricks and mortar. Progress? I wonder.

One building stands supreme still, after over 150 years, St Peter's Church and still a very important part of life for many people. From a little village school, Earley St Peter's has grown into a modern thriving part of the community. St Peter's Hall is home to many organisations and very smart it is, but secretly I treasure memories of the original hall where, as a small child, I was taken at Christmas to the bazaar known as *The Forest of Christmas Trees* where I was given a present of either a book or a toy by Father Christmas.

Mrs Mycock

My husband and I moved into The Cottage, Elm Lane in 1972. The Cottage was built in 1969 in front of old cottages called Coppice Cottage which dated back to the 17th century. They were pulled down when the modern house was completed. The previous occupants were the Franklins who also worked for the Colebrooks. Twelve months after Mr Franklin died we moved in. My husband had been working as a gardener for the Colebrooks since the early sixties at the Spinney and latterly at Hillside House. He also helped with other jobs around the farms.

There was a well in the grounds but we were unable to find it. The Franklin's grandson was a trainee blacksmith in the farm buildings almost opposite The Cottage. I well remember the horses being shod and being trotted up and down the lane.

Ours was a tight knit community. Opposite us were the farm buildings, where the cattle were over wintered, the farrier was next door with Male's Veterinary Surgery behind. Beyond the farrier were two Coppice cottages, a modern bungalow, Rose Cottage a black and white building which was very old and at the end of the lane where the swimming pool is now being built, a lovely detached house that had superb views across the Loddon Valley. Next door to our cottage were Copse House and Copse Lodge, the latter had its own driveway leading onto Radstock Lane. The Colebrook's built Hillside House in 1965–6, about the time that they sold Elm Lane Farm including the Spinney to Reading University.

Members of the Males family, who formerly had a veterinary practice on Friar Street in Reading near where Sainsbury's is now, owned the Vet practice at Westcroft. The lovely late Victorian house, Westcroft, was let out in the 1960s onwards. It was used to make a horror film but we never did see it! I invited Mr Dawson from Trelawney to see if he thought that the blue cedar in front of Westcroft was worthy of saving, whilst we were watching it the contractors pulled it down!

Around the Spinney the two fields were called Little Spinney and Big Spinney, Gun Sight Field (there were two gun emplacements in there during the war) along Elm Lane. Green Lane is now

Chalfont Way alongside ASDA. The field at the back of Redhatch Copse was Spring Meadow.

Hillside House was built in 1965–6 and the inside was influenced by the Spanish home of the Colebrooks. I enjoyed living there, walking the lanes. Mr Colebrook was a very good and generous employer.

We saw muntjac deer in the garden once, we fed foxes and plenty of hedgehogs visited us. We once had the pleasure of watching the vixen and her cubs in the field. It must have been autumn as the cubs were playing on the straw bales.

But this idyll changed on the 1st June 1978 when earthmovers were brought on enormous low loaders along Elm Lane and a hole was punched through the hedge near Westcroft; the ASDA development had started and Elm Lane was blocked for four hours. We had to endure this heavy traffic moving along Elm Lane and up the lane opposite us for months whilst my husband fought to persuade the authorities to put a temporary path across to the site from Cutbush Lane.

Margaret Fairburn, St Peter's School, 1937–1940

I started at St Peter's School in the summer of 1937 when my father's job brought us from the north of England. My first memory of the school is of walking along Church Road on an early summer morning with my mother and sister. It was a quieter and more rural scene than it is now, with the cricket ground on one side and glimpses of green fields between the houses on the other. We crossed the railway bridge, in at the school gate and after my mother had a brief talk with Mr Rutter, the Headmaster, we were in.

So what was the school like in 1937? The area where the present school stands was our playground – a large unpaved area, dry and gritty in the summer, often largely underwater in the winter and divided down the middle by an iron fence. The boys had the half nearest the road and the girls the side alongside Solly Joel's playing field, which in those days had a line of large lime trees.

Here we played hopscotch, skipping and round games like Oranges and Lemons. We swept up the dead flowers from the lime trees into little house plans with doors and gardens and played house.

Meanwhile the boys played football, fought or swirled around the playground in an ever-growing line abreast shrieking, *Does anybody want to join on*? We girls were quite glad of that railing between us sometimes. When a teacher came out and rang the big heavy handbell, we all lined up and marched into the old Victorian school.

What was that like? Well there was one large main classroom which could be divided in two by folding glass doors, a smaller classroom beyond, and two more big classrooms at right angles to the main building. It was in one of these that I spent my first year at the school, and I think it must have been at about this time that three new classrooms were built with a corridor joining them to the main school. During the building, I learned a new word, scaffolding, painfully drummed into me one day when I tore around the corner as you do when you are seven and made violent contact with it with my head and was sent home dazed and bleeding, with a new word in my vocabulary.

My classroom was large and lofty with a pitched beamed roof, painted brick walls and high windows, impossible to see out of without a stepladder. On the windowsills were vases of wildflowers and beans growing in jars of pink blotting paper. The walls were decorated with pictures of wild animals of many lands. I remember especially a fierce Tasmanian Devil with a great red mouth and yellow fangs. I decided definitely not to go to Tasmania.

My teacher's name was Miss Hinckley and I enjoyed her lessons on the whole, although my maths then as now was weak. Our reading books contained extracts from great works of literature. I remember a story about the child Cosette from *Les Miserables* gazing at a doll in a shop window, and a gripping tale from Australia called *Lost in the Bush*.

We had spelling lessons with large pictures draped over the blackboard of high streets and houses and gardens with long lists of words connected with them.

In geography lessons we made models of the Arctic with half-eggshell igloos and little china Eskimo from the Christmas cake sitting on flour snow, or Dutch scenes with little wheelbarrows of red plasticine cheeses. All this delighted us in a way that may seem very simple to a modern child, but we had a long way to go before television brought us natural history programmes and cheap travel brought almost every country in the world within our reach, although I often wonder how much our modern travellers in search of sun, sea and sand know about the places they visit, or even if they know where they are on the map when they get there.

When lessons got boring, one could gaze up at the high windows, and if it was a fine, sunny day imagine that the clouds were standing still and the classroom was a big ship sailing to foreign countries – not Tasmania of course.

We sat at old double wooden desks each furnished with two china inkwells filled with liquid ink, into which we dipped our metal pens, mopping up the excess with blotting paper and little cloth penwipers. Of course at the end of the day a great deal of this ink had transferred itself to our hands, faces and clothes, but there was no alternative, we were going to wait a long time for Mr Biro to come up with his invention.

Our teacher sat facing us at a high desk, the waste paper basket beside her and a few feet away a large coke-burning stove which kept us more or less warm in the winter. The stove was kept burning by Mr Shackleford, the caretaker, an impressive looking elderly man with a big, white moustache, and his entry with a bucket of fuel was a welcome diversion during lessons.

The school toilets were in the far corner of the playground and if anyone asked to be *excused* during a lesson, Miss Hinckley would ask the pupil to knock on Mr Shackleford's door with a request for more coal, and also to tell her the time by the church clock. I am sure that Miss Hinckley had a watch and used these trips for a little practical education, but I usually decided it was better to wait for playtime than to request one of these trips across the playground and risk getting the time wrong.

So my time at St Peter's went on, with new teachers year by year, Miss Grenon, Miss Timms and Mr Fisher, a dark-haired young teacher from South Wales, who read us stories on a Friday afternoon if we had worked well. He sang beautifully and tried to teach us to do the same, but often complained that we were *a whole tone flat*! A new Headmaster arrived, Mr Willoughby, who was a brilliant teacher and got the best out of the older pupils with his enthusiasm and encouragement.

School was much involved with the church with frequent visits from the Vicar, Christmas Carol services in church and the annual celebration of St Peter's Day with a half-holiday.

I do not remember school assemblies, but I still remember the graces we sang at the end of morning and afternoon school:

To God who gives our daily bread,
our thankful song we raise,
And pray that he who gives us food
will fill our hearts with praise.

Then there was a quick dash home for lunch, no school dinners then, although the little bottles of school milk had arrived, not free but costing tuppence-halfpenny per week, and drunk through a natural straw. At the end of afternoon school we sang:

Lord keep us safe this night,
secure from all our fears.
May angels guard us while we sleep,
till morning light appears.

Then there was an amen and a noisy rush for the door and home to tea, or maybe to play on the swings in Solly Joel's and be scolded for arriving home late. Nobody was collected from school in those days, except the five-year-olds. We all ran home together, playing marbles in the gutter if it was the marble season (not to be recommended in today's traffic) still less the game of jumping on the rubber pad in the road to make the lights change at Earley crossroads!

In September 1939, we all came to school with our gasmasks slung around our necks in cardboard boxes and identity bracelets on our wrists in case of air raids while we were at school. There were no air raid shelters at school at the beginning of the war, so a system of dispersing the pupils in an air raid was begun. We were all given a nearby house to run to in the event of a raid and we had several practices. We were told to run to the house and stand quietly on the doorstep till recalled. My house was a pretty house with a large tiled porch at the top of St Peter's Road and I always secretly hoped that the alert might sound one day and I could see the inside of this house and meet my kind hosts, but it never did. Indeed we were very lucky in Reading and had only one serious raid throughout the war.

In 1940 I was eleven years old, and at the end of the summer term I left St Peter's School. My memories of the school are very happy ones, with very clear and vivid memories of the teachers who helped me at such an important stage of my life. Good luck St Peter's and may you have another successful 150 years.

M. Cooper

Until the Gough-Cooper housing estate was built in the early 1960s, Maiden Erlegh House and the surrounding land still had quite a rural feel to it.

The approach to the mansion was along Maiden Erlegh Drive, lined with large houses built between the wars. Its fine dark reddish dome was visible above the trees across the fields from the houses in Beech Lane when we lived there as children in the 1940s. At the bottom of the field behind Beech Lane lay the lake with damp reedy margins, and at the Beech Lane end, a series of little grotto-like caves through which ran the stream which fed the lake. Behind the mansion stood a large stable yard built of black pitch covered timber in the style of barns in Berkshire with mossy red tiled roofs. They were approached from behind the mansion, in the thirties and forties along Betchworth Avenue. Where the new 1960s houses began there was a five-barred gate and a track of maybe 200 yards with fields on either side leading to the stables. The stables lay on the right of the track. On the left, a drive led to substantial redbrick stables and a house occupied by Mr James Black who schooled show Hackney horses.

At the beginning of the Second World War the stables were leased to the Reading Co-op to house the horses and floats which delivered milk to a large surrounding area of Earley and Reading. My father was the Transport Manager so I often went to the stables with him especially at the end of the day when the milk floats were returning, and the great horses being taken out of the shafts and led to the drinking trough in the middle of the stable yard before they were relieved of their harness and groomed in the luxurious stables where Solly Joel's racehorses had once been housed. It was a wonderful sight to see these working horses, literally in a lather after a hard days work being groomed and fed and watered by the stablemen led by Mr Dave Rodger, who in his earlier life had a successful career showing horses.

None of this, the lovely farm buildings, the beautiful working horses, which nowadays would be a heritage sight worthy of a Sunday afternoon visit, impressed the then residents of Betchworth Avenue – they complained of the clip-clopping of the early rising milk horses for disturbing their slumber! I wonder which the current residents of Betchworth Avenue would prefer today – the horses or the endless stream of cars.

In the field to the right of the track near the stables was quite a large round pond. I wonder what happened to that. In the stable block there was also a forge where a blacksmith came regularly to shoe the horses and behind it, a little cemetery of sporting dogs, all with their named headstones.

Around the mansion, at that time being run as a private boys' school, were fields and rides, now covered by roads and houses, where I used to ride my grey mare Pat nearly every day, and where I now walk my border terrier.

Anyone returning to Earley after a long absence would, of course, be amazed by the changes that have happened in the last thirty to forty years but would be so pleased to see the lake and the woods being so well looked after and so much enjoyed by everyone.

Mrs B. A. Brooks

Rose covered cottage, York stone bungalow and countryside abounding... the family's dream for retirement. In reality, in 1964 my parents moved to a semi-detached house in Earley, lovingly nick-named by us as *The Dolls House.*

Having scoured the Southern counties for the ideal home, we returned to my mother's roots. A number of strong ties drew us back; my grandparents lived in Southampton Street, a three story Victorian house with my grandfather's barber shop below. Sadly, that house has now made way for offices.

My parents were married in St Giles Church and, during the war, members of my mother's family lived in both Purley and Woodley. The aerodrome was very much in existence then and the drone of aircraft was commonplace.

Some holidays were in Purley with my aunt and, as a small child, I loved our trips into the centre of Reading ... running up and down the paths at St Mary Butts, calling our names under the tunnel in Forbury Gardens, laughing at the echoes, hearing the voices of the prisoners in Reading Jail, paddling in the Thames at Purley. Despite the war, these were joyous days. Returning to live in Earley brought back all these memories and it was moving to return to places that I had not seen since I was a small child.

My uncle was a builder in Woodley and procured a plot of land in Earley, building two houses. One of these was then to be our home. Other than past thoughts, one of the reasons we liked the area was that there were so many contrasting features. Designs of many of the houses in the road varied considerably, countryside close by and yet public amenities within a short distance.

When we moved to Earley in 1964, walks to green fields were only a matter of minutes away... no supermarket, no motorway. Local shops thrived in Silverdale Road, the butchers, bakers, greengrocers and general store.

The consternation that abounded with the news of the motorway was very evident. However, it was a relief when people realised that it would be more of an asset than an inconvenience.

Trips along Mill Lane and Gypsy Lane to reach the motorway in the early mornings were often fraught as, with heavy rain, the ditches filled quickly and the lanes became flooded. However, the days of no streetlights and country lanes were far more preferable than the busy roads and built up areas we all experience today.

During the first years in Earley I spent weekends with my family, travelling down from Waterloo. I fondly recall when returning to Earley Station on Sunday evenings, the gas lamps being lit and, in the winter, a roaring fire in the waiting room. It created a mysterious aura, reminding me of the film *Brief Encounter* and it was with sadness that we witnessed the demise of gas lighting.

Having both the lake and the University grounds within a short distance has been a bonus, but fewer people in the 1960s enjoyed the lake. It became almost as if it was one's private property. Taking friends' children down there, it was fun to explore. Scrambling down slopes to come across large clumps of kingcups, knees that got covered in mud and were quickly washed before returning home. (And that was me!) On one occasion we were fortunate enough to see a kingfisher, its beautiful colours holding us spellbound.

In the 1960s there was a stream emanating from a pond in Beech Lane, running past the bottom of our garden, eventually leading into the lake. Sadly this has now dried up but it has left us with the legacy of a number of quite friendly toads that visit our garden.

Again, walking through the University grounds in the spring one can forget the built up area that lies just outside the perimeter; although the roads then were far less busy than they are today. Having, over the years, watched houses being built, gardens that are now mature, there still remains a rural atmosphere. Also we have the improvements to the lake, the gardens full of colour from spring to autumn and yet modern amenities close to hand. I have and, hopefully, shall continue to enjoy Earley past and present for many years to come.

Ruth Coles

My father lost his own farm during the 1930s agricultural depression and so was employed running Lower Wood Farm. We were there about 1932–6. My mother thinks that it belonged to Red Hatch Farm, but it later was part of the Shinfield Grange estate. Further questioning of my mother reveals that the farmer at Red Hatch was a tenant of the Palmers; Lower Wood was part of his farm, and young stock was raised there for his dairy herd. We walked to Red Hatch farm each day to collect milk. We had a suckler herd and a few pigs and poultry. My mother says that the house was built in 1666 (date over the front door) and that the big walnut tree was planted at the same time. Water was from a hand pump in the scullery. The older section, at the left-hand side of the picture (page 79) was used for shooting party lunches – I think by the Palmers – from time to time, but I think my mother had to make tea. There was a terrace of five or six cottages on the Shinfield side of Mrs Quelche's cottage – one was a printer's workshop.

I remember snakeshead fritillaries growing in a water meadow by the old Arborfield church.

We went to Reading by bus from the Merry Maidens having walked up Beech Lane past Mr Black's stables. We very occasionally walked to Earley St Peter's, but it was a long walk. I didn't start school until we moved to Old House Farm, Shinfield, and we went to St Mary's, Shinfield. Much later, during the war, my father's WWI wound meant we had to leave farm work altogether. He became a milk recorder. We had to leave our tied house, and live in rooms – first in Loddon Bridge Road, possibly no. 544 and later in Meadow Road, Earley with Mr Wyer. We were there in 1946, on VE Day. Then we were able to buy a house in Reading.

Ruth Coles with her parents in front of the farm buildings at Lowerwood Farm, 1935.

Michael Holt

By 1933 large parts of the Erleigh Court Estate had been sold to builders for development. My mother and father bought one of the first houses to be available in Erleigh Court Gardens from the builder James McClelland. For them the mortgage on a property worth about £550 represented a considerable investment and involved much sacrifice for many years.

My father was employed at Huntley and Palmer's and my mother before her marriage worked as a secretary at Knills a local printing firm. They both lived in the Newtown area in Reading and in planning the move to what is now North Earley, they were following a mobility trend for movement outside the Borough boundary to secure a three-bedroom house. I recall their memories of first moving into the house when it was still surrounded by fields and when the white gates at the entrance to the drive to the mansion house were still in place even though Erleigh Court had been demolished. Sidmouth Grange itself continued to exist for many years and the local bus stop at the junction of The Drive and the A4 was always until recent years described in timetables as Whitegates.

Although their house had gas, water and electricity upon occupation there was no surface water drainage or foul main drainage. This appeared to be because of a lack of a local infrastructure. Surface water drains were installed in the road in about 1938 and the work caused much concern because not only did the then concrete road bear the scars of the excavation for many years to come but also the much loved ornamental trees on the grass verges were destroyed by the digging equipment and never replaced. The work was accompanied by a hut for the night watchman who cooked his breakfast on the coke fire. Whatever happened to night watchmen?

The lack of a foul drainage system meant that for many years each house had at the bottom of its garden a cesspit which had to be emptied frequently by the District Council. The need for the emptying was notified by means of a postcard being posted to Shute End at Wokingham. The main drainage network planned for the area was clearly delayed because of the outbreak of war in 1939. However early in 1946 the District Council embarked on the installation of the sewers. The construction work was carried out by a firm called French and Co. and in the early days of the scheme the manual labour force was provided by German prisoners of war. Before the scheme was completed they were replaced by an Irish work force and some quite sophisticated equipment. Connections to the main sewer were the responsibility of each householder and it was not until about 1948 that these were completed and the fleet of Dennis sewage emptying vehicles owned by Wokingham Rural District Council became redundant.

However life in Erleigh Court Gardens in the period from 1933 until 1939 appeared to be idyllic. There was a mix of young and older families in sparkling new houses and a feeling of belonging as part of a new community was created. At the junction of the road with the Drive stood a telephone kiosk and a post box, both still exist in modern form in the same location, but are subject to frequent vandalism.

Only two houses in the road possessed private telephones, and the public facility with its buttons A and B to push and a set of directories was much used.

A policeman in uniform would cycle down the road each day and stand outside the telephone box from 11am to 12 noon! At 2pm each day in the summer, except Sunday, the Walls Ice Cream vendor with his *stop me and buy one* logo would appear on his three wheeled pedal driven vehicle and ring his cycle bell to attract attention. A representative from the Reading firm of Baylis would call once a week to take the grocery order and this would be delivered in the brown van on Fridays. At least four dairies served the area as well as bakers and butchers in their vans or horse drawn carts.

Just around the corner there were four shops and two more within walking distance at the top of the road. These included a newsagent, grocery and provision stores, post office, chemist and a wool and baby clothes store.

The adjacent Southern Railway lines were being equipped with a third rail and an electrified service started to run from Waterloo to Reading Station in the late thirties. Also from May 1939 a gleaming new fleet of trolley buses appeared. These were provided by Reading Borough in place of trams but turned at Liverpool Road as they were not allowed to operate outside the Borough boundary! However above all the excitement about modern and clean forms of public transport appeared the dark clouds of war.

Mrs Elsie Parlour

Until the 1920s only very rich people bought their own homes, then almost overnight developers started to build estates all around London and large towns. They were nearly all semi-detached at around £500.

I came to live in Earley in 1933 in one of the first to be built in Erleigh Court Gardens, so named because they were being built in the kitchen gardens of Erleigh Court.

It was just off the A4 which at that time was a fairly quiet road, although it was the main road from London to Bath. There were no roundabouts or dual carriageways. The trial grounds of Sutton and Sons was a blaze of colour every year. Not Suttons Seeds as it is wrongly referred to now.

All around was open country, lovely walks along footpaths, over stiles, by streams and through woods. It is all gone now except South Lake in Woodley and High Wood. I sometimes think that London has more open space and parks than around here.

We were very fortunate during the war when a German plane dropped a number of bombs which landed not as intended on the railway but harmlessly in the gardens of our houses.

We were not so fortunate in 1970 when I and the family were living in Mays Lane, we and several hundred other people had our homes flattened so that Berkshire County Council could build the A329M.

Norman A. Parlour added that unfortunately several workmen, I think it was four, were killed when the formework for the bridge over the Loddon collapsed when the concrete was being poured throwing the workmen and tons of concrete into the river.

Graham Parlour: I was born in Erleigh Court Gardens in February 1945. I remember seeing a look-out shelter for looking out at London Road and the railway line at Suttons Seeds, for any war time invasion about the area. When I moved up to Mays Lane, Mays Cottages were standing at the end by the railway, further around in now Courts Road there were tennis courts and a wooded area behind the tennis courts. At the corner of Mays Lane there was a garage called The Blue Garage. On High Tree Drive was Reading Cricket Ground where many a famous cricketer has played, such as Ken Barrington. At the bottom of Maiden Erlegh Drive was the mansion which had been owned by Sol Joel, I remember looking around it before it was sold and pulled down. At the lowest point in Beech Lane there were some flint caves which were used as icehouses. At Earley Station there was a house standing to the entrance to South and North Lake Estate which has now been pulled down. There were houses at the top of Pond Head Lane and also on the top of the hill into Woodley, and they too have now been pulled down.

Maureen Baggaley

The land near Loddon Bridge now occupied by a Garden Centre was a centre for recreation before the war.

The Loddon Swimming Club had a clubhouse holding dances on Saturday nights, two or three tennis courts and swimming fixtures, training and water-polo being held in the river.

A group of the members were in the Territorial Army and were called up for service in August 1939.

During the war the club closed and on returning after the war the old members then formed the Reading Swimming Club.

After the war the clubhouse, now derelict, went and various tea-rooms and cafes opened on the site.

The following memories are taken from various publications

Leonard Quelch *(taken from an article in the* Evening Post *of 30.5.84)*

I was born at Hurst in 1917 and lived with my mother and grandparents in cottages near Lower Wood Farm where my grandfather was head cowman for Mr George Hatch. In those days, the area was little changed from when the farmhouse was built centuries earlier. Before I was 10 I worked in the fields for Mr Hatch and I was a beater when Mr Eric Palmer held shooting parties on his land at Lower Earley.

I went to Earley St Peter's Church of England school when I was five and left at 14 to help on a milk round in the Earley – Woodley area. I was a very active lad and ran the two miles to school and then ran home when lessons were over. I remember that Miss Gash was the first teacher in the infants and Mr F. J. Rutter was the headmaster when I left. Mr Rutter did not approve of the milk round job: he wanted me to be trained as a stonemason. In 1939 Mr Rutter became the first headmaster of Woodley Secondary Modern School and he will still be remembered by many who went to St Peter's and at the school at Loddon Bridge Road, Woodley.

At school I took part in maypole and sword dancing and excelled at soccer. I became captain of the school football team and still have a photograph in which I am proudly wearing a captain's badge on my jacket lapel. I was also selected to play for the Berks and Bucks FA boys' team. Another youthful interest was fishing in the Loddon, which flowed at the bottom of the farm garden. I remember that when the river flooded the farmhouse was surrounded by water.

In 1940 I was called up to serve in the Devonshire Regiment. Later I worked for Adwest Engineering at Woodley for 19 years until I retired more than a year ago.

I lived in the Lower Earley area in the 1920s and 1930s when there were no public roads from Cutbush Lane to the River Loddon. I recently visited the area after a thirty-year gap and was not prepared for the disappearance of the meadows and other landmarks I knew as a boy. I found difficulty in getting around the biggest private scheme for housing, shops, offices and industry in Europe.

Reminders of the rural past were few in the development. Car-cluttered closes had replaced the cattle and cornfields.

It was a different world from the one I remembered.

Harry Chapple *(first published in 1969 in the* Reading Chronicle*)*

My recollections go back to before I left Earley National School [Earley School]. I was born in Earley, my father was signalman at Earley Station and we lived for a number of years in a bungalow in Ginger Terrace, on the Wokingham Road.

I used to go over the rear of Maiden Erlegh Terrace and watch the racing when meetings were held on the Course which extended over an area now covered by Hillside Road, Sutcliffe Avenue and Mill Lane.

About 1903 Maiden Erlegh Estate was bought by Mr Sol Joel from a Mr Hargreaves. Soon after the purchase a Croydon firm started working on the estate. Apart from redecoration, they laid a drainage system with filter beds and built stabling and garages. They also cleaned the lake and built an island in the centre, then they built a powerhouse.

The Clerk of Works was a Mr Will Toogood. After all the work was completed, Mr Toogood started in business on his own. His works were on the corner of Belle Avenue and Whiteknights Road. When I left school in 1906, I worked as an electrician's mate and assisted in the wiring of the Stud

Farm at Lower Earley. We ran an underground cable from the power station at Maiden Erlegh to the farm across the lawn's side of the lake and through the paddock. About this time the old Maiden Erlegh racecourse was given up. With others, I dismantled the grandstand, marking the sections and loading them on to three trucks which were towed away by a steam traction engine.

The old stand was to be re-erected on Newbury Racecourse. But rather in the manner of the old style comedy, things did not turn out quite as planned. They had trouble getting the dismantled stand underneath the telephone wires at the course entrance and the driver of the traction engine was fined for causing a smoke nuisance.

Then came a change of job – though still close to home. I became an assistant at the powerhouse. The plant consisted of two horizontal steam engines, two Newton dynamos and a chloride battery. The whole place was kept spotlessly clean; all copper and brass highly polished and lino on the floors.

On special occasions, when Mr Joel came down, we had to run during the evenings – especially the Sunday before race meetings, when there was a large party, including all the racing nobility. A large marquee was erected on the lawn and wired for lighting. Mr Joel used to show his friends around the powerhouse and always had a friendly chat with me. He was very generous to his employees and when he had a good win he always gave an extra week's wages.

I remember when Mr Hutt, the head coachman and chauffeur, was returning from Mr Joel's London residence and saw the stables of *The George* at Loddon Bridge on fire. This was the chance they had been waiting for. He picked up Mr Chapman, Mr Smith and myself and we brought the engine to the fire. I was the stoker. The Wokingham Brigade turned up as well. When everything was brought under control, the landlord brought out food and drinks and we completed a very pleasant evening's work. This was the only time to my knowledge that the engine was used. The insurance company also rewarded us for our services.

Every year Mr Joel gave the Earley School pupils a treat at Maiden Erlegh. There was tea, swings, roundabouts, coconut shies and entertainment.

Mr Joel, of course, donated the Sol Joel Playing Field – opened by the Duke of York (later King George VI). Also there was a luxury swimming bath panelled in marble. The water was heated by a boiler which was my job to look after.

I left Mr Joel's service about 1912, when a diesel engine replaced the old steam power in the plant. I saw the old steam plant taken out and towed away; the old, faithful friends which had given such good service for at least ten years were scrapped. Never to my knowledge had they caused any trouble.

I went back to work again for Mr Toogood. But not for very long on this occasion. The First World War was just around the corner. I volunteered for service and eventually joined the Royal Flying Corps as an Air Mechanic.

I had always been interested in aircraft. After being de-mobilised in 1919, I returned to work for Mr Toogood. Shortly after his return, Mr Joel's diesel, the one which had replaced the steam engine at the plant, broke down and I was one of those who came to his rescue.

We approached a Major Ingram, whose residence was at the top of Wilderness Road. He had an electric plant at the corner of Wilderness Road and Beech Lane. Major Ingram was only too pleased to help out. We ran overhead cables across the road on trees to the power plant and, by this means, we were able to keep a certain number of lights going and charge the battery.

Another amusing incident that I recall was the time that the windmill at Maiden Erlegh developed trouble and a new bearing had to be sent from Canada. When eventually it arrived, myself and a colleague had the job of fitting it. Unfortunately, my colleague dropped the bearing into a pond. There was just a round hole in the green slime where the bearing had submerged. Mr Toogood arrived and was not too pleased about what had happened. However, he borrowed a boiler suit and went into the pool to recover the missing bearing. After several attempts he managed to find it.

After I left Mr Toogood's employment I went to work for Cox and Sons, electrical engineers and builders.

Throughout the Second World War I worked again in the aircraft industry, this time for Miles Aircraft. My last employers were Duran and Co. of King's Road, Reading. I retired in 1963.

It is, however, to those old days in Maiden Erlegh that I look back with most interest.

May Day at Earley St Peters *(extract from* Berkshire Within Living Memory *produced by the Berkshire Federation of Women's Institutes)*

The crowning of a May Queen, maypole dancing, English country dancing and Morris dancing, were a part of school life at Earley for many years, until 1958.

A May Queen was chosen by secret vote of all children in the third and fourth year juniors at St Peter's school from the fourth year girls. She had six attendants (girls) from her own age group, and four boys, one of whom was the herald, and four little flower girls chosen from the first year juniors. Parents provided long white dresses.

In the weeks before and immediately after Easter, each class learnt a country dance to perform on May Day, which was usually held on a Tuesday at the end of May in the Manor House gardens, by kind permission of the owners. Even the youngest infants performed a simple dance and to the top infants was given the privilege of maypole dancing. The girls wore long dresses and the boys wore smocks and felt hats – owned by the school. These young children took their dancing very seriously and wove the intricate patterns with, sometimes, heartstopping accuracy. In addition the older boys performed traditional Morris dancing, taught by the headmaster.

On the morning of May Day, children could be seen coming to school laden with armfuls of garden flowers. These [flowers] soon filled baskets with long round handles or made circlets for the attendants' head-dresses. The weather always seemed to be beautiful.

Chairs were carried across the road and set out on the Manor House lawn, a piano was trundled out and the children dressed in their prettiest summer frocks or clean white shirts went across, class by class, ready for the march past. The Queen was crowned usually by a local dignitary and the dancing demonstration began. It was a wonderful day for children, teachers and parents who flocked to the ceremonies. I cannot now remember whether the march past opened or closed the afternoon but every child took part.

12 Earley – the Future

And what of the future?

Transport: A new station is promised for the Thames Valley Park. All important routes through Earley in the past have been east-west but that may change if a bridge is built across the Thames taking the A329M into Oxfordshire and so relieving the mediaeval bridge in Sonning. Our roads are very full and many different methods are being tried to improve matters. Attempts are being made to slow down traffic, to discourage the use of cars for short journeys, to increase cycling lanes and to encourage walking. We can only hope that, as our roads become quieter and more attractive to walk along, we can follow in the steps of Mary Mitford!

Housing: Almost all of the available land within the boundaries of Earley has been built on. A few houses will be squeezed in and extensions added to existing houses.

The Population: In the 20th century the population increased dramatically from a few hundred to over thirty thousand. We assume that it will remain constant.

Community Facilities: At the end of the 20th century new facilities included a new police station, cinema and skate park and in the first years of the new millennium a swimming pool, water sports centre by the Thames and a new community building (Crescent) are being completed.

Environment: Over the past half century the fields and meadows have become covered with roads and houses. The Town Council is concerned that the remaining wildlife habitats and open spaces should be preserved and where possible improved. To this end the council has restored the Oakwood wildflower meadow and the Maiden Erlegh Environmental Interpretation Centre has been built. Hedgerows and roadside verges give shelter to a variety of wildlife and these are being maintained so that they can provide suitable habitats; the verges can be cut less often and hedgerows can be restored and new ones planted. Residents can also become more aware of their environment and provide suitable habitats in their gardens.

Official opening of
The Interpretation Centre,
Maiden Erlegh Nature Reserve,
4 November 2000.
left to right:
Grahame Hawker *(Senior Ranger)*,
Richard Raymond *(Town Clerk)*,
Helen Bowden *(Ranger)*,
John Davies *(Placement student)*,
Alan Hughes (partially hidden) *(Electrician)*,
Dominic Murphy *(Builder)* and
Paul Ferdinand *(Architect)*

References

Reference List

PRO Public Records Office
BRO Berkshire Records Office
RLSL Reading Local Studies Library
VCH Victoria County History

Personal Communications

Pettitt, J. 1998 *Oral account given by Mr J. Pettitt*
Pettitt, J. Topography of Earley, written account unpublished
Rowley, G. 1999 Written account

Primary Sources

A rate granted to Mr Nathan Goddard the Overseer of Earley in the Parish of Sonning from Easter to Michaelmas 1801 at 4/4 in the pound rents BRO/DP113/12/15

Appointment of Overseers BRO/DP113/18/4

Beating the Bounds BRO D/EDO E23

Census returns 1841–1891 RLSL

Draft Tithe Map 1844 BRO D/EZCo P2

1820 Enclosure Award for the Liberty of Earley BRO D/R113/26C

Enclosure of Earley 1742 BRO D/EDO E33

Lay Subsidy Rolls PRO E179/73/121–141

Loddon Bridge Toll Gate. Windsor Forest Turnpike Trust BRO D/EGL/O1

Parish of Earley, Charity Accounts containing an account of Barker's Charity, Englefield Charity, Earley Poor's Land Allotment 1853–1902, Earley Charity, Liberty of Earley House

Poll of Recusants for 1657 in Berkshire BRO EN/1/2/12

Release and Sale of Brickneys House 1689 BRO D/EZ 7/21

Removal Orders BRO D/P 113/13/1

Removal Orders BRO D/P 113/13/2

Removal Orders BRO D/P 113/12/1

Settlement Certification BRO D/P29/13/4/39

Sonning Parish Records. Baptisms 1603–1828, microfiche, RLSL

Survey of the Parish of Sonning 1617 BRO D/EZ 38/1

Tithe Apportionment in the Survey of Sonning 1773 and 1783 BRO

Will of Richard Smith BRO D/A1/122/129

Wokingham Union Minutes Book 1836–38 BRO G/WO/1

Wokingham Union Minutes Book 1846–49 BRO G/WO/4

Wokingham Union Minutes Book 1849–51 BRO G/WO/5

Maps

Draft Tithe Map 1844 BRO D/EZCO P2

Enclosure Map of the Liberty of Earley BRO D/P/113/26a

Map of Earley by the cartographer Edward Blagrave. 1669 RLSL

Map of Earley Meads (late 18th) BRO D/EDO/P3

Map of the Manor of Whiteknights. 1826 copy of a 1756 map by Josiah Ballard BRO D/EBb/P1

Ordnance Survey 1:25000 scale 1870

Ordnance Survey Explorer 159 1:25000 scale 1998

Ordnance Survey Series One Inch

Pride, T. 1790, *A Topographical map of the Town of Reading the County adjacent to an extent of ten miles*

Rocque, J. 1761, *Survey of Berkshire* (2nd and 3rd sheets) RLSL

Sonning Enclosure Award BRO Q/RDC 97A

Directories

Kelly's Directory 1930

Kelly's Directory 1936

Kelly's Directory 1940

Rusher's Reading Guide and Berkshire Directory 1807 *VII*

Snare's Berkshire Directory 1847

Newspaper articles

Advertisement for Leighton Park, *The Times* 24th June 1886

An ancient economic centre, *Reading Mercury* 1936

The Town Council have an earth hunger, *Berkshire Chronicle,* 16 and 30 October 1886

Boundary changes – So Parish Doubles in Size, *Reading Chronicle* 18 October 1985

Bridge Disaster, *Berkshire Mercury*, 26 October 1972

Burying a problem on site, *Evening Post,* August 1988

Cattle Markets, *Reading Mercury,* 30 May 1840

Daily Mail Weekend, 5 February 2000

Dormer, E.W., The White knight, *Reading Mercury,* 2 July 1904

Dormer, E. W., Perpetual Rent Charge, *Reading Mercury* 15 March 1930

Interview with Harry Chapple, *Reading Chronicle,* 11 April 1969

Interview with May Staley, *Reading Chronicle,* 21 October 1983

Howlett, C., Earley in the last fifty years, *Reading Mercury,* compiled by E. M. Tull, 1937, RLSL

Leonard Quelch, interview, *Evening Post,* 30 May 1984

Maiden Erlegh Spring Steeple Chases, *Berkshire Chronicle,* 7 February and 7 March 1903

Malcolm, D., *The Times,* 1931, RLSL

Repeal of Corn Laws, *Berkshire Chronicle*, 1855, 19 May

Review of the volunteer corps of Berkshire on Bullmarsh-Heath, July 26, *Reading Mercury,* 27 July 1799

Solly Joel's Old Place, *Reading Chronicle,* 2 June 1978

Suttons Seeds site – plan for factory causes uproar, *Berkshire Mercury,* 5 May 1977

Underhill, F. M., History of Earley Parts 1, 2, 3, 4 and final part, *Reading Chronicle* 20, 1981

Journals

Antiquarian Notes of Berkshire, 1885 *1* RLSL

Berkshire Archaeological Journal, 1960, Hand Axe, *58,* 52

Berkshire Archaeological Society Journal, 1911, 17

Dormer, E. W., 1927, The Ancient Common Fields and Common Mead of Earley, *Berkshire Archaeological Journal,* 31, 193–198

Dormer, E. W., 1931, Mockbeggar Farm, Earley, Reading, *Berkshire Archaeology Journal,* 36, 81–85

Electrician, 1943, Obituary: Baron Hugo Hirst, 1943, January

Entomological News, 1923, Obituary: Canon W. W. Fowler, xxxiv, October

Entomologist's Monthly Magazine, 1923, In Memoriam, The Rev W. W. Fowler, 1923 July

Harris, W., 1977, Maiden Erlegh Fifty Years Ago, *Maiden Erlegh Residents' Association Newsletter*

Hatherly, J. M., Carter, L.M., 1979–80, The Medieval Parks of Berkshire, *Archaeological Journal,* 70, 67–80

Pettitt, J., 1985, The Hamlet of Little Hungerford, *Berkshire Old and New,* 2, 16–19

Pollock, C. K., 1911, The Manor of Earley Regis otherwise Earley Whiteknights in the County of Berks, *Berkshire Archaeological Journal*, 17, 59–62

Prior, G., 1972, Canon W. W. Fowler, 1848–1923, *Amateur Entomological Society Bulletin*, 31

Rutland, R. A., Greenway, J. A., 1970, *Archaeological Notes from Reading Museum*, 65, 4

The Entomologist, 1923, Obituary: Canon W. W. Fowler LVI, August

Sonning Parish Magazine, Centenary Edition, July 1969

Tate, W. E.,1943, A Handful of English Enclosure Acts and Awards relating to Land in Berkshire, *Berkshire Archaeological Journal*, 42, 56–90

Books

Alexander, A., 1985, *Borough Government and Politics: Reading 1835–1985*, London: George Allen and Unwin

Ayres, V., 1988, *Stupid as Oxen*

Barnes, I., Butterworth, C. A., Hawkes, J. W. and Smith, L., Excavations at Thames Valley Park, Reading 1986–88, 1997, *Wessex Archaeology Report*, No 14

Benham, 1843, *Benham Excursions to Reading and Berkshire*, Enclosure Acts MSS, Volume II part 1

Boyd, D., 1978, *The Running Horses – A Brief History of Racing in Berkshire from 1740*, Berkshire County Libraries

Bricks and Mortals: Story of Reading's Buildings, 1994, Reading: Corridor Press

Butts, D., 1980, Barbara Hofland, 1770–1844, M Phil Thesis, University of Sheffield

Caird, J., 1851, *English Agriculture in 1850–51*

Clayton, W., *The Earley Years. The story of the formation of the Earley Home Guard Social Club, 1944–1966*

Coates, C., 1802, *The History and Antiquities of Reading*, RLSL

Coates, C., 1810, *A Supplement to the History and Antiquities of Reading*, RLSL

Cobbett, W., 1967, *Rural Rides 1822–1830*, Harmondsworth, Middlesex: Penguin Books

Dils, J., 1998, *Atlas of Berkshire*, Reading: BRO

Doble, 1961, *History of Shinfield*, RLSL

Dormer, E. W., 1912, *Erleigh Court and its Owners*, Reading: G. A. Poynder

Dormer, E. W., 1944, *The Parish and Church of Saint Peter, Earley*, Reading: C. Nicholls

Endowed Charities, London: HMSO 1910

Farrar, H., 1984, *The Book of Hurst*, Buckingham: Barracuda Books

Gelling, M., 1972, *Place Names of Berkshire*, Cambridge: English Place-Name Society

Hanna, L., 1994, *The Story of Earley St Peter's*, Earley, Reading: St Peter's PCC

Hawes, H. (Compiler), 1999, *A History of the Shinfield Players and the Shinfield Players Theatre*

Hobson, W. (Ed), 1995, *Newton, Reading The Inside Story*, Reading: Newtown Local History Project

Hofland, B., 1819, *A Descriptive Account of the Mansion and Gardens of Whiteknights, A Seat of His Grace the Duke of Marlborough, with illustrations by T. Hofland*, T. Hofland

Holt, J. C., 1977, *The University of Reading*, Reading: University of Reading

Homer-Woof, G. H. R. and Jones, P. J., 1981, *Postal History of Reading Volume 1*, Reading RLSL

Homer-Woof, G. H. R. and Jones, P. J., 1982, *Postal History of Reading Volume 2*, Reading RLSL

Hurry, J. B., 1901, *A Guide to Reading Abbey*, Reading: RLSL

Hylton, S., 1996, *Reading at War*, Bodmin, Cornwall: Alan Sutton Publishing Ltd

Leadam, I. S. (Editor), 1897, *The Domesday of Inclosures 1517–1518*, London: Longmans, Green and Co

Lloyd, F., 1977, *Woodley in the 19th Century*, Reading: Reading Libraries

Lynch, D., 1989, *Chariots of the Gospel: The Centenary History of the Church Army*

Maggs, C. G., 1993, *Branch Lines of Berkshire*, Berkshire Books

Man, J., 1810, *The Stranger in Reading. Letters from a traveller to his friend in London*, RLSL

Mavor, W. 1809, *A General View of the Agriculture of Berkshire*. In: The Victoria History of the County of Berkshire, vol. 1

Mayer, L., 1958, *Ace of Diamonds: The Story of Solomon Barnato Joel*, London: F. Muller Ltd

Meaney, A., 1964, A gazeteer of early Anglo-Saxon Burial sites

Morris, J. (General Editor), 1979, *Phillimore Edition of Domesdsay Book. Volume 5 Berkshire (Morgan P County Editor)*, Chichester: Phillimore and Co Ltd

Mullaney, J., 1987, *St James Catholic Church and School in the Abbey Ruins, Reading*, Reading: Caversham Bookshop, St James' Parish

Perkins, A., 1977, *A Book of Sonning: The Story of an English Village*, Chesham: Barracuda Books Ltd

Phillips, D., 1980, *The Story of Reading,* Newbury, Berkshire: Countryside Books, revised 1990

Phillips, D. (editor), 1985, *Reminiscences of Reading: An Octagenarian*, Newbury, Berkshire: Countryside Book

Rackham, O., 1993, *Trees and Woodland in the British Landscape,* London: Weidenfeld and Nicolson

Robertson, 1840, *A Tour Round Reading,* RLSL

Robinson, S. C., 1947, *Earley S. Nicolas – the Story of the Building of a Church*

Rudd, J. and Rudd, S., 1990, *A Village Post Office,* Twyford, Berkshire: Twyford and Ruscombe Local History Society

Rylands, W. H. (Editor), 1907, *The four Visitations of Berkshire*, PRO

Scott, V. G. and McLaughlin, E., 1984, *County Maps and Histories Series, Berkshire*

Simonds, E. M., 1985, *The Woodley Album*, Reading: Coles and Sons Publishers Ltd

Smith, E., 1957, *The History of Whiteknights,* Reading: University of Reading

Soames, M., 1987, *The Profligate Duke,* London: Collins

The Monumental Inscriptions of Reading Cemetery Berkshire 1843–1995, Berkshire Family History Society, 1997

The Past in progress: The Archaeology of the Thames Valley Business Park, Salisbury, Wiltshire: Trust for Wessex Archaeology, 1991

The Victoria History of the County of Berkshire, vol. 1, *Geology and Agriculture*, London: St Catherine's Press, 1923

The Victoria History of the County of Berkshire, vol. 3, *Sonning Hundred,* London: St Catherine's Press, 1923

Verey, A., Sampson, S., French, A. and Frost, S., 1994, *The Berkshire Yeomanry: 200 years of Yeoman Service,* Bodmin, Cornwall: Allan Sutton Publishing Ltd

Waters, L., 1990, *Rail Centres*, Shepperton, Surrey: Ian Allan Ltd

Watts, E., 1998, *Copybooks to Computers: A Celebration of 150 years of Earley St Peter's School,* Earley, Reading: Governors, Earley St Peter's School

Young, F. A. Jr, 1979, *Guide to the Local Administrative Units of England*, vol. 1, *Southern England*, London: Royal Historical Society

(Some of these references are available at the Offices of Earley Town Council)

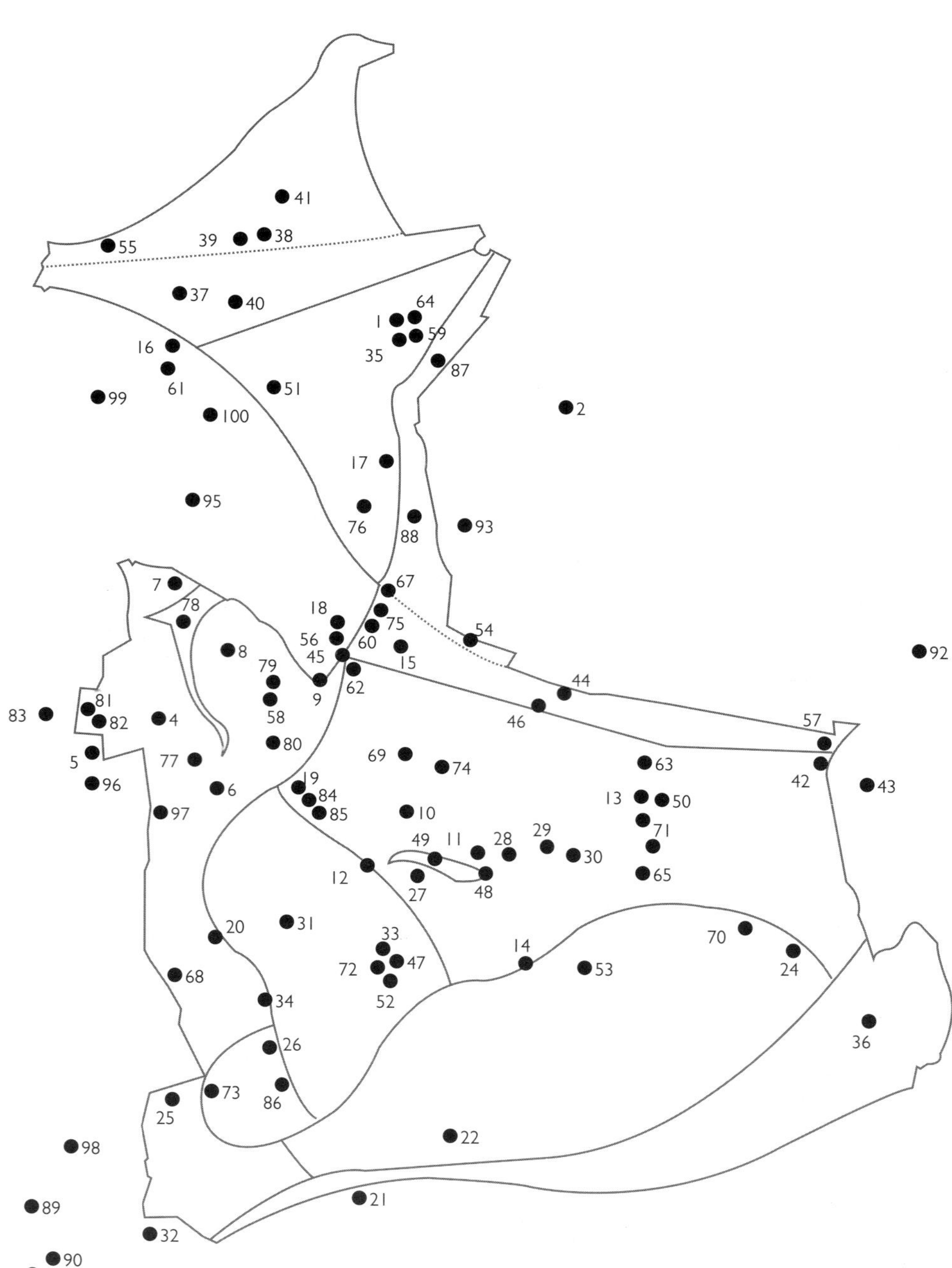

Location Map

Map showing the location of many of the features referred to throughout the book.
Scale 1 : 25000

Key to Location Map

Chapter 3: Earley's Manors and Estates

1 Erleigh Court (*site of*)
2 Bulmershe Court (*site of*)
3 Whiteknights House
4 Whiteknights Park House
5 Blandford Lodge
6 The Wilderness House (*site of*)
7 Foxhill House
8 Erlegh Park House (*site of*)
9 The Gate Lodges (*listed buildings*)
10 Maiden Erlegh House (*site of*)
11 Ice House (*site of*)
12 Flint Grotto (*site of*)
13 Maiden Erlegh Racecourse (*site of*)
14 Maiden Erlegh Stud Farm (New Farm) (*site of*)
15 Sol Joel Park

Chapter 4: Earley's Development

Land use

16 New Farm (*site of*)
17 Larkins Farm (*site of*)
18 Earley Heath Farm (*now* the Manor House)
19 Home Farm (*site of*)
20 Elm Farm (*site of*)
21 Upper Farm (Upper Wood Farm)
22 Lower Earley Farm (Lower Wood Farm) (Rushey Mead)
23 Marsh Farm (*site of*)
24 Sindlesham Farm (*site of*)
25 Hillside Farm
26 Coppice Farm (*site of*)
27 Oakwood
28 Old Pond Copse
29 Moor Copse
30 Old Lane Wood
31 Redhatch Copse
32 Pearmans Copse
33 Radstock Cottages (*Listed building*)
34 The Spinney
35 Sidmouth Grange (formerly Earley Court Farm) (*site of*)

Industry

36 Sindlesham Mill
37 Sutton's (*site of*)
38 Earley Power Station (*site of*)
39 Ideal Casements (*site of*)
40 Sutton's Business Park
41 Thames Valley Business Park

Transport

42 Loddon bridge
43 Loddon Turnpike Tollgate (*site of*)
44 Earley Station

Earley's Early Centres

45 Three Tuns Crossroad
46 Little Hungerford

Chapter 5: Earley's Community Buildings and Institutions

Local Government in Earley

47 Radstock House
48 Maiden Erlegh Local Nature Reserve
49 Maiden Erlegh Lake
50 Meadow Park
51 Culver Lane Allotments
52 Radstock Lane Community Centre
53 Maiden Place Community Centre
54 Mays Lane Cemetery

Earley's Public Houses

55 The Dreadnought
56 The Three Tuns
57 The George

Earley's Churches

58 Chapel of Earley St Nicholas (*site of*)
59 Chapel of Earley St Bartholomew (*site of*)
60 Earley St Peter's
61 Earley St Bartholomew
62 Our Lady of Peace and Blessed Dominic Barberi
63 St Nicolas Church
64 King's Church – Hilltop
65 King's Church – Brookside Christian Centre
66 Trinity Church

Schools

67 Earley St Peter's
68 Whiteknights Primary
69 Aldryngton Primary
70 Hawkedon Primary
71 Loddon Junior and Infants
72 Radstock Primary
73 Hillside Primary
74 Maiden Erlegh

Other Community Buildings and Institutions

75 The Porter Institute
76 Woodley Hill House
77 The University of Reading
78 Whiteknights Lake
79 Temporary Office Buildings
80 The War Room
81 The Cole Museum of Zoology
82 The Ure Museum
83 The Museum of English Rural Life

Chapter 6: Earley's Community Groups

84 Maiden Erlegh Bowling Club
85 Whiteknights Indoor Bowling Club
86 Sutton's Bowling Club
87 Earley Home Guard Social Club
88 Reading Cricket and Hockey Club (*site of*)

Chapter 7: History on the Edge

89 European Centre for Medium Range Weather Forecasting
90 Meteorological Office College
91 Shinfield Players Theatre
92 Dinton Pastures Country Park
93 Highwood Local Nature Reserve
94 Holme Park and Reading Blue Coat School
95 Mockbeggar Farm (*site of*)
96 Leighton Park (Pepper Farm) (*site of*) and Leighton Park School
97 Shrublands (Briggins) (*site of*)
98 Crosfields School
99 Reading Cemetery
100 Palmer Park

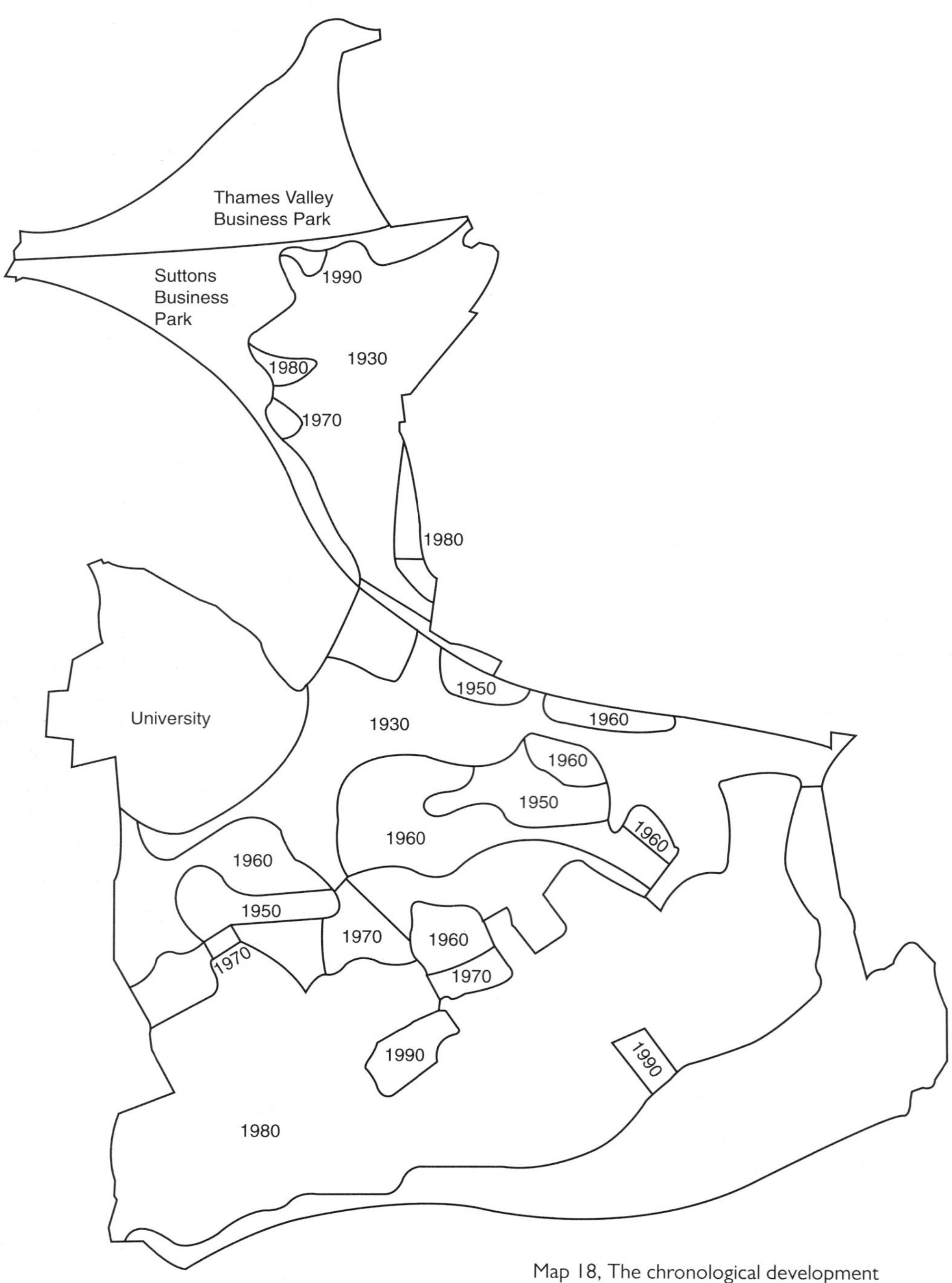

Map 18, The chronological development of housing and industry in Earley

Glossary of terms

Acre originally meaning a field; it was the size that a yoke of oxen could plough in a day. It was standardised by statute for official use as early as the reign of King Edward I.

Desmene Land of the manor held in the lord's own hands (villein tenants as part of the obligation in return for their holdings, had to work on the demesne lands).

Escheat the reversion to the lord or the Crown of an estate e.g. when the tenant died without heirs, or where the heir had not yet attained majority, or where the tenant had committed a crime and forfeited his estate as a consequence.

Escheators were appointed by the Crown to collect any revenues from escheats.

Fisheries rights to fish, these could be rented out.

Furlong originally a furrow length in the open fields and sometimes a measurement of area i.e. a rectangular block of strips. It eventually became standardised as a measurement of length (one-eighth of a mile).

Glebe Land assigned to the Incumbent of a parish as part of his benefice and the endowment of the church.

Hide originally the amount of land supporting one family. It varied from 60 acres (27.2ha) to 180 acres (81.6ha) depending on soil quality. Later it was equated with the amount of county tax that a community was responsible for. Whole counties were divided into hides.

Hundred (of Germanic origin) a subdivision of a shire; used to denote a group of a hundred warriors; also the area occupied by 100 families or equalling one hundred hides. A hide being the amount of land necessary to support one peasant family.

Liberty A Liberty is part of a unit (such as a parish or manor) granted special rights in government or administration, subject to the paramount authority of the holder of the unit. It is not known when the term was applied to Sonning Parish but it was certainly in use in the eighteenth century and possibly came into common usage when the parish became the normal administrative unit in an increasingly burdensome local responsibility for the Poor law and Settlement law management. Each had the right to hold their own vestry meetings under the supervision of Sonning in the late eighteenth century and the right to elect their own overseer, highways surveyor and constable (Lloyd, 1997).

Manor an administrative unit.

Metecorn an allowance (usually of corn) made to servants.

Parish A medieval unit, initially solely ecclesiastical rights and obligations. From late 16th century civil responsibilities imposed upon parish and when parliamentary constituencies were restructured in 19th and 20th centuries, defined in terms of governmental units comprised of parishes. Thus in time the parish became a fundamental unit in the civil, parliamentary and ecclesiastical organisation of England, important both for royal and local government.

Peculiar *Eccl.*: a parish or church exempt from the jurisdiction of the ordinary or bishop in whose diocese it lies: *in Canon Law:* a jurisdiction proper to itself, exempt from, or not subject to, the jurisdiction of the bishop of the diocese.

Plough arable land for plough team i.e. area of open field.

Quit claim a release and disclaimer of all rights, interest and potential legal actions from a grantor to a grantee.

Quit rent a payment made by tenants to their lord to excuse themselves from the customary manor services. It was abolished in 1922.

Recusant those people who would not swear an oath abduring the papacy.

Slave someone held as a prisoner or against a debt. He worked on the Lord of the manor's land and was tied to it.

Smallholder (bordar) a villein cottager and therefore one of the lowest ranks in the feudal system. He was allowed to cultivate some land to give him sustenance, but he was obliged to perform menial work for the Lord either free or for a fixed sum.

Tithe in a parish one tenth of the profits from the soil went to the church, this was a tithe. They were divided into Great and Small tithes. In the Parish of Sonning the Lords of the Manor collected the Great tithes and the Incumbent (Vicar) the Small tithes. By the 1836 Tithe Commutation Act tithes could be commuted to a rent-charge based on the prevailing price of wheat. The rent-charge was abolished in 1925 and the Tithe Act of 1936 extinguished them altogether.

Villager (Villein) unfree tenant. In return for his land holding he was obliged to perform a variety of services and pay a range of fines; this holding was at the will of the Lord and the tenant could be deposed from it. His usual holding was about 30 acres (13.6ha).

Virgate 30 acres.

Yeoman a tenant farmer with substantial income/assets.

many of the definitions were taken from *The Local Historian's Encyclopaedia* (John Richardson, 1981) Historical Publications Ltd.

Units of measurement

units of length

inch	one twelfth part of a foot
foot	12 inches
yard	3 feet
furlong	220 yards (one-eighth of a mile)
rod or rood	$16\frac{1}{2}$ feet
perch	$16\frac{1}{2}$ feet
mile	1,760 yards (eight furlongs)

area

1 acre	4,840 square yards (0.405 ha)
1 rod/rood	$\frac{1}{4}$ acre
1 perch	$\frac{1}{40}$ rod

List of Subscribers

Mr K. F. Colvert
Mr Northeast
Paul Kurowski
Mr P. Hyslop
L. G. E. Aburrow
Andrew Long
Mrs Ruth Pomroy
Mrs N. Gay
Mrs D. Terrell
Mrs M. Wellman
Miss D. M. Woods
Mr & Mrs F. Putman
Mr & Mrs Palmer
Sara Scanlon
Mr & Mrs Prior
Miss T. M. Charlton
Mrs P. Fowler
Mr & Mrs Kisiala
G. H. Westall
Mrs P. J. Smart
Mary Blustin
Daphne & Jim Phillips
Dennis Butts
Mrs Mollie Marsh
Elizabeth Vincent
Renee Smalley
Ada Little
Marjorie Culham
Peter Little
David Little
Alexandros Hind
Miss J. Rupert
Mrs K. Paterson
Mr Steve Caddy
Jenny Lissaman
Mr & Mrs Norton
Mr & Mrs Haggerty
Mrs S. Timms

Mrs Barrow
Mr & Mrs De Fraine
Wokingham Library
Fiona Rolls
Mr Terry
Kathy Goodwin
Mrs J. Allen
Mr R. Emptage
Mrs P. Teagle
Mr D. Wright
Mrs J. Clark
Mr R. Brown
Mr J. Eastwell
Mr A. Borland
Mrs A. Burnett
Mrs C. J. Braine
Mr R. E. N. Boulton
Patricia Edwards
Mrs M. Voake
Mrs E. Spratling
N. Harlow
P. Medcraft
R. E. Ames
Mrs P. Bell
Mrs M. Smith
E. D. Pendlebury
Mrs J. Eager
Mrs M. A. Richardson
Mrs P. Tribe
Mrs H. Witt
Reading Library
Mr R. Horvath
Mr H. Dickinson
Mrs Marion Walters
Mrs D. Stratford
Mrs M. Holloway
Mr D. Box
Mrs E. Coles

Mrs J. Lomer
Mr B. Fozard
Mrs Pam Scoble
Mrs Janet Audain
Mr A. Pollard
Mrs J. Lynton-Buchan
Paul & Alison Swaby
Mr Philip Markham
Mr & Mrs R. N. Terry
Carol Whelan
Gordon Rowley
A. Empson
Helen & David Hitchcock
Mr R. P. Dowling
Mr R. W. Stringer
Mrs A. Forkes
Mrs Mavis Avery
Mrs B. S. Painter
Miss Sheila Jennens
Mr H. G. Albertini
P. D. Cole
Mrs M. E. Ross
Mr B. R. Jones
Dr N. J. Brock
Mrs Angela Beales
Mrs M. Lewin
James & Anne Nalty
Tim Holton
Mr D. J. Smale
John & Veronica Lewer
Elizabeth Glaister
Mr S. Beck
Mr W. J. Illsley
Mrs E. West
Mr C. Tillin
Julie Boulton
Grahame Hawker
Mrs B. Yates

Mrs M. Jobson
Mrs S. C. Little
Mrs F. Jones
Terry Huggins
Mr Michael J. Holt
Mrs M. A. Knight
Mrs Pennicott
Mrs F. M. Rogers
Mr W. E. Baker
Mrs R. James
Mr & Mrs C. Dodsworth
Mrs J. P. Kelly
Mr & Mrs R. Baxter
Mrs G. E. Coward
Mr N. Winham
Mrs D. M. Groom
Mr & Mrs D. A. Double
Barbara & Edward Stansfield
Mrs A. J. Bates
Mr K. Hillebrandt
Mr Geoffrey & Mrs Dorothy Bartlett
Mr Colin Parker
Mr H. Jones
Ian & Sarah Miller
Mrs L. Jinks
Mr G. Parker
Mrs W. Ballard
Mr E. E. Clift
Mrs S. Gilbert
Mr G. Kalsi
Phyll Parsons
Mrs J. Mill
David Wilson
R. D. & H. Nicholson
Mrs T. L. Jackson
David & Judi Stanley
Mr G. Kitch
Mr & Mrs Westacott
Julia & Richard Tredgett
Sidney & Pamela Plenty
Roy & Margaret Carter
Mrs S. Leach
Mr A. Langdon
Dr Philip Stothart
Richard & Janet Jennings
Bernard & Mary Kiff
Mrs M. Grozman
Richard & Jane Halton
Penny Goldsmith
Margaret Pocock
Eileen & David Coles
A. G. Male
Mrs P. D. Williams
Mr M. R. N. Ball
Mr & Mrs Butler
David Parker
J. V. Mildenhall
Mary Sutherland
Colin & Dayle Mair
Mrs V. Robinson
Mrs Surinder Dosanjh
E. Watts
H. C. Watts
J. W. Watts
W. D. Watts
David J. Rowe
Mrs P. J. M. Hooper
K. T. Ackerman
J. Malpas
Mrs J. Allen
B. A. Brooks
S. Brown
Anne Rees
Alice Taylor
Betty Neville
Audrey Bridges
Richard Raymond
Mr Roger Tayler
Doris Taylor
Mr & Mrs Burnett
G. Parlour
A. Edmonds
Elizabeth Henderson
J. Cobbold